D1085205

STARTING OUT:

Class and Community in the Lives of Working-Class Youth

STARTING OUT:

Class and Community in the Lives of Working-Class Youth

Victoria Anne Steinitz
and
Ellen Rachel Solomon

TEMPLE UNIVERSITY PRESS
Philadelphia

Temple University Press, Philadelphia 19122
Copyright © 1986 by Temple University. All rights reserved.
Published 1986
Printed in the United States of America

Library of Congress Cataloging-in-Publication Data

Steinitz, Victoria Anne.
Starting out.

Bibliography: p.
Includes index.
1. Youth — United States — Attitudes — Case studies.
2. Labor and laboring classes — United States — Case studies.
3. Class consciousness — United States — Case studies.
I. Solomon, Ellen Rachel
II. Title.
HQ796.S8265   1986   305.2′35′0973   86-5808
ISBN 0-87722-430-7 (alk. paper)

To our children,
Anna, Becca, Fara, Jessie, Sarah

and in memory of
Lois Kalb Bouchard

Contents

Preface

This is a very different book from the one we had in mind when we began our work. Then we were, respectively, a faculty member and a graduate student at the Harvard Graduate School of Education in the early seventies, celebrating that heyday of youthful protest while we examined it.

Our questions centered on the relationship between adolescent questioning and social class. From our experience and reading, we were alert to differences between the social classes in the United States — differences in access to education, money, and power, differences in values and priorities. It seemed to us then, as it did to some others, that the ideals and activism of white high school and college radicals were consonant with their middle- and upper-middle-class values and realities.[1] Raised to expect that they would hold power in a society that promised justice and equality to all, they were sensitive to hypocrisy and the betrayal of those ideals. Confident that they would be successful, they had little to lose in questioning the American Dream of individual competition and turning instead toward more communitarian visions of "the good life."

We wondered if their working-class peers were raising similar questions. In portrayals of working-class life by Gans and others, we saw a subculture of people who had never bought into the American Dream. They lived in "urban villages" where personal relationships were valued more than achievement, continuity more than change, and the welfare of the group more than the pursuit of individualism. Were these values now leading working-class youth to join in questioning the morality of American society? Did traditional working-class skepticism about progress and politics lead them to agree with radical critiques of unequal power and opportunity? What of their aspirations for themselves?

Now we write these questions dispassionately, but at the time we very much hoped to find radical working-class adolescents. Fortunately, our criticism of the politics and methodology of most survey research put us on guard against asking questions that would elicit the answers we wanted to hear. We wanted to avoid imposing our interests upon the young people we interviewed and deliberately did *not* assume that political and social issues were central to their thinking. We planned for long, intensive interviews with a small number of youth and took care to begin with open-ended questions that would capture their interpretation of personal and social realities. Only then did we move on to probes about specific issues.

We also wanted to counteract the images of power and distance that our Harvard connections might evoke for working-class youth. We promised them anonymity, for the administrators of the high school in the nearby town of Hillford had agreed that we could use their file of high school seniors without revealing names or findings. We told prospective interviewees part of our motivation for doing the study: our recognition that many professional educators wanted to change the schools, but that few had actually sat down and listened to students talk about their needs and interests. We were completely honest in saying that we considered them the experts on their experience and wanted to hear whatever they had to say to us.

The care we took paid off. Almost as soon as we finished interviewing, we realized how wrong our assumptions had been. The working-class seniors of Hillford were concerned about the wisdom of the war in Vietnam, but they had not become questioners of the morality of American society; they were confident that the United States would soon recover its basically sound direction. They believed that great strides had been made toward racial equality through civil rights legislation. Their own attention was focused on getting out of high school so they could go on to further education and achieve their goals. Their optimism was grounded in their belief that opportunities were available for hard-working young people like themselves.

We found it hard to give up our search for working-class radicals. We explained to ourselves at first that the ideologies of Hillford seniors were not typically working-class because, in our rush to interview youth in an easily accessible high school, we had chosen a community unlikely to produce working-class dissent.

The income of the working-class population of Hillford was relatively high, and many owned their own homes. A substantial number of white-collar workers and owners of small businesses lived in the community. Many of the parents of our interviewees had spent their childhoods in the ethnic urban villages of Boston and might well have interpreted their move to Hillford as evidence that American society was open to all those who tried. Working-class people encountered no dominant group of upper-middle-class people in Hillford, and the major university on one edge of town was considered another world. We thought that the questions raised by Hillford seniors about America reflected their feelings about their huge, modern high school, which had opened the year before: it was too big, anonymous, and they often felt lost in the halls. But they were proud of it — its Olympic-sized swimming pool and music practice rooms — and they viewed it as a tangible sign that they were growing up in a community that was making progress.

We thought that if we found a more typical working-class community, we might yet discover youth who were questioning the American Dream. Yet the very characteristics of Hillford made us pause. We had to ask what a typical working-class community might be and if, in seeking one, we were not denying the complex realities of contemporary working-class life.

Gans collected his data in the late fifties, as the urban village and its stable working-class subculture were under siege by gentrification projects, called at the time "urban renewal." Urban villagers had been forced to move out into a variety of places; other working-class people had lived for generations in suburbs, small towns, and rural areas. Whether the general upward mobility since the Second World War had destroyed a working-class subculture was being debated: some observers argued that working-class people had undergone an *embourgeoisement*, the transformation of their values into those of mainstream consumerism, while others believed that class differences remained deeply etched into the American landscape.[2]

We had come to a new conception of our work. We decided to face head-on the question of working-class diversity and to look for contrasting communities in which working-class adolescents were growing up. We would explore the impact of these different kinds of communities on the personal and political development of working-class youth. Thus, this has become a book about the relationship between adolescent development, community, and social class.

Our task now was to think through what sorts of working-class adolescents to interview and in which communities. We decided to find those youth who—because their IQ's were listed in school records as above average—might have been treated as promising by their teachers and parents and thus might now have the option of becoming upwardly mobile. These young people, we reasoned, might be setting goals for a future that was not a replica of their parents' lives and would thus have to assess the openness of the social structure to their hopes and consider the range of power and privilege in American society.

Given the exploratory nature of our work, we were less concerned about finding representative communities than places that contrasted vividly. We asked which structural dimensions of community life might be most influential in the development of working-class youth. We concluded that there were three, and decided to vary the socioeconomic composition of the communities, their size, and their relative proximity to the city.

We wondered whether promising adolescents who were part of the working-class majority or minority in a community would differ in their experience of ambition.[3] Would youth in a more homogeneous working-class community face conflicts between traditional values and the values of mainstream America? How would being part of the working-class minority in a more affluent place affect the standards adolescents used to judge their parents' accomplishments and the comparisons they made between their own and others' life-chances? We thought that the relative size of a community might influence whether its young people experienced consistent or conflicting messages about how they should behave and where they should aim, and whether they had become identified with school and community activities. Finally, we wondered whether urban working-class youth might feel more directly touched by state and national political debates and more enriched by diversity than those in less urban communities.[4]

These considerations led us to the high schools of Cityville, an old, largely working-class city close to Boston; Townline, a predominantly middle-class suburb also near Boston; and Milltown, a small working-class town 25 miles from Boston and surrounded by affluent suburbs. In each school, we sought to interview 20 seniors, 10 young men and 10 young women.[5]

The first set of interviews took place in the months before high school graduation, a pressured time for seniors. Our lives became frantic too as we planned the interviews to suit their schedules, in between school and their part-time jobs and other activities, in empty classrooms, guidance offices, in neighborhood youth centers, our homes and theirs — wherever they felt most comfortable. These young people seemed candid and responsive. They appreciated the opportunity to talk at length to an adult who took them and their ideas seriously. Many of the interviews were more like wide-ranging conversations, lasting several hours and punctuated by our questions and by the changing of tapes on the tape-recorder.

We found the interviews rich in what they revealed about how these young people had learned the lessons of community life — absorbing the examples and warnings of parents, siblings, and neighbors, taking cues from the "action" on the street corner or in the schoolyard, drawing morals from their dealings with school authorities and bosses — and from these interactions had developed their hopes, sense of well-being, and political stances.

As we analyzed the interviews and began to report our findings, we wondered what had happened after high school during these young people's first forays beyond their communities and into late adolescence. Most had been headed for colleges or technical schools, and we wanted to know the fate of their hopes and expectations. Had their visions of the good life been sustained or transformed? How did they now view their original communities and the new contexts in which they studied and worked? Had their conclusions about the social order changed, and what did their new status as voters mean to them? We decided to interview them again, four years after high school, and when we contacted them, almost all sixty agreed to meet and talk with us.[6]

In the chapters that follow, our accounts of the thinking of these working-class adolescents draw on their own words and need no further explanation. But we alert the reader to two instances in which the text may confuse unless what was going on during the interview is kept in mind. In the first case, we showed the young people interviewed three photographs, asking them to tell us what each picture brought to mind and then what meanings they thought it had for their own lives and for life in America. One was the "kitchen picture," which shows a well-dressed couple standing at the counter of an immaculate, modern kitchen. Another was the "commune picture," a photograph of a large group of adults and children standing and sitting closely together, facing the camera dressed in the informal "hippie" garb of the period. The third was the "high-tech picture," a photograph of some sort of technical studio in which men in business suits are busy working at the screens of computer terminals or standing and conversing.

The second instance occurred near the end of the interview when we asked the young people, "What do you think is important in determining whether someone gets ahead or not?" After hearing their spontaneous views, we asked their opinion of several alternative explanations. We then described a series of proposals for legislation, asking what they thought of them, and who they thought would favor and oppose them.

Although we have struggled toward a whole understanding of the lives of these working-class adolescents, we have been unable to discuss fully all the topics that arise from the interviews. Thus, although we discuss gender differences within each community and in the sample as a whole, our discussions are suggestive rather than exhaustive. Similarly, we describe the powerful role of ethnic differences in Townline, but we do not undertake a full-scale exploration of ethnicity. Doubtless readers will find other topics incompletely addressed, but it was only when we accepted our limitations that we could complete the book.

Ours has not always been an easy collaboration. We have seemed at times the most unlikely partners, opposite in intellectual styles and emotional habits. And yet the frustrations have been greatly outweighed by our deep satisfaction in working together. One reason must be our mutual commitment to give voice to the life-stories the young people of *Starting Out* shared with us. Another is our essential respect and love for each other, which have grown during this arduous journey. We have learned together that struggle can be worth it.

To the young people of Cityville, Townline, and Milltown, whose perceptions of self and society form the core of this book, we owe the deepest thanks. We hope our work is an adequate response to the trust they placed in us by speaking with such care and honesty about their lives and ideas.

We thank the original members of the first Learning Environments research team on adolescent ideology at the Harvard Graduate School of Education: Prudence King, Ellen Shapiro, Jim Sleeper, Don Oliver, and Jean Wu. We owe a special debt to Prudence King, who did the Milltown interviews and whose doctoral dissertation on Milltown was a rich resource for us. We were substantially helped by grants from the Spencer Fund for research costs, the Milton Fund of Harvard University for transcription costs, and a Faculty Development Grant from the University of Massachusetts for the preparation of the manuscript. We could not have undertaken this study without the cooperation of the administrations of the high schools of Cityville, Townline, and Milltown.

There are many whose friendship and support have made our work possible: Melanie Barrou, Joan Bolker, Stan Bolster, David Bouchard, Jean Briggs, Judy Cheng, Leo Cleary, Eleanor Duckworth, Fred Erickson, Helen and Jay Featherstone, Steven Fraser, Kristine Gerstner, Jude Gregory, Phil Helfaer, Peter Jenner and the Old Firehouse Restaurant, Pauline and Patricia Hickey, Herbert Kelman, the Lanesville Women's Group, Peter Lenrow, Eva Miller, Jean Baker Miller, Anita Mishler, Kiyo Morimoto, Lisa Joel, William Perry, David Riesman, Phoebe Schnitzer, Jim Schoel, Michael Schudson, Jeanne and David Shub, Walter H. Solomon, Velma Sowers, Carl Steinitz, Eva Travers and Bob Whitney.

To Anne Smith, our warmest thanks. In addition to her continual encouragement, she has typed draft after draft with virtuosity and patience.

We feel fortunate to have our book published by Temple University Press. Michael Ames welcomed our manuscript, communicating to us thoughtful criticism as well as his faith that the revisions would make the book, what we wanted it to be. In copy editor Jane Barry and production editor Candice Hawley we found respectful and expert advisors to whom we are very grateful.

We thank especially William Greenbaum, whose generosity and belief in our work have given us courage throughout, and Elliot Mishler, whose perspective and support lightened the burden of completing the manuscript. We are indebted to two accomplished writers, colleagues and dear friends, Pamela Daniels and Lois Bouchard, who gave us vital encouragement and responded to the manuscript at critical points. Pamela's editorial suggestions have resolved many an impasse and contributed greatly to the manuscript's clarity. We dedicate this book to Lois, who died tragically in 1984, and to our children—whose lives are interwoven with our work and who can scarcely remember a time when some version of *Starting Out* was not being written.

STARTING OUT:

Class and Community in the Lives of Working-Class Youth

1

Adolescence, the American Dream, and the Developmental Vision

"I wouldn't be me if I hadn't grown up in Cityville."

Like Joe Mendoza, the young people who speak through these pages believe that their personal lives and their theories about the world have been deeply influenced by what they learned at home and in the schools, neighborhoods, and workplaces of Cityville, Townline, and Milltown.[1]

From life in each place, adolescents arrive at different "social identities," in Robert Lane's fine phrase:[2] they draw different conclusions about what lies in store for people like themselves and thus what it is appropriate to hope for, personally and politically. On the social maps they create of their communities, they place "fault lines" that divide allies from enemies, people they can count on from those they distrust. They encounter casts of moral and political characters from whose actions they draw lessons about privilege and power. In addition, they learn their communities' interpretations of the history of their times and how to judge the significance of the news and newsmakers.

Social identity evolves from the individual's life in groups. In focusing on community as the formative basis of group life—influencing family as well as school and neighborhood—we emphasize a crucial, yet rarely studied, aspect of development.[3] Most adults we know—of every social class—look back at the place where they grew up as a powerful influence on how they came to regard themselves

1

and the social world. Yet research on development is remarkably placeless, assuming some generalized individual growing up in an undifferentiated or aggregated (though occasionally regionalized) America.

The role of social class in development is also neglected and, in addition, badly distorted. When researchers do investigate class, they usually treat it as an abstraction, lifted out of place and time. Thus, one hears or reads little about the impact of community on the formation of class-identity, and there is hardly any literature on the diversity of working-class experience in different communities.[4] Moreover, we believe that the upper-middle-class bias in mainstream developmental theory has produced a stereotypical portrayal of working-class families as deficient settings, incapable of providing children with the requisites for positive growth.[5]

The social identities of promising working-class adolescents in each community are based in their positioning of themselves in relation to others: in Cityville, these young people see themselves as part of the school-oriented group, fortunate in having been encouraged to plan for the future, but also sharing, in fundamental ways, the circumstances of all Cityville youth; Townline working-class youth, Jewish and Irish, see themselves as on the disadvantaged margins of a favored, affluent community; and Milltown youth view themselves as in the midst of a friendly, familiar small town inhabited by decent, hard-working people "in the middle."

These social identities are emotionally charged. Young people's views of themselves in relation to others are accompanied by strong feelings—feelings of vulnerability in Townline or confidence in Cityville; feelings of comfortable acceptance in the consensual community of Milltown or angry or fearful marginality in the polarized community of Townline, and feelings about the distribution of privilege and power in American society—anger in Townline, resignation in Cityville, or remoteness in Milltown.

Early in our research, we were convinced of the importance of our focus on community but also troubled by questions it raised about the relative values we were placing on community and social class as formative influences in the lives of working-class youth. We wondered if we were saying that community life is so powerful that it changes the nature of social class in each place. Did we believe that working-class youth in America are more fundamentally community-members than members of their socioeconomic class?

As the work progressed, we came to see these questions as simplistic, based in the linear, input-output models of influence so common in the social sciences. These models assume that the individual is passive, bombarded by competing forces that researchers seek to place in rank order according to their strength of influence.[6] In contrast, we based our research in the belief that individuals are always actively constructing meaning from whole experience. From this perspective, class can only be experienced in context.[7]

Thus, in pointing out the substantial differences in the social identities that emerge for working-class youth in City-ville, Townline, and Milltown, we are demonstrating the contextualization of class in process, showing how the realities of working-class life — scarcity of money and resources, parental jobs that have little dignity and security — become meaningful as individuals live their lives in particular circumstances, times, and places.

Such a contextualized conception of class — as a basic but fluid force in everyday live — is given by Connell, Ashenden, Kessler, and Dowsett in *Making the Difference*.[8] They suggest that class (and gender) are structuring processes of power rather than rigid systems of power: through these structuring processes, "social life is constantly being organized (and ruptured and disorganized) through time" (1982, p. 180). We take this to mean that although class relations are structured by the differential access to money and power of groups in society, individual members of a class construct their interpretations of social class through their actions in specific contexts and times.

Just as working-class life has been treated as monolithic and undifferentiated by place, it has been viewed as rooted in a subculture whose commitments are antithetical to the values of mainstream American culture: economic and geographic mobility, and the inner development of the individual. Our interviews open a window onto the worlds of contemporary working-class life beyond the urban village, in

3

which promising working-class youth confront mobility as an option.

Promising accurately conveys the situations of the youth we portray, for they consider their abilities and hopes part of the promises they make to their families, and they interpret the ideology of American society as having promised them access to the opportunities they seek. Being promising, they start out with the task of figuring out how to achieve more security and dignity than their parents have known.

When Joseph Kahl (1953) looked at the development of ambition among boys in the working-class subculture of the 1950s, he saw that young men who studied hard had to forsake their lives in the peer group, acceding instead to their parents' wishes that they become achievers. And in Herbert Gans's (1962) work, the sharp distinction between working-class and middle-class life meant that only working-class youth who became separated from peer-group life — through either special gifts or lengthy illnesses — became ambitious.

The gulf between working-class values and those of mobile America is movingly explored in Sennett and Cobb's *Hidden Injuries of Class* (1972). They argue that it is impossible for upwardly mobile working-class people in the United States to evade the double bind in which they are doomed to feel like failures if they do not move up the ladder and to disrespect themselves if, betraying their working-class origins, they do.

Our data complicate and extend this argument. On the one hand, we report working-class experience in the seventies, when higher education had become a widely accepted norm in working-class life; few of the adolescents of Cityville, Townline, and Milltown imagined that going to college would take them into worlds alien to their parents. Life in each community lent different interpretations to ambition, setting a different scope and different criteria for success. Thus, for example, promising working-class youth in Cityville saw few contradictions between their wanting to go on to college and remaining close to their families and non-college-going friends; as we show, they intended to "become somebodies while remaining themselves." Townline youth encountered no gulf either, but faced instead a complicated dilemma because they feared that moving up might mean that they would become like the materialistic Townliners they disliked; for them the problem was not to stay as they were but to come up with better alternatives. Yet we show as well how these working-class adolescents, as they move out of their communities during the four years after high school, tend to blame themselves when they encounter difficulty. This self-blame, less rooted in the communal injuries described by Sennett and Cobb, leaves these young people especially vulnerable, since they are unable to articulate for themselves the values they do hold and share with others.

We caught these working-class youth at two particularly interesting historical moments.[9] High school seniors in the early seventies, they had seen on television and in newspapers, images of youth in rebellion against the war in Vietnam, of women in revolt against conventional sex roles, and minorities seeking their rights. We show how these young people experienced these events through the filters of their community — how, for example, in Cityville, although social protesters were viewed as alien, their message came to signify hope for a new generation; how, in Milltown, national events were felt to exist in another universe; and how, in Townline, "the movement" was endorsed by adults at the high school and perceived as patronizing by working-class youth.

Born of the rising expectations of the Great Society, social protest had waned by the mid-seventies, the time of the second round of interviews, and the Watergate revelations, the oil crisis, and an economic recession had set a general tone of skepticism and limitation. We learn from these adolescent accounts how those who are born with little power or privilege — and who have come to want more — deal with unforeseen difficulties, including the broken promises of education. We learn how they sustain their hopes and redefine the role of college education, how they reinterpret explanations for inequality, and whom they blame for the obstacles they face as they begin their adult lives.

Connell and his colleagues include gender alongside

class as a central structuring process of power and say that the situations of the working-class schoolboy and schoolgirl "cannot be lumped together as if there were just *a* working-class situation. Both class and gender are historical situations, riddled with tension and contradiction" (1982, p. 180).[10] We agree. Just as we insist that each distinctive community presents working-class youth of both sexes with a different life-situation, we show how young men and women in each place contend with different and changing assumptions about the proper roles for men and women.

We have discovered strong similarities between conceptions of women and of working-class people in mainstream social science. In the same way that having ambition has too long been considered antithetical to traditional working-class values, it has until relatively recently been considered a masculine prerogative.[11] The deficiency theory of working-class development parallels the deficiency theory of female development, and women, like working-class people, have been conventionally portrayed as constricted by their inability or unwillingness to free themselves from their relationships. By subordinating their own choices to the needs and wishes of others, they are believed to limit their development.[12]

In the next section, we attack the inadequate and biased concept of development that underlies these portrayals. Here we point out that in looking at the development of promising working-class young women, we are affirming what has too long been unacknowledged—that is, that contemporary young women have ambitions in their own right and that the processes through which these ambitions develop are worthy of investigation.[13]

Until recent critiques of mainstream research on stratification, young women's aspirations have been measured by the occupations they hope for in their future husbands.[14] So taken for granted has been the assumption that a woman's socioeconomic status is a function of her husband's occupational status, that girls' mobility aspirations were assumed to be manifest in their desire to marry up—that is, upward mobility for a woman was measured by comparing her father's occupation with her husband's.

6

The women's movement was an emerging, visible force when we conducted our first interviews. Some radical analysts compared the status of women to that of blacks and other minorities, as victims of a capitalist imperialistic society in which patriarchy reigned. At the same time the term "silent majority" was coined, and in media coverage of the alleged political backlash of hard-hats and other white workers — including the then-new television program "All in the Family" — patriotism was linked to traditional sex roles. Edith Bunker might disagree with Archie but would never challenge their basic arrangement, and it seemed doubtful to many observers that working-class women would find their concerns addressed in feminist ideology.

We show that the feminist challenge was heard very differently by the working-class young women in each community — as exaggerated and shrill in Milltown and Cityville, as true but incomplete in Townline. But most of these young women saw their mothers' lives as full of frustration and struggle, situations of entrapment that they were determined to avoid. In each community — at different points in their lives and in very different ways — these working-class young women were taking seriously not only the necessity to prepare to work for income but also the intrinsic value of a career as the means to more interesting and secure lives than their mothers had known.

Our work challenges the powerful tradition in mainstream social science that sets forth a single optimal route to development and assumes that working-class adolescents are doomed to miss it. Following this optimal route is necessary if the individual is to fulfill what we have come to call the *developmental vision* of social science, a vision of what the good life is and the sort of person who can best live it. According to this vision, the ideal individual develops through an education of widening horizons and increasingly complex choices, gradually becoming confident enough to take risks and choose among options.[16]

Personal confidence leads individuals to political confidence. Through increasingly complex interactions with others, they come to understand different viewpoints while pursuing their own interests. They develop what political socialization theorists call a sense of political efficacy — the belief that they can influence the workings of government — and a sense of allegiance to America: they believe that all benefit from the give-and-take of the political process. But they remain critical citizens, alert for anti-democratic trends.[17]

Most developmental theory does not conceive of development as part of the individual's life within communities or other groups. Instead, development is assumed to occur as a result of separation from the collective, from one's original contexts: to become truly individual means becoming free from ties that bind.

And the ties of early relationships are almost always characterized as binding: the interests of the individual are assumed to be in inevitable opposition to group life. To develop fully, the individual must separate from family, peer group, and community: choosing for oneself is presumed to be more mature than acting on behalf of others; moving on is preferable to staying put; individual feedom of choice is set forth as the highest good.

The developmental vision assumes that growing up in the United States fosters ideal development. The American experience is characterized as one of change and challenge, with unparalleled opportunities for personal growth and political freedom. In America, it is possible for the individual to move beyond traditions of past, place, and group life, which are viewed primarily as impediments to the development of individuality. Affluence is assumed to nourish the possibilities for development: money buys the choices that clear the way to personal and political growth. American cultural heroes have been those who pursue the American Dream, those who "light out" ahead of the rest for the new frontier. If they are fortunate, moving on eventually leads to moving up and rising above the group.[18]

In this vision of the heroic life, adolescence is a critical stage because it is then that the individual develops the cognitive capacity to step — at least in imagination — outside the particular context of childhood. Anna Freud (1958) portrays the new cognitive powers of adolescence as good protection

8

against the instinctual drives of puberty: through their obsession with ideology and utopian possibilities, adolescents distance themselves from their families before seeking new sexual attachments.

In the work of Erik Erikson, the ideological capacity of the adolescent becomes a complex and adaptive aid to development in a post-industrial society in which previous forms of identification based on ethnic, class, or occupational roles have become inadequate, and the adolescent must evolve a psychosocial identity that is more than the mere sum of childhood identifications.

As Erikson sees it, the contemporary adolescent must deal simultaneously with the past — "trying to free himself [*sic*] from parents who made and partially determined him" — and the future — "facing membership in wider institutions which he had not yet made his own" (1958, p. 114). The hope necessary to imagine and move into the future can grow only if the adolescent can "convince himself that he has chosen his past and is the chooser of his future" (p. 114).

To arrive at this conclusion, the adolescent turns to the ideology of his society for nourishment and confirmation, and the American youth finds there an idealization of the free-standing, separate individual and learns that to be successful, he must become his own person. Erikson believes that if adolescents have enough time detached from the need to make final choices, if they are granted a psychosocial moratorium in which to experiment with ideas, ideals, relationships, lifestyles, and work, they may arrive at commitments that feel self-propelled, generated by their own needs and talents and emerging from their unique identities. And they may be able to "convince themselves that those who succeed in their anticipated adult world thereby shoulder the obligation of being best" (1968, pp. 133–34).[19]

Just as American heroes are depicted as risking loneliness and danger in order to forge ahead, the adolescent of developmental theory is seen as questioning, searching, distinguishing himself from others. As Eriksonian heroes transcend the psychosocial givens of their day by resolving their conflict and pain into a new formulation of identity, frontiersmen advance civilization through their own efforts, stopping

9

finally to dig in and establish new settlements on their own terms.[20] This eventual settling means the end of adolescence.

There is little evidence that most adolescents are questioners, just as it is likely that most Americans have been settlers rather than explorers.[21] But the attraction of the developmental vision — powerfully resonant as it is with the American Dream — has been strong, and students of adolescence have focused their attention upon those who are restive and singular. "Youth in any period," Erikson notes, "means first of all the noisier and more obvious part of that subrace, plus the quiet sufferers who come to the attention of psychiatrists or are brought to life by the novelists" (Erikson, 1968, p. 26).[22]

White working-class youth have seldom been considered distinctive enough to command attention, and when they have been considered, they have been held up against the ideal of adolescence and judged developmentally stunted and ideologically deprived.[23] Rather than seeking to separate and strike out on their own, rather than pursuing questions and challenges, working-class youth are described as wanting to conserve what they have and get by.

Their parents are similarly judged. Although most white working-class people came to the United States in search of some element of the American Dream, they are portrayed as living outside its progressive and expansionist traditions. Working-class life is depicted as antagonistic to the aims of the developmental vision — too constricted by the extended family and peer group to promote individualism, too traditional to encourage independence, too authoritarian to accept questioning.

Working-class youth are assumed to grow up in peer-group societies that are governed by economic scarcity and tribal relationships: they live in extended families that enforce conformity of behavior; their fathers do repetitive work and must remain subordinate to the boss, requiring in turn obedience from their wives and children. Working-class people are assumed to project their fear and insecurity upon the "outside" world. Unable to feel a part of larger mainstream society and its political process, they focus their attention on their immediate world and define the rest as lying outside, a province reserved for "them."[24]

Ironically, while becoming ambitious is considered a developmental step up, working-class youth who go to college are viewed as too pragmatic to be properly adolescent, intent on studying only what will be useful to them in their quest for advancement. Becoming college students is also thought to make them marginal: feeling "tenuously included" in middle-class culture, they are assumed to be too dependent on the existing order to raise political questions, too bound by necessity to dream.[25]

It is not surprising that those who wield power in a society consider themselves to be most highly developed and go on to judge other social groups against their norms of developmental adequacy. By the standards of the developmental vision, working-class people — and women and members of minority groups — appear to be not only less economically and politically favored but also personally deficient.

The use of deficit theories to account for the persistence of inequalities is a form of Social Darwinism, maintaining that those who succeed deserve to. An example is Knutson's analysis of studies of the effect of personality variables on social outcomes, in which she reports a "relationship between psychic competence and social and economic status," claiming that "advantage in one sphere of society is inevitably correlated with advantage in other spheres" (Knutson, 1974, p. 15).[26] We agree with Pease, Form, and Rytina (1970) that such a view reflects the "evolutionary liberalism" of most American stratification literature, which holds that "amorphous classes emerge as a consequence of individual mobility which represents the process of natural selection of those who are socially and biologically most 'fit'" (p. 128).[27]

From these analyses, the corollary easily follows that those who do not succeed have only themselves to blame. This conclusion is bolstered by the use of research instruments that incorporate the perspectives and values of the upper middle class. Despite decades of criticism of their biases, these standardized tests continue to be used.[28] And so, working-class people consistently score higher on the F (authoritarianism) scale, lower on traditional measures of personal and political efficacy, lower on scales of moral development and on measures of psychic needs. These measures rest upon a set of interrelated assumptions that obscure the differences in power among members of different social classes and end up ascribing positive pyschological qualities to those who have wealth and power, and negative qualities to those who do not.

The first assumption is that American society is open and responsive to the individual efforts of its citizens, and that individuals who do not believe this have failed to develop trust. The propensity of political socialization researchers for measuring political attitudes with questionnaries that resemble civics tests compounds the problem.[29] Children who respond that individuals can make a difference and that citizens ought to participate in the political process receive high marks, whereas skepticism about individual efficacy and the opinion that the society is rigged and change unlikely are judged psychologically unhealthy. It is rarely acknowledged that children whose social circumstances include less actual power may be giving realistic answers.

A second assumption is that the factors that contribute to development are known and that contexts can be rated as to how much they promote or inhibit growth. Invariably working-class settings turn out to be less conductive to growth. Perhaps the most blatant version of deficit theory is Stanley Renshon's claim that "money can provide growth potential." The difference between being born into "a high SES family" and "a low SES family," Renshon explains, is the difference between living in a system of expanding choices or limiting choices:

> By "expanding system" we mean that one is more
> likely to acquire the attitudes, skills, and
> resources to develop and expand one's personal
> development and life horizons. By "limiting
> choice system" we mean that the development of
> certain attitudes, skills, and resources will not
> reach that critical level needed to increase both
> one's life choices and chances. (1975, p. 48)

Money per se is not usually singled out as the key factor, but deficit explanations all start from the premise that, as Connell et al. put it, "Members of lower status groups failed because their homes weren't up to it. There wasn't enough ambition, or stimulation, or loving-kindness, or patience, or whatever in their homes" (1982, p. 26).[30]

The third assumption is that most Americans agree on definitions of the good life and the successful person. This assumption of a shared community of meaning promotes the illusion that test items mean the same thing to all people — and that the items are equally meaningful to all.[31] The measures result in ratings of developmental adequacy based on the values and aspirations embedded in the developmental vision, and thereby legitimize attempts to judge as less developed those people who hold other values or who have drawn other meanings from their experience.[32]

The value of "self-contained individualism" (Sampson, 1977) dominates the American cultural ethos and the developmental vision. As Sampson says, "The person who most separates self from the group is seen as embodying that ideal most strongly" (p. 776). This value runs counter to the ideals of people who believe that *development through relationships* is the critical route to maturity, who hold that responsibility to others is necessary to the realization of the self.

Working-class people have traditionally pursued this ideal; so have many ethnic groups and the majority of humankind — women. The developmental vision is an upper-middle-class ideal, and it is also male. It is the young man who has been encouraged to set out alone, just as male pioneers were enjoined to leave women and children behind in order to seize the main chance. As Jean Baker Miller (1976) and Carol Gilligan (1982), among others, have pointed out, tending to others' needs has been seen as part of women's work, devalued as a developmental pathway in its own right, but taken for granted as the necessary background for male achievement.

A theory adequate to explain the development of personal and political beliefs and behavior must stand at a critical distance from the prevailing ideology of society and recognize that the dominant value system serves to rationalize existing inequities in the distribution of money and power (Habermas, 1970). It must take into account that working-class Americans, like everyone else, construct explanations of the social world and justifications for their own behavior that are based both in their varied experiences of the way the world actually works and in the public meaning systems available to them for interpreting their experience.[33]

These explanations and justifications do not emerge simply through a process of passive socialization in which youth are imprinted with attitudes and behavior appropriate to their circumstances. Instead, we assume that the process of meaning-making mediates experience. Individuals actively try to make sense of their lives, and it is through their interactions with others that the world of social reality is jointly constructed. (This theoretical perspective makes it possible to envision people using their understanding to transform their realities.)[34]

We aim to contribute to critical theory an understanding of the evolving social identities of the promising working-class youth of Cityville, Townline, and Milltown. We show how their interpretations of social class emerge through their discovery of their positions in the structure of life within each community. Adolescents in each place draw different conclusions about their life-chances and arrive at different conceptions of personal and political maturity.

Yet we show as well how, within their communities and in the wider worlds they enter after high school, these young people confront the values and judgments of the developmental vision. Predominant among these values is the ethic of individual responsibility, which, we believe, fuels their personal hopes while making them vulnerable to self-blame if their efforts fail. In addition, we show that because they judge their political behavior by the conventional definition of the good citizen, they blame themselves for not becoming involved in electoral politics and do not recognize the political significance of the actions they do take in their own realms of reality.

From our perspective, many of their ideals — for example, care-taking and cooperation — are worthy, and we believe that attaining a sense of interdependence with others, rather than becoming an autonomous, free-standing individual, should be an ideal aim of development. And we see links between their socially responsible behavior in their immediate worlds and the prospects of the larger society.

As political educators we ally ourselves with all those committed to the struggles of young people facing the dominant ideology of self-made individualism from positions of relative powerlessness. In doing so we confront and struggle with the dilemmas of advocating a radical stance from relatively privileged positions. For example, is it possible for working-class youth to deepen their awareness of the systemic nature of inequity without diminishing their hopefulness about their own life-chances? Can they recognize the compatibility between their individual aspirations and their collective interests without feeling that they are jeopardizing their own futures? And what collective efforts would they find meaningful to join? We discuss these questions not in universal terms, but rather in light of the specific issues faced by the youth of Cityville, Townline, and Milltown, and the interpretations they have created of their lives.

Cityville in the 1970s

The working-class adolescents of Cityville grow up in a densely packed city that borders one edge of Boston. In Cityville's four square miles, 99,000 people live, mostly in two- and three-family homes.

Most Cityville adults work at blue-collar jobs, some in the community's many small foundries, trucking firms, and bakeries, others in nearby communities.

Cityville has long been a place to settle for each generation of immigrants who leave the "urban villages" of Boston. In 1970 the Irish and Italians who first went there to work in the railroad yards and steel plants of the 1890s were in the majority. Since the 1940s a steady stream of newer immigrants from Italy, Portugal, and Greece have come and stayed. Many who move into Cityville, including students at the prestigious private universities nearby, are attracted by its relatively cheap apartments, and 66 percent of the city's dwellings are rental units.

Parochial as well as public schools serve the children of the many neighborhoods of Cityville. Young people in the public school system — nine elementary schools, two junior high schools, and the single high school — face a good chance of failure: 40 percent of Cityville High School students become dropouts, of whom 71 percent are unemployed. Only 15 percent of those who graduate continue their educations.

In 1970, after 40 years of political control by Irish and Italian politicians, a reform mayor — a Protestant minister — was elected. In 1971 a series of highly publicized articles in the Boston *Globe alleged widespread payoffs in previous administrations and led to indictments of several former Cityville mayors and city councillors.*

16

2

CITYVILLE:
Becoming Somebody
and Staying Oneself

Joe Mendoza
"I'm going pretty straight so far"

> *How do you see yourself?*
> I don't know — it's kind of hard to say what
> people think of you, 'cause you don't know what
> they're thinking.

> *What do you think of yourself, yourself?*
> I don't know — I think I'm pretty straight. I'm
> going pretty straight so far.

When Joe Mendoza is asked to talk about himself, he
speaks as someone used to seeing himself through the eyes of
the people around him. What has made him realize the importance of going "straight" to college? Joe thinks that some-
time near the start of high school he began to heed his parents' warnings: "They always had the idea that you had to go
to college, and they pounded it into my head." Joe's older
brother graduates from college this year and will be an accountant, but their younger brother still resists. "My little
brother thinks you can get through without the college stuff.
He thinks so, but it's pretty hard. He hasn't been around long
enough to know what work is."

In Mr. Mendoza's work life, Joe has seen a powerful
example of what happens to people who don't go to college:

My father always says, "What, do you want to have to work like *me*?" 'Cause he comes home dead tired. That's a rotten job. He should get another one, 'cause he's old now—54. Oh, Jesus, he comes home and he coughs and this rotten stuff comes up. When he started in insulating five or six years ago, he had to wash his hands every day with gasoline to get the tar off, and his hands were always getting red. His skin on the back of his hand is all stretched out and shiny. It's a rotten job.

Joe's mother once mistakenly mixed his father's work clothes with the family wash. For a week she, he, and his brothers itched and burned from the insulation fill.

There are other painful ways in which his father's job seeps into the life of the Mendoza family, other consequences of a non-college job that Joe hopes to avoid when he is older. Joe wants to be able to "express" his feelings to his future boss; otherwise, he imagines, he'll explode at his own wife and children the way his father now does:

Like my father's boss really gets my father teed off, and he holds it inside him. I can't see that, 'cause the guy gets home and he's edgy on us, and you know, we don't even see him all day till he gets home, and he yells at my mother and everything, and that's kind of hard on us.

You want to be able to speak back to a supervisor?
Yeah, I want to tell him how I feel, 'cause you hold all that stuff inside of you and it's going to do something to you after a while. My mother's always been that way, and she has an ulcer. My father—I think he's ready for a nervous breakdown, 'cause he comes home, and he's mad at us. I would like to—if someone gets me teed off and it's not my fault—I'd just tell them straight off. Why should he get mad at me when it's not my fault?

Do you do that with your father now?

> If I ever talked back to my father that way, he'd
> kill me. He'd push me right in the mouth. But
> that's not really so bad, 'cause after dinner he
> usually calms down. And anyhow I know that it's
> not me or him — it's the pressure he's working
> under, that the boss puts on him.

The past five years have taught Joe many lessons about his family's helplessness to control their fate. The pressures and pain of Mr. Mendoza's job are not what he imagined his work would bring him at this point in his life. For many years he worked as a carpenter in a small construction company in a nearby town. The boss and his fellow workers had an understanding that someday they would all share in the ownership and profits of the company. But, Joe says, the boss died suddenly and his wife challenged the will and gained complete ownership of the firm. Bitterly disappointed, Mr. Mendoza at 50 had few options when he began looking for work. His vulnerability on the job was matched by the helplessness of the whole Mendoza family and their neighbors when they saw the state highway program demolish their neighborhood and build an artery of an interstate highway over what had been their homes. The Mendoza family had almost paid off their mortgage but received such a small settlement from the state that "we had to start all over." Joe talks bitterly of the failure of the neighborhood petitions and legal actions and believes that ordinary people are powerless when they deal with the authorities. "They didn't even listen to us, to what we were saying. They don't care. Once they get something set, they're going to do it."

When he thinks about his own future, Joe hopes to escape the conditions under which his father has suffered and the limitations of Cityville life. At 17, he looks forward to "getting a good house, a good wife, and having a lot of kids" and living, surrounded by "a group of friends," somewhere "in the country" where there is fresh air and lots of room. "A man should not live alone or be one of those playboys or anything like that."

The key to achieving his hopes lies in his future work in electronics, a field Joe has pursued ever since his uncle started him off with speakers when he was eight or nine; now the tenant in his family's house lets Joe use his shortwave radio. Joe thinks that electronics will make it possible for him to "expand more, instead of a regular job that you do every day. You'd be going further — research. You'd be learning new stuff." Joe wants to be free from his job in electronics as well as interested in it. He imagines that his future wife wouldn't like his having to work late, and that he would object to working Saturdays "because I like being around kids."

He expects that his own future family will be more spontaneous in day-to-day life and less rigid in their thinking. For example, he will allow his children and wife to eat when they want rather than making everyone wait, as his father does, until they are all assembled. About his life in general, Joe says, "Mine will be more free 'cause my parents were brought up and they just followed *their* parents in thinking they had to do certain stuff at a certain time just because they were told they had to do it." Joe feels part of a more open generation, one that thinks differently about old taboos, "like drugs and sex —I don't know why, like other people, like my parents, you can't even talk to them about it."

Yet this is the only point at which Joe puts his parents into a fixed category of "older people" from whom he feels different. On most issues that arise as they all watch the evening news together, he and his parents agree. He admires them as stern and loving guides to the future, as people who have cared enough about him to insist that he smarten up and head for work that will make his future better than their past:

> They are rational people. They get the pretty
> straight way of life. They won't do anything
> unless they know it's right to do it. Like they
> won't invest in a car if they know it's a junk box.
> They always check everything out, and that's the
> way I would like to be, 'cause you can get
> screwed so easily now. They can palm off bum
> products on you and you won't even know.

Like his parents, Joe intends not to be caught unawares. "If I can get through college and get my degree, I think it will turn out. Now I've got that push behind me."

In accepting "that push," Joe finds himself now looking

for summer work that will pay his tuition at the technical school that has accepted him for next year. He would like to work in a factory but is not yet eighteen and will have to "stick to something like a stock boy" for the time being. When he was a high school freshman, he imagined quite a different summer after high school graduation. "This is going to sound kind of stupid—I thought cross-country bike riding was the thing. Me and three other kids, I thought. No cars, just a pack on your back and Wheeee! Take off for California, right?" A few excursions into New Hampshire showed him what that trip would require. "In those first years I thought you could do it in a week, but now I've heard of kids doing it in a month. It's a long haul." For now, Joe is committed to the long haul of achievement, confirming the struggles and hope of his family.

"You know the kids better than you know your own brother"

It is at home that Joe's future has taken shape and has been gauged against his father's past and his brothers' possibilities. Yet much of Joe's time has been spent with other kids—outside the house where he now lives and, for most of his life, on the corners and streets of his old, now demolished, neighborhood.

Joe mourns the loss of the kids in his old neighborhood, even though some of them are part of the new group with whom he hangs out on Friday nights in the empty lot near his house:

> I grew up with all those kids, and when you break up like that after being together for so many years—like you know the kids better than you know your own brother. When you break up, you feel completely lost, 'cause you don't know nobody, and now you have to start all over and make new friends and everything.

Joe says he has met two kinds of kids at Cityville High. Most are "pretty straight," planning and working toward their future jobs; the rest are "goof-offs," who "don't give a damn about anything. If they're lucky, they'll get a good job.

21

If not, they'll go down the drain." When Joe talks about his friends, however, he does not describe them in terms of their ambition or lack of it, but in terms of what they do together. "Some like hockey, some like different sports, but most like the same music — hard rock music. Everybody likes going drinking Friday nights."

Joe does not judge his friends by the standards of achievement he sets for himself, and because he is in "a special section" of the General course, "sort of like the College course," he hardly sees his friends during school. Joe says at one point that "the majority of my friends want to go to college," yet later, when he talks angrily about the effects of the tracking system on students in the lower sections of the General course, that is where his friends turn out to be.

Joe is incensed about how unfairly his friends are treated. In contrast to the "College kids," who get the best teachers, Joe believes that the "General kids" get the worst deal. "I think that the city has something in their mind, like when a person is in General C — that would be something like sheet metal — they think when you're in there, you're a dummy and you're going to drop out of school. So right away they put in a lousy teacher. That's stupid." Joe says that the kids who get such treatment end up feeling that they aren't smart enough "to go out and be on some kind of job," and that the tracking system is unjust. "If you've done badly in junior high, they put you in the low sections. Now that's stupid, 'cause everybody in junior high school goofs off, right?"

Being an ambitious kid, one who is college bound, is for Joe Mendoza a distinguishing mark, a sign of personal character. Joe tends to extend the college insignia to all his friends, despite their low positions in school. In making this judgment Joe is saying that his friends are dear to him and that he considers them people of character, different from the "deadbeats" and "goof-offs" he has seen. Joe feels that his friends are likely to "become somebodies" despite the judgments of uncaring school personnel. He does not imagine that his future will diverge from theirs.

"Slip them a couple of hundred and they'll shut up"

The compassion, wariness, and strong belief in equality, opportunity, and hard work that Joe expresses in describing his friends and his hopes also emerge when he talks about American society. Joe cares about the future of the country and sees deep divisions of interest and power between rich, middle class, and poor. Joe believes that large, wealthy corporations —"the companies," as he calls them—have gained illegitimate power over politicians and over national life. He worries about the growing pollution of the environment and the ability of the companies to thwart the passage of laws that would penalize them for polluting. Joe feels that corruption pervades local politics as well and is exposed only when "some reporter breaks his way in there and sees what's going on." Joe is critical too of a legal system in which those who have "money and political pull" go "scot free," whereas "if you're a poor guy and can't afford a lawyer, you're going to be spending the rest of your life in jail."

Joe wishes things would change for the better, but he is pessimistic. No one in power was willing to listen to what members of his old neighborhood had to say against the highway bulldozers, so he imagines that someone his age who voiced an opinion against "the politicians" would be "kicked out" without a hearing. "The only time they will listen to you is if you bring them to court."

Joe clearly identifies with "the people" in their efforts to have their needs met and to keep the companies and politicians honest. He believes that what Congress does usually benefits "the middle-class guy," and this means that "the poor guy's probably getting screwed out of something." "Middle-class people," he believes, "have more of a chance at stuff. They have the money — no, not the money, but they have a chance to try and get it, 'cause they have the charge accounts. They're more likely to get accreditation than poor people. I think that poor people are being deprived of the right kind of education."

Joe cares about poor people. He feels that they should have more than they do, but he is also concerned that hardworking individuals be rewarded for their efforts. Thus, when he is asked what he would think of a law that would set limits on the amount of money families could make and keep, and would distribute all extra income to the poor, Joe is enthusiastic but immediately cautious: "That would be great. It would help out the poor people a lot. But then the poor people might figure, 'Why should we work when we can get this other guy's stuff?' This guy who's working like a dog!" Joe imagines that the poor would vote for such a measure, but that no one else would, and he thinks that the poor would also vote for another suggested law, that everyone in America get the same income. Joe himself opposes this one. It wouldn't be fair, he argues, for a janitor to make the same income as a research scientist or "some smart guy." He imagines that "the middle and upper classes wouldn't like that law too much, because it would pull them down."

Joe suspects that the desire to take the easy way out is strong in everyone—people at the top and people on the bottom of the social ladder. When he is discussing how the companies buy off local and national politicians, he claims, "All they have to do is slip them a couple of hundred and they'll shut up." And then he adds, "But that's natural—I would do it too." In the same way, Joe can picture himself in the position of someone on welfare and imagines how easy it would be to want never to work again. "One day when I'm missing from school, I just stay home. The next day I don't feel like going back. I figure that's like welfare. Once you get it, you're not going to want to go back to work. You figure you've got the food on the table and everything." Joe believes that welfare should be available "for people who really, really need it," but he is reluctant to endorse proposals for income redistribution. Giving people money they have not earned, he thinks, would destroy their incentive to work in their own behalf.

Joe believes that individuals are substantially helped if they have money and connections, but he also believes that there is "equal opportunity" in most places. "If you are serious and not just goofing off," he explains, "I think everybody has a chance to try any job he wants to try. Right now, the way I see it is that if you try hard, if you want to do something badly enough, you're going to do it. You're going to get through all the obstacles and everything."

"Someone's going to get greedy and take advantage of the people"

Joe first responds to the "commune picture" by saying, "Well, it kind of shows everybody free and more happy like, but I don't know — these people are *out* of everything. I don't want to be like that — just living completely alone, off the land." And then Joe is asked if the picture has anything to do with the way America is going.

> I think it's going for a change. No more strict stuff — more freedom.

> *Do you think this is a good thing?*
> Freedom is only good when — you know, you
> can't have a lot of it, 'cause if you have a real lot
> of it, everything will all come to pieces. You've
> got to have somebody chiding you, keeping you in
> place, but not putting a lot of pressure on you.

When Joe talks more about the commune and also about the food co-op that flourished briefly in his former neighborhood, we hear how skeptical he is about the chances for social reform. Joe imagines that people founded the commune because they were "fed up with all that's going on. They can't stand living in the city with all the pollution, all the corruption. And they probably just want to try it out to see if it can work." Joe thinks that if "everyone pulled their own weight and helped along, it would last," but there would be many difficulties. For one thing, other people "would come and look at them as if they were in a zoo. 'What are these people, nuts, trying to live like that?'"

And Joe remembers the downfall of the food co-op in his old neighborhood:

> We used to belong to one. That was fantastic.
> You'd get good food at low prices 'cause there
> was no middleman. The middleman screws you all
> the time because he jacks up the prices. You buy

> direct — each week one lady would go to pick up
> the orders and distribute it. . . . It was started by
> a lady across the street, who later moved. She
> called us, we called my aunt, we all got in. But
> then the thing fell apart. It just caved in.

Joe is not sure exactly why the food co-op failed, but he
imagines that the inevitability of human greed had something
to do with it. "I don't know, but every time you get something
like this, someone's going to get greedy and take advantage of
the people. And I think that's probably what happened."

Just as Joe Mendoza wants to achieve direction without
pressure, just as he wants equality without giveaways, he
values freedom only when it exists without license. Human
beings, he believes, are easily led astray. They are vulnerable
to bribes, to sloth, and to giving up. Joe has much hope for
himself and other young people who work hard in a time that
is more favorable than his parents' time was, but he has little
optimism that, given the nature of human nature, fundamental social problems will be resolved.

The Nature of Ambition in Cityville

Joe's story is one of the starkest of all, portraying in bold
strokes the central themes in the lives of the promising working-class youth of Cityville. No one but Joe has a father whose
job gets under the actual skin of his wife and children, but
almost everyone tells of the importance of a father's work to
the life of his family. Joe's parents are particularly insistent
that he "straighten up," but all these youth know that their
parents are resolved that their children's fates will be better
than their own. In his pride at having become ambitious —
unlike the many youth in Cityville who "don't care" — Joe
speaks for almost everyone else.

Not all the promising young men in Cityville are as certain as Joe about the kind of work they want, but they all share
his desire to avoid the back-breaking and morale-crushing
jobs of their fathers, to escape being dependent on the whims
of bosses and the fluctuations of the economy. They are considering careers in accounting, architectural draughting,

banking, aviation, electronics, and law enforcement; there is a would-be doctor, lawyer, dentist, and worker on an oil tanker.

The promising young women of Cityville want their future lives to be less limited than their mothers' have been: "I see my mother cooking meals and making beds, and that's all." They want to develop interests and work of their own, postponing the marriages and children that, if they come too early, fill up the rest of one's life. College is the unquestioned prelude to the more independent lives these young women envision for themselves: after college graduation they will begin their careers and then, once they have made a good start, they will take time out to marry and have children, returning to work when their children enter school. Most of these young women plan to become public school teachers, but some consider becoming airline stewardesses, secretaries, physical therapists. One young woman, whom we will later meet, hopes to be a doctor.

It has become important to all these youth that the jobs they consider for themselves lie within the realm of what is possible. John Coutermarsh, who thinks he might become a lawyer but hasn't yet decided, speaks for most when he says, "I never set any big goals I knew I couldn't reach." This is a statement of pride for Cityville youth, not an admission of cowardice or sloth. Becoming practical is considered an achievement; it indicates that one cares enough about oneself and one's parents not to take chances with one's life.

Just as Joe Mendoza regards his dream of a cross-country bike trip as a childish thing, now to be put away, so do others make their peace with their future plans. When Joan Leahy talks about how she gave up her "fantasy" of becoming a forest ranger, it is with relief that the saner voice of her mother has prevailed:

> She brought out the impractical sides. "Where
> are you going to find this sort of thing?" And, "It
> costs more than going to teachers' college." Or,
> "What are you going to do when you get out — go
> to some park and say, 'Hey, do you need a
> ranger?'"

27

Joan now plans to become an elementary school teacher. Like Joe and several others, she worries about her younger brother, who still dreams impractical dreams. And she joins her voice to her mother's in a chorus of guidance to him.

> He's really funny — he got off on a loony, you know. He got really interested in philosophy and he was all for it. "Well, you gotta know what you want to do." So he says, "I guess I'll take a liberal arts course." And so she was upset about that, 'cause there aren't many people who are going to pay you to do *that*. You can't sit around. I think he should get a job too. You can't philosophize for a living.

Most of these young people believe that their parents have "cared" enough about them to "push" them in the right direction. In accepting that push, in deciding to become "somebodies," they feel they return that care. Even when they have misgivings about the routes their parents propose or the advice they give, they are convinced that their parents speak with their children's interests at heart and out of first-hand knowledge of how the real world works.

Going to college — whether to four-year or junior colleges or to institutes for technical training — is the next step urged upon these young people by their parents. For all of them, college is an option that must be seriously considered. Not only is further education promoted by parents and teachers as the means to a good job and financial security, but having proved oneself able to go to college is an insignia of distinction, a sign of personal character.

But unlike the young women, many of the young men are unsure whether they should actually go to college; unlike Joe Mendoza, they have not found a clear career direction and a school to prepare them for it. Some are not sure they want a "college-type job"; they suspect that they will prefer working with their hands to sitting behind a desk. Others are interested in college subjects but cannot see how studying them will lead to a job. As one young man puts it, "I don't think anyone is going to pay me to write history." All the young men who are skeptical about college fear to waste any time and money on schooling that will not pay off. Yet they cannot help feeling that not going would deprive them of an option that society values and that they have earned.

We can see this uncertainty in Dave Greene, who has found models for the kind of person he wants to be in his mother's brothers. Dave's uncles are carpenters who stand at the center of a large, vibrant family. Dave wants his future life to be like theirs, filled with activity and family: he wants to build a house "with my own hands" for "fifteen kids. That's why I need a lot of money." Dave imagines that he would enjoy working as a carpenter or a mechanic and says that his grades have dropped in the past year: "I don't have as much confidence in my brain as I do in my hands." But he thinks he will probably attend a private liberal arts college next year for two reasons. First, his uncles have told Dave how vulnerable they feel as carpenters: "They fear that something will go wrong with their legs or their backs." The second reason is his father's urgent desire to see him in college. Mr. Greene worked for years as a salesman for a plumbing supply company, spent a year in the hospital with severe heart problems, and was then, according to Dave, "let go" by the "rich people" in charge of the company. Now, with the help of an old friend, he has found steady money and some security through a union job in the boiler room of the subway system. Mr. Greene is so eager for his son to go to a good private college that he is willing to pay the steep tuition.

A similar leaning toward college is expressed by Tim Johnson, who used to think he'd like "being behind a desk, like an accountant or something," but now thinks he'd prefer manual work to "beating my brains out against some figures." Tim makes good money at his part-time window-washing job and likes it. "Even in the cold, we do windows up until Christmas outdoors. I like work where you have to put yourself out a little bit and you come home and you're tired. It feels good." It also, from what Tim has learned, makes you good money. Tim is impressed by the salaries made by the firemen who work beside him, moonlighting on their jobs. "A fireman doesn't seem like the greatest life, but one guy's got a new Buick, his wife drives a three-year-old Chevy. He has his own home, his own trailer." Tim's girlfriend's father, a welder, tells Tim how well he could do if he came to work with him. "People say, 'Oh, an ironworker, poor slob up there trying to get those rivets in in the freezing cold.' But they make 300 dollars a week. You might make a lot more than a poor executive banging his head, getting an ulcer behind his desk." But other people in Tim's life press him to get a college degree before making any final decision. His boss —"he's like an uncle to me"— refuses to give him a full-time job for next year. "He thinks I should go to college, so he's sort of giving me a little shove." Another person who encourages him is a doctor for whom Tim has done odd jobs for many years. Most important to Tim is the experience of his mother, who works as a bookkeeper and who felt that she "couldn't take the pressure" of being head bookkeeper in her company because she lacked the experience of college and a degree. Mrs. Johnson tells her son that college will give him the confidence to handle life. Tim thinks that he will try it: "Because I know that once I get out of school, if I don't go to college my first year, then I'll never go back."

Keeping Connected

These young peoples' ambitions are to find good jobs and make something of themselves, and to keep connected to their lives in Cityville. They do not want to become different kinds of people, nor do they want to separate themselves from those they now know and love. The modesty of their ambitions helps them feel that they are not presuming or reaching beyond what hard-working young people might reasonably hope for.

Remaining oneself while becoming somebody does not leave you open to the charge — a serious one in Cityville — that you are a selfish or pushy person, that you think you are better than others. Most of these promising youth feel that they are different not only from "goof-offs" and "dead-beats," but also from the "snobs," the kids who think they are "upper than us." John Coutermarsh describes this sort of person when he talks about members of the leading clique at the high school: "They've got very large mouths and are always pushing to the front. They make sure that they serve their own interests first. Being different just for the sake of being different." John imagines that these students want to graduate "first in their class" and then go on to become "president of the board" of something. They want to have the power to influence others — "to push other people, well, not to push, but to *suggest* things to others." And John thinks they will succeed. "They'll get their own way, they usually do. But I don't think they'll go as far as they expect. They'll go far enough."

This image of selfish and aggressive ambition is despised by these young people. They are afraid that high ambition makes one prey to the standards of others and requires that one forfeit independence and integrity. When Bob O'Neil thinks about how nice it would be to move out to the suburbs for their space and quiet, he worries about the pressures his older brothers feel there to "keep up" with the neighborhood. Bob vows that if he ever does make that move, he will keep his mind on who he is and what he really wants.

Remaining oneself means that one can continue to be involved with the people one cares for, to maintain the relationships that have brought one pleasure and hope. Most of these young people remember vivid childhoods in the neighborhood, where they met playmates who were to become life-long friends. The corners, streets, and backyards were full of noise and movement — the shouts of children playing stickball and street hockey, the steady background rumble of cars and trucks going by, the whistle of the trains that cut through the city, the cries of squabbling children, and the yells and calls of their mothers. At first they played with friends all day long and then — when some went off to public school and others to parochial school — looked forward to being back in the neighborhood just as soon as school was over.

If parents were friendly with other adults in the neighborhood, children grew up feeling part of a small network of supportive people. At "the Point," Tim Johnson's family and the others looked out for one another. Work was unsteady. "Did you get paid today?" they would ask each other. And if the answer was no, the entire family would be carted off for supper at a neighbor's house. When Tim's family moved from one house to another in the Point, "It was like a parade. Everyone would pick something up and carry it over." And parents were able to take a few days' vacation in the summer, leaving their children at each other's homes and then returning the favor the next weekend. In John Coutermarsh's neighborhood, the sharing focused—and still does—on bargains. "All the people in my neighborhood—like if one person finds a great buy in applesauce, she'll buy a ton of it and spread it around. Then the next week, the other person will buy something else."

What is familiar is not always benign—one learns whom to avoid in the neighborhood as well as the friends one can count on. The individual bully encountered in childhood later becomes part of a group of neighborhood toughs. Several young men were challenged to fight over and over again by the "corner boys" on their blocks. Fred Meegan's experience is typical: he was 10 when he first had to face those boys, and as he grew older, he began to define himself as different from them:

> They were always getting into fights. I got into
> fights but not all the time. And seems like when I
> walked into the neighborhood, it was them
> against me. They drink every night. I go out
> drinking occasionally but never splurge. They
> miss a lot of things. Sort of limit themselves to the
> corner or the poolhall.

As promising young people get older, the neighborhood confronts them with another danger—heavy drugs and those who use them. Many have smoked some pot, but most think of themselves and their friends as social drinkers who steer away from drugs:

> Down at the park there's kids that take dope, kids
> that have been shipped home from Vietnam for
> dope. One kid died just a few weeks ago. He
> OD'd on heroin. But most of the kids I hang
> around with, they're through with dope. The
> only thing they do is drink.

32

When one young man found out, the summer before his senior year, that his close buddies had become regular drug users, he was horrified, and still feels overwhelmed by shock and a new loneliness.

Tim Johnson's family moved away from the Point several years ago, but because he makes enough money from his window-washing job to have a car, Tim drives over every night to hang out with his friends at the park across from his old neighborhood. There is "a mixture of all kinds of kids — from 13-year-olds to 21-year-olds — at the park. Each kid has his own group. The older kids stick with themselves, and the kids who take dope don't try to get others on it. We drink up in the back of the park. We don't bother anybody." Tim explains that the older kids protect the younger ones. "If an 18-year-old picks on a 13-year-old, the 18 or 19-year-olds will talk to the kid and make him pay damages." But if a younger kid has trouble with someone his own age, no one intervenes: "A kid should be able to handle that."

Tim's close friends are a group of 10 to 15 kids, many of whom have known each other since they were children. Once the group decided to help one member become more outgoing. "This kid was so shy he worked the night of his senior prom. A couple of kids got together and decided they had to pull Pete in and get him going. They took him bowling and got him to hang around with them. Now he drinks — he was never like anybody, he never did anything — but now he goes out with girls." Tim's friends pool their resources — a few have cars and the others help pay for gas — and they all look out for each other. "If I have a problem — with my girlfriend, my parents — if I need money — if you have a problem you're ashamed of — among all of us, we find some way to help out. It's like, say you're in Vietnam, you become extremely close to the ones you're buddying with. You're like brothers."

Life in the neighborhood gives many Cityville youth an early sense of place, where adults and children live in close, lively, and sometimes problematic relationships. A second source of early continuity with other people is the family — and family in Cityville usually means more than just parents and siblings. It is common for young people in Cityville to live upstairs or downstairs from grandparents and to feel in constant touch with the lives, problems, and celebrations of aunts, uncles, and cousins. Dave Greene's family is typical: his father's mother lived in his home until she died; his mother's large family live and work in or close to Cityville and often gather at her parents' house, just around the corner from the Greene's. When Dave was young, the whole family spent their summer vacations together in a large house in Maine. "When I was small," he remembers, "everywhere you looked there was a cousin."

Most of the young women depend less on the neighborhood for their friendships than the boys do: they do not seem to hang out as much on the corner or in playgrounds and parks. It is in the family that they make the early important friendships in their lives. For a few young women, the closeness they feel to their first cousins mirrors their mothers' closeness to *their* sisters. Lois Gendreau's cousins down the street are "like sisters" to her, and her own mother's ties to *her* sisters remain strong. The Gendreaus once moved out of Cityville to Lakewood, 28 miles away, "because my father thought he'd like to try country life." Lois has fond memories of Lakewood; she loved having land around their house and skating in winter over the "little swamp" in the backyard. From having to ride five miles each way on the school bus and taking responsibility for many household chores, she feels that she "grew up a lot that year." But her family moved back to Cityville the next summer. Mrs. Gendreau had become ill and felt too isolated from her sisters.

Like the neighborhood, one's family is familiar and appreciated, but not always easy. Dave Greene loves his mother's family, but his father's mother made his life at home hellish. He believes that she hated him and blamed him for the mental retardation of his little brother. Several of the young women hold their grandmothers responsible for the unhappiness of their mothers and for problems in their parents' marriages. One young woman describes the abrupt decline in her family's income when her father was cheated out of the family business by his brothers-in-law. Another tells of the difficulties caused by the presence of her aunt and cousins as tenants in the downstairs apartment of her family's house.

For young people with older brothers and sisters, the

family provides further lessons about paths to follow and paths to avoid. Bob O'Neil is the youngest of nine children and has decided not to go work for the telephone company, where his father and two of his older brothers have worked for years. "My older brother Charlie, he's worked his way up and now he's a foreman, but I think he's really as high as you can go and he's in his thirties, so it seems like he's stuck." Another older brother has taken a more entrepreneurial tack and now works as a free-lance draughtsman. Bob thinks he'll try that route and plans to enroll in the technical college that this brother attended.

Older siblings serve not only as role models, but sometimes as important sources of support. John Coutermarsh is also a youngest child. "I will be the first one to go to college, and that kind of gives me the distinction. Everybody takes an interest in what I do. When I bring home a report card, everybody runs to see it, you know." He is buoyed by the enthusiasm of his four much older brothers. "They didn't go to college, and my father didn't go to school, and they all want me to make up for it."

The conclusion these Cityville youth have drawn from life in their neighborhoods and families is that it is important to sustain relationships that have already been tried and tested and found good. They have seen that when families move from one Cityville neighborhood to another — because of evictions, obnoxious landlords, a chance to get a better apartment or to buy a house — the old important relationships between adults and children endure. As they face the end of high school, these young people do not intend to say good-bye to the people for whom they care or the kinds of people they have themselves become.

Linking the Generations

Just as continuity in relationships is valued, continuity between the generations is an important part of these young people's view of the future. In hoping to go farther than their parents did, they are realizing their parents' dreams, and they view their parents as worthy of respect for having done as well as they did. They take a historical perspective and generally interpret their parents' struggles and personal limitations as appropriate to the previous generation — one that followed the Great Depression and required that its children quit high school to help support the whole family. Similarly, they explain their parents' moral rigidity and closemindedness as products of that historical time. These Cityville youth feel that they have become mature enough to sympathize with the problems their parents have had — on the job, with alcoholism, with understanding the looser moral standards of today.

Looking ahead, these young people easily talk of themselves as future parents. And they consider the consequences of their choices for their future children. When Joe Mendoza talks about how he wants his life to be different from his parents', he thinks of a kitchen free of his father's domination and free of the dirt that comes from working with asbestos, a room where his own children will eat and talk more freely than he can now. Just as they feel they confirm their parents' lives through their own achievements, these young people feel that they are working so that their own children's realities will be better than theirs have been.

Tim Johnson hated the indifference and hostility of his alcoholic father but two years ago — before his father died — he realized that his father had been a victim of diabetes and hard luck, and forgave him. Tim says that he himself wants "a successful life." When he thinks about what will be most important to achieving success, he decides: "It takes two. If you're going to be married you have to find someone who will help you. You don't want to come home and be tired and have someone tell you you're useless. A little pat on the back won't hurt." And then he adds, "I think I'll end up like my father. Not a drinker, but I've seen pictures of him when he was younger and he looked like me. And people always say, 'When Tommy was in his twenties, he'd do anything for you.' He was a great guy and people really like him, and that's what I want — people to really like me."

Tim wants his future to be an improvement over the life he has now:

Money is a worry to everyone. I just don't want it
to be a problem. When I was younger, things
were really bad, tight living. But now they've
gotten better. It's not my mother's fault — we
can't overspend really. But we never go without
anything we need, like she's going out and buying
a dryer. But she always worries about bills and
whether she can get them paid. We talk a lot
about bills. She has to talk to someone and I'm
the oldest. My father left no insurance. I just
want to have a life where money will be no problem.

Part of Tim's strategy for his future is to buy a house. "We've
never owned our own home. My mother had chances to buy
but she never did, and now they've gone out the window. And
that's one thing I want to do — buy a home from the beginning. When the kids are older, I'll have a place for myself
without rent."

Tim is unsure where his house and family will be. Like
many others, he assumes that for the sake of his future children, he should live in a more suburban place than Cityville.
"I've thought about it and I want to live in some place like
Yardley or Fremont, a nice cozy place where it's quiet, no
trucks zooming by every night." But life in Cityville has been
good to Tim, and he adds, "But then if I moved out of Cityville
I'd go crazy. Kids in Cityville — you see them playing baseball, hockey in the streets. You go up to these other places and
it's dead. The birds chirping, that's about it. I couldn't take
that."

The Challenge of Cityville High

When these young people remember the start of high school,
they think of the jolt they felt at confronting for the first time
in their lives a large and indifferent institution. Before this,
they had left the familiarity of neighborhood and family for
small elementary schools — public and parochial — and then
moved on to much larger junior high schools. But it was not
until they entered Cityville High that they felt overwhelmed

by the experience of being anonymous, known only by the identification numbers and the labels—"college," "business," or "general"—they were given. They tell of scheduling mix-ups that took weeks to unravel, of teachers who had long ago stopped trying to teach, and of administrators who ignored their requests for help.

One young man chose to step outside his family's tradition of parochial schooling precisely because he wanted to face the challenge of being "more on my own" in high school. Taught only by nuns and meeting only the Cityville kids whose parents sent them to Catholic schools, Bob O'Neil felt sheltered. He believes that he was exceptionally unprepared for the first weeks at Cityville High, but his account speaks to almost everyone's experience:

> Coming in to the school, people would say, this is your student number and you do this and you do that. Like they give you courses that you didn't even sign up for because you couldn't fit in with another class. . . . So I go down to the guidance office—there's just hundreds of people waiting to get in to see her. She's old. You try to explain to her. But she just has what's in front of her. She doesn't know what happened to you or nothing. So all she can go by is your number and your records, so she says, "Here's your schedule."

Bob felt the same sense of impotence in class: "Sometimes you just feel like telling the teacher where to go or something, but you don't. You sit there and he makes you look stupid by yelling at you and you just sit there. You can't do nothing."

Floundering during his first semester, Bob flunked several subjects and then switched from the College to the General course. Since then, he has regularly made the honor roll and is convinced that learning to make his way through Cityville High has helped him accomplish a major goal—taking responsibility for himself. The impersonality of the school continues to take its toll on him: his guidance counselor knows him still "only through my grades" and has neglected him. Only recently she told Bob that to enter the technical college he has chosen for next fall, he will have to go to summer school to take courses he never knew he needed. Those young people who managed to find someone to give the right advice or inspire them to learn feel very lucky. A single guidance counselor, who had once been a teacher and was exceptionally caring, was cited by several of them as having saved their high school careers.

Most teachers at Cityville High are remembered as boring, irrelevant, and inclined to go through the motions — reading from textbooks, giving quizzes, and keeping order in the classroom. A few younger teachers are cited as vivid exceptions who cared enough about their students to risk the administration's disapproval by discussing important, interesting issues in the classroom and helping their students learn to think. One is now in trouble with the head of his department and another was recently fired for being "too radical" in her Problems of Democracy classes. Students who drew up a petition to have her reinstated were ignored, reinforcing the general conviction that Cityville High School is an unresponsive place where only a few exceptional adults care about what students think and do.

But despite their criticisms of Cityville High, these young people feel that they have accomplished a great deal during their high school years. They think of high school as the means to ends that are crucial, and they place a high priority on learning to cope with difficulty. Part of their sense of success comes from having overcome the obstacles they faced in making their way through.

During high school they have also learned where they stand in relation to a larger universe of young people. They confidently make use of a set of categories to describe the range of youth from all over Cityville whom they have encountered. Most of them identify a small group of cheerleaders and star athletes who are part of the "leading crowd," a smaller, more marginal group of "freaks" and "brains," and a large majority of "regular kids," a group within which most of them enthusiastically place themselves. High school has also given them another system of distinctions — the labels applied by the school to young people on the basis of its assessment of their probable futures. The youth in our sample feel that they have stacked up well in these terms; almost all of them feel that as part of the College track or the "top sections" of the Business and General tracks, they have been considered promising and given advantages.

They regard the tracking system as unfairly stereotyping students and creating rigid distinctions: it is impossible to take classes outside one's track, and except in homeroom, where students are seated alphabetically, one sees only students in one's own track. These Cityville youth believe that the very students who need the most help become lost in the General track with its inferior courses and teachers. Like Joe Mendoza, these young people are glad to be in the better part of a school that is not all that good, but are concerned about the treatment less favored students receive. They fear that without good teaching, such students will tend to "accept whatever comes along," stagnate in their lives, or, worse, turn to drugs and drink.

Being ambitious and bright is satisfying, and these youth feel that they are making gains on the future. But they have also learned that doing very well in school can be a burden. One young man heading for a career in accounting switched from the College to the Business track so that he could learn accounting methods; no longer permitted to take College English, he found himself bored by his Business English class, snubbed by his former classmates in the College track, and resented by his classmates in the Business track, where he gets "all As." He also resents the discrimination against Business-track students in the computing of rank orders for his class: his As are worth fewer points than College-track As. Few others star in all their classes, but most have learned that "breaking the curve" is resented. "If you flunk a test, you have plenty of friends. If you get the highest marks, you have no friends at all until the next test."

For the young women school has been a crucial arena for gaining independence. They have become involved in school-sponsored activities—the Drama Club, yearbook, the National Honor Society—and they have made new friends in those activities and in their classes. Although the girls are as critical as the boys of the teaching and guidance offered at Cityville High, their activities and friendships at school have aided their attempts to move beyond their mothers' prohibitions. One young woman tells of the difference it made in her life when she became friends with the girl seated next to her in homeroom class, who had lived in another town and was more sophisticated than she, and whose friendship gave her the courage to confront her mother, "who wants to keep me a little girl." Another young woman, given the part of "Hate" in a school play, found it a chance to be "bad" in a legitimate way and a help in her fight against her mother's attempts to make her "the perfect little lady."

For almost all the young men, school is considered a separate matter from the rest of life; High school is perceived simply as a necessary step toward the future: "The purpose of high school is to get a piece of paper for the purpose of getting a job; in order to get the piece of paper, you have to accept the things the school forces on you."

Even for those who, like Joe Mendoza, have become interested in school subjects related to their prospective careers and put in many hours on homework and special projects, it is the time spent with friends that stands out in their minds as most important. Plans for the future, school labels, parental expectations — all these are considered irrelevant to life with friends. When Bob O'Neil thinks of what is important to him, he talks of his plans for the future and about his neighborhood friends, most of whom remained in parochial school. He talks of what they do together, the sports they play, the "riding around at night." He says that he alone among them has "shaped up" and begun to take the future seriously, but that fact does not matter to him. He says approvingly, "None of them are real smart anyway. They know that. They just try to be themselves."

Work and Love

Work and love, two new experiences of the past few years, have given many of these youth chances to discover — outside the authority of family and school — more about themselves and what they want.

Everyone thinks a great deal about the work he or she

wants to do in the future, and many put in long hours now on part-time jobs like scooping ice cream, selling in stores, loading supermarket merchandise. The two types of work are seldom related: only Tim Johnson, who thinks he might like to continue washing windows and cleaning offices, and Tina Stelluto, who would like to teach dancing after high school, see their present jobs as possible rehearsals for the real thing. Right now most of these young people work so that they can save a portion of their earnings for college tuition and have some money of their own to buy clothes and other things they want.

What comes along with the job, however, sometimes turns out to be as important as the money. Proving that long, sometimes boring hours can be endured, that struggles with unfair employers can be waged, that one can be competent and get paid for it — these are considered accomplishments. Sometimes employers and fellow workers become advisors on how to "wise up," and when they've worked a while at their jobs, these young people may themselves advise younger, newer employees. Tim Johnson, whose father was a helpless and hostile alcoholic, found an encouraging "uncle" in his boss, and several other young men whose relationships with their fathers are troubled have looked, usually less successfully, for supportive bosses. The money that goes into savings for the future bolsters attempts to gain respect from parents. And occasionally it is spent with the same results. One young man tells of how his father taught him to become independent. "For years he said I couldn't have my drums, because he wouldn't have all that noise in the house. Finally I saved up the money to buy them and took them up to my room, shut the door, and started to play. All he said when I came down for supper was 'What took you so long?'"

In romantic relationships some of these young people also find important lessons for their development. For many, such relationships are still something to look forward to, and a few young men worry that they should already be more comfortable with girls. But most of the young men and women date and meet members of the opposite sex at parties. For those who regularly see only one person, that person's preferences and desires may be a significant influence.

42

We can see the influences of boyfriend and work in the life of Tina Stelluto, who thinks her development took a critical turn in response to both. Up until the tenth grade, Tina was concerned with "what everyone else thought" and with being "the most popular girl." She was a cheerleader and felt that as a member of the elite crowd of students in student council, varsity football, and the cheerleading crowd, she could dress and behave only in ways prescribed by the group. She dated a basketball star and spoke only to other luminaries. As a sophomore she achieved the coup of being invited to the senior prom.

Her present boyfriend, Jim, was never part of the leading clique, and Tina turned him down when he first asked her out. But soon after the prom, Tina got "bored" with the popular scene and tired of her senior date. "I started dating my boyfriend, and that was the end of all those kids." Tina says that this change in her life came naturally. "It just happened—I got sick of all the make-believe." And Jim has strengthened her resolution. "He didn't like me to fool people. He thinks I should be myself." For example, if Tina wore dungarees because "everybody else did," Jim would say, "That isn't you." Her present girlfriends, like Tina herself, "don't feel they have to belong to anything or put on any acts. You can talk about anything. You can disagree with each other."

Tina feels that her new independence and maturity also have roots in another aspect of her life—her work as a dancer. Having "taken" and taught dancing for six years, she became part of a line of chorus girls last year in a Boston night club and was sent to New York City one day to buy costumes. Tina has become savvy about the world of "showbiz"—the financial side of it, the endurance it demands, and the experience of being continually propositioned by male customers. "This sounds kind of conceited, but I feel more mature in a way than most kids at the high school. Not because I'm smarter, but because I've been through more."

The money she makes from dancing buys Tina clothes and the chance to go on to college. Her deepest wish is to open a dancing school right after she finishes high school. "I don't want to go to college, really. I'd rather open a dancing school, but they always fall through." So Tina thinks she will become a schoolteacher unless the present scarcity of teaching positions gets worse. Her father would prefer that she become a nurse, "where I can always get a job." But Tina feels that she can make her own choice because she has saved enough money to pay for college.

At the same time that Tina is making her college plans, she worries about a future with Jim. "He's kind of mixed up. He doesn't care about anything. At least I care about school and my job right now." Jim has done "lousy" in high school and dislikes both of the two jobs he has now, in a supermarket and a hardware store.

> He doesn't know what he's doing. If it ever
> comes to marriage, I don't know what I'm going
> to do with him. Because who could have a half-
> decent income unless he's lucky enough to get a
> good job, and I don't see how he is. He doesn't
> care. He just goes out to work and works. I'm
> making him sound lousy. He isn't really lousy.

Tina's relationship with Jim points to an interesting paradox. Although almost all the young women are sure that they do not want to get "trapped" into early marriages, many have steady boyfriends whose lack of seriousness about the future makes them wonder about the effect that marrying these boys would have on their own lives. And although most of the young men stress how important the women they marry will be to their future success, only Tim Johnson has a steady girlfriend. She is a year older than he, working in an office where many of her colleagues are married. "She's got marriage on her mind," Tim says, "but I tell her, if she wants to marry me, she'll have to wait. I'm not ready to get serious."

The Costs of Being Different: Aiming High, Taking Risks

When being practical signifies that one cares for oneself and others, it is not easy to take big risks. The stakes are high enough already for these Cityville youth who know how important their future jobs will be and how hard their parents have struggled to bring them to this point. They want to know before they start out how one step will lead to the next. They have kept their ambitions within reach and within the limits of what is familiar to themselves and their parents, for they plan to move ahead with the blessings and support of those who care for them.

A few tell of wanting to move higher than the rest do, or of dreaming dreams that are not shared by others. In the life-stories of two would-be doctors and one young man who gave up dreams of being a revolutionary, we see the consequences in Cityville of having and not having support for high aspirations, and the vulnerability that results from trying to become "somebody" when one feels different from everyone else.

Tony Sambataro is the most ardent striver in the sample; he works 25 hours a week as a soda jerk and is so diligent in his studies that he has scarcely any time left to spend with his neighborhood friends or family. Tony feels that he is sacrificing "everything" now so that he can pay his tuition at a private college, and he expects to continue this relentless schedule until he has become a doctor. He chose this route at the start of high school when he suddenly realized, "If I don't do good now — that's it. This is my last chance." Tony thrives on being challenged. He is angry at Cityville High for not moving him up into the top English class, a place he believes he has earned. "It's not that I feel I've got to be the best at everything — it's just that if I feel I can do something, I want to be able to do it. Don't just keep me down like a vegetable!" Though the college he plans to attend has a fine reputation and has promised Tony $1,200 toward next year's tuition, he wonders if he should have aimed higher and applied to a more prestigious university.

Tony's high ambitions are sustained not only by his family but by his visions of what he will do when he finishes medical school: he plans to move with his parents to Italy, where they have bought a house in their hometown. There, Tony believes, he can both work as a doctor and spend "a reasonable amount of leisure time in the sun." The Sambataros immigrated to Cityville when Tony was two; they have spent vacations in Italy and keep in close touch with relatives who live near them in Cityville. Life in Italy, Tony feels, is closer to nature, less focused than American life on accumulating material goods.

Tony draws support from his family's life together; his belief that he will join them in Italy affirms the Sambataros' sense of what's important. Tony admires his father:

> My father never went to college. He's a simple
> man, but he's *happy*. He has his family, his own
> house that he owns. Sure he has his worries,
> everybody does. He works very hard and he has a
> great feeling of accomplishment because he has
> worked very hard—long years too. And I can't
> see anything wrong with it all. And the man
> didn't go to college and he has a great life.

Yet Tony says that if he were to become a mechanic like his father, he would chafe under the lack of challenges: there are no promotions for mechanics to seek.

Tony feels that he is accompanied now not only by his family, but by his friends, a group of boys in his neighborhood who for many years have played sports together and kept out of the path of the troublemakers on the block. "It's a great bunch of kids from way back. We'd do anything for each other." Tony says that his work leaves him no time now for these friends, but he still considers them important to his life.

Becoming a doctor is a goal that brings Barbara Lockhart no support from others; her ambition is much less clearly held and more complicated than Tony's. Barbara's family wants her to be a teacher and threatens to withhold the $3,000 they have saved toward her college education if she persists in her plans. Barbara lives with her mother, who is deaf and has trouble speaking, in an apartment downstairs from her grandparents. Her grandmother, the "matriarch" who "dominates the family" at 72, runs whist parties for her friends. Barbara's father, an alcoholic who does occasional work as a mechanic-carpenter, left the house years ago. "He's living—I guess you could call it that." Barbara feels that for years her family tried to "wrap me in cotton wool"; they wanted her to stay "the perfect little lady" and to "be a teacher, never get married, to stay at home and take care of my mother."

Through high school Barbara has struggled to become a less sheltered person, one who does not simply respond to the expectations of others. She believes that at first teachers and the other students thought of her as the "class genius," but soon she realized that "school wasn't going to go on forever" and stopped worrying so much about getting As. She feels more thoughtful now and more expressive of her own thoughts, except at home, where "I act the way my mother wants me to — a little lady, good manners automatically." She feels more adventurous than she used to and cites as influences upon her a teacher who asked her to argue about underlying causes in history and a friend who is "more liberal" than she about "Women's Lib." Barbara feels different from the energetic, active kids in her accelerated classes, the kind who "will get anything they want — they can do anything," and also from the apathetic kids who "are waiting for fortune to hit them, who will settle down, have unhappy marriages, never try to get anything, and think they deserve it." And she thinks of herself as different — first by upbringing, now by choice — from most people she knows:

> *How do you see yourself?*
> I'm rather weird. I'm not normal. I stay home a
> lot by myself. I read a lot. I've gotten used to
> being different — I cultivate it now. If everybody
> came to school in jeans, I might come in a fancy
> dress. I can't generalize — I'm just a weird
> person, not popular, talkative, or normal.

Barbara is in the habit of thinking about people's underlying motives, including her own. When she reflects about her ambition to become a doctor, she explains that at first it was a "substitute" for having her own family, a way of being satisfied that she was helping others and enjoying her work, rather than simply working for money. Recently, while working in the candy department of a large department store, Barbara met Tommy and began the first romantic relationship of her life. Being involved with Tommy separates Barbara from her family even more, for he comes from a family that her grandmother considers beneath theirs. Their relationship also presents Barbara with the possibility that someday she might have her own family. As she prepares to leave high school, she is 'confused":

> In my future I have visions of a small house in the country — a nice, quiet existence. If I marry my boyfriend I'll be happy doing anything. But I can't really be sure about anything. I'm going to wait till I get out of restricted high school. I'm going to change — everybody does at this age. I'm going to get some experience and then see where I am. I'm confused. I still want to be a doctor, but I don't see how I can do it.

Barbara's conflicts are unique, for in order to become the sort of person she wants to be, she has had to distance herself from her family as well as cope with her sense of being unusual among her peers or, as she puts it, "weird." Barbara is not sure she "has what it takes" to become a doctor — either enough determination or enough money. She is only sure that she must be able "to stand on my own — to get away from my mother and grandmother" — if she is to accomplish anything. And she is convinced that if she has children of her own, she will raise them to be more independent people.

Pursuing high ambitions without the support of others is difficult in Cityville, where having goals typically brings one closer to rather than farther away from one's parents and does not interfere with one's relationships with peers. Another sort of vision is judged impractical in Cityville, and its pursuit alienates one from others. Revolutionary dreams led Greg Hynes to become a high school activist, the only young person to become deeply involved in the student protest movement then at its height.

Greg traces the origins of his political interests to his father's "political maneuvering" in Cityville local politics and to his ninth-grade social studies teacher, who helped him to see "that there were some very bad things going on." At first Greg "didn't believe it," but gradually he began to go to anti-war demonstrations and soon started to organize actions

48

in Cityville "with a bunch of students who wanted to change things at the high school, then the city, then the country."

Their activities on the local level failed. His comrades in the movement began to "just get together with friends, talk, and get stoned," and Greg's only experiment with LSD really "bummed me out." When the activists did act, they found very few sympathizers at Cityville High. Publication of their radical paper, *The Agitator*, led to "hassles" as well as indifference: "People looked at it and saw the same old rhetoric. It just doesn't do any good. All they care about is getting out of school and making some money." Greg came to feel that the capitalist system in America requires that there be underdogs, and that "as long as the majority are happy, nothing can get done. I decided to give up on the world and be happy myself."

Now Greg has deliberately become self-interested, pursuing what he sarcastically calls "the American Dream." He will go to college and train to be a dentist, a job that "doesn't take too much out of you" and is the quickest way he can think of to make money. He wants to marry and have kids and live in a rustic "chalet" in New Hampshire.

In deciding to want what everyone else wants, Greg took leave of the "pseudo-intellectual part of myself that thought because I was in the College course, I was better than everyone else. Now I don't think anyone is better than anyone else." He has also become critical of his former activist friends, whom he now sees as conformists rather than revolutionaries. They wear "mod and dirty clothes," say "what everyone wants to hear, quoting Chairman Mao. They don't harm anyone." Greg considers them very similar to the "in-crowd" in being always concerned about what others think of them.

Greg thinks of himself now as a loner who has learned his lesson about the costs of going along with the crowd. But he still feels vulnerable when he is with people who do not share his views: "It's easier to act like them and not get criticized." As long as he can maintain his distance from the pressures that others place upon him, Greg feels confident that he can achieve his goals. He has already been accepted at a prestigious nearby university, with a partial scholarship and the certainty that he can get federal loans. After he becomes a dentist, Greg plans to leave Cityville. "I want to get out of here, away from the people here. I want to get to a place where you can decide for yourself how you want to live. In Cityville you have to be what others want."

Greg's parents and he disagree about everything, except that "the sky is blue." His sister is the only one of his three much older siblings that he can talk to. Although all the Hyneses and Greg's teachers always assumed that he would go on to college, his parents have worried about whether he would have a steady job. In the past he wanted to become a marine biologist, but he has become convinced that in order to make a secure living in that profession, as he ironically comments, "I'd have to go into the navy and make a disease!" His father works as a mason in a local dairy, and Greg says that his parents "think I should be a bricklayer. But they're a little satisfied now because I'll be a dentist and have a steady job."

When he himself becomes a father, Greg intends to follow different guidelines from his parents' way of leaving "kids alone until they do something wrong" — "I never did anything wrong, so I never got any attention. I got a quarter when I got good grades on my report card." He also does not buy his parents' view that "if you have enough to eat, a job, watch TV for 10 hours a day, and obtain lots of materialistic objects, then you're doing great." Greg doesn't blame them: "If I had grown up in the Depression I'd be the same way." But Greg believes that he is a child of another era and wants to make his own choices.

"We" and "They": Explaining the Way Things Are

Barbara Lockhart's and Greg Hynes's sense of uniqueness is itself unusual. Most of these Cityville youth have developed a strong sense of being like others: they feel an abundance of "we's" in their lives and often talk in terms of "we" and "us." The "we's" with whom they feel allied are perceived to be decent, hard-working, ordinary people who care about their relationships with others.

These Cityville youth have also encountered other sorts —neighborhood toughs looking for a fight, people pushing up to "the front," indifferent school officials, corrupt politicians—and their self-definitions have been forged in part in opposition to these others. They view selfish, uncaring people as alien, to be avoided whenever possible. From their own and their families' dealings with Cityville officials, they have concluded that those in positions of authority do not care about ordinary people. Even Marlene Raneri, a student leader and one of the few students to express enthusiasm about Cityville High, has come to that conclusion. As a member of the student-faculty board that supposedly has the power to make suggestions for improvements at the school, Marlene discovered that "the board always had to go to the school committee, a bunch of old people that don't want change. They're just big business men. They don't have to *go* to this school."

The conviction that "they"—the people who control things—are of a different breed is even more central to these young people's views of the world beyond Cityville. Although many have taken part in classroom discussions of societal issues—the war in Vietnam, civil rights, problems of pollution and poverty—that larger world has seemed remote. But no matter how politically informed or interested these youth are, they all hold theories about how society works. When they think about the United States, they think in terms of a political system governed by people and institutions that are alien: the country is run by "them."

"They" are perceived as "rich" and "powerful" people whose interests override those of "the little guy." "They" include big business men and the heads of corporations whose only concern is making money, no matter what the cost to others. "They" control the elected representatives to Congress, who claim to care about people like these young people's parents, but who actually pay attention to them only when an election occurs. The Mafia and the big unions too are viewed as contributors to the inaccessibility of the system to ordinary people.

But most Cityville youth take it for granted that government is always unjust and unresponsive; they blame this state of affairs on "the way things are." America is no worse than other countries; it may even be a bit better. The root of the problem is the greed and exploitation that are characteristic of rulers and rich people in all times and places; people like themselves and their parents have never had a say.

And yet these youth have some hope that the future will be better: they believe that their generation rejects materialism as a ruling motive and aspires to more humane principles. They feel themselves to be less prejudiced than their elders and less willing to accept the "status quo." They believe that some leaders in the sixties were willing to listen to calls for change, and their earliest political memory is grieving the death of John F. Kennedy, when they were nine years old.

Most of these Cityville youth — unlike Greg Hynes — have faith in "the people," particularly in young people. For example, they favor the proposal that all citizens be enabled to vote on each important national issue because they believe that politicians are too corrupt to represent their constituents' interests. They criticize their parents for "complaining" and "squawking" without coming up with concrete suggestions for change and intend to be more politically active, uncertain about exactly how, but hoping to get involved when something meaningful comes up.

Despite this faith in themselves and their hope for change, they perceive the political system to be corrupt and impenetrable. For example, they believe that if "an honest man" ever could break into politics, he would soon be contaminated. As one young man explains, "You'd have to get an honest person in the government somewhere" to bring about the changes he thinks are necessary, but "I don't know how you'd fit him in there." Another fears that by the time members of his generation can be elected, it will be too late to save the country.

There is also a gap between the recognition of pervasive inequalities in American society and the belief that those inequalities will not seriously affect their own futures. These young people agree that the sons and daughters of the rich have a head start toward success, inheriting wealth and power whether or not they are capable or work hard. But these youth believe that it is "the poor" whose chances are blocked by the inequities in the American system, and they consider "the poor" to be somewhere else, not in Cityville. In Cityville, people scrimp and struggle, and families down on their luck sometimes go through very hard times, but these youth say that Cityville is a long way from places like Appalachia and the urban ghettos and slums where the poor "don't really have much of a chance."

They believe in their chance to succeed in getting what they want and support this conviction with their determination to achieve only what lies within their reach and their own definition of success. Cityville youth do not intend to be influenced by the standards of success held by "them." Most want to avoid being in situations where others could "look down" on them, and only two have applied to the elite private university nearby. One plans to go: Greg Hynes, who, as we have seen, is the only person who wants to turn his back on Cityville and all those within it. The other, Joan Leahy, says that although she has applied, she will not go, not only because it costs so much, but because she would feel uncomfortable about the way she talks and acts—and she hates "snobs."

Reaching too high is also perceived as dangerous. Several talked about a recent graduate of Cityville High who studied so hard to get into Harvard that he lost a lung. Once there, he flunked out. The moral Cityville youth draw from this tale is that rather than trying to measure up to alien standards, it is far better to be satisfied with what you can achieve on your own terms. Joan Leahy is adamant on this subject. Joan badly wanted to take guitar lessons, but her family could not afford them. She practices on her own. "It may not sound like much," she says, "but it's good enough to satisfy *me*." She responds to a question about "money and connections" in the same spirit:

> If you've got money you've got a lot better
> chance at getting ahead. Your father or your
> relations back you. You've always got them to fall
> back on even if you don't make it. And if you

don't have money and connections, well — I'm
not going to be a failure. I'll be a success to
myself! Maybe not to other people, but for my
own needs.

So these young people find it possible to recognize the
power of societal inequities, on the one hand, and, on the
other, to insist that these inequities are not really relevant to
their own lives. Fred Meegan, one of the most beleaguered of
all these youth, agrees with everyone else that "money and
connections" are important in determining whether a person
gets ahead. "Yes," he responds, "this is true, money and
connections do help a lot. There is not really equal opportunity, but the important thing is you've got to keep trying,
keep plugging for the little guy." As Fred insists, "the worst
dump has possibilities." These Cityville youth have staked
their futures on struggle, on overcoming obstacles and limitations. Struggle is the common factor in the lives of the "we's"
they care about. It is the mark of a decent person that he or
she has *tried*.

Seeking futures that can be judged by their own standards of success assures the promising youth from Cityville
that one can stay "oneself" as one becomes "somebody."
These Cityville youth value caring and believe that striving is
moral only as long as one tends to the important people in
one's life. They are convinced that wealthy people are lonely
and emotionally impoverished, because to amass money and
power, a person must neglect relationships with others. They
imagine that wealthy suburban adolescents who don't have to
work for their college tuition pay the price of alienation and
drug use for their privileges. Almost everyone views the
"kitchen picture" as an example of the materialistic values
that have overtaken America: such a kitchen would not be
found in Cityville, for warm family relationships could not be
sustained amid so much high polish and order.

The Morality of Individual Effort

When these young people talk about what is important to
their everyday lives and when they are asked to describe
social groupings in America, they speak of themselves as part

54

of a "we," people whose development depends upon the care and concern of others. In addition, as they have become strivers toward the future, they have come to believe in their own capabilities and to think of themselves as individuals as well as part of the "we." Although they are convinced that the social system cannot be altered, they also insist that individuals have the power to better themselves. Thus, as they prepare to leave high school, they believe that the system cannot trap them, because for individuals who work hard and set their sights on what is possible, there must be hope.

Despite their anger at the injustice of inequality, these young people are ambivalent about whether and how the social system should be made more equal. Although they are outraged that "General students" at Cityville High are treated as if they were dumb and usually give up on themselves, these promising youth do not want the tracking system altered, for they are not sure that they have themselves been well prepared for the hard work of college and feel that they have needed all the help they have been able to get — and more. They wish that there were more resources to go around, not that what is scarce should be redistributed.

Another reason for their reluctance to change the tracking system is their belief in individual efficacy and the worth they attach to every individual, regardless of his or her status. Despite their conviction that the futures of General-track students are limited by the school system, these young people also believe that what happens in the future is "up to the individual," to his or her efforts and choices. Even as they criticize the mistakes school staff make in assigning people to the General track, they have a vague notion that these students may have chosen to be there. They hold open the possibility that individuals in the General track will be able to get what they want from life — if they try hard enough. Committed as they are to moral equality, they feel strongly that no one should be judged better or worse than anyone else on the basis of being interested in college rather than business or manual work.

These young people feel themselves to be sensitive to the "squashing" effects of poverty on the poor, whose interests they almost unanimously support. In their view the poor are the chief victims of an illegal and immoral political system. Yet these Cityville youth also believe that it is through struggle, not hand-outs, that a good life is won, and they find it hard to imagine that poor people as individuals would be helped rather than undermined by outright gifts of money. The same belief in the value of hard work makes them respect the gains of wealthy people when these young people think of them as *individuals* rather than as collaborators in the economic system. They would be reluctant to limit or take away their money. Many of these Cityville youth are outraged by the fact that some people have an income of a million dollars while so many go hungry, yet they believe it is possible that large sums of money are made by dint of hard work, even if the hard work took place in previous generations. "Rockefeller was no slouch," says Fred Meegan. These young people do not envision themselves in positions of great wealth, but they do believe that their hard work will bring them what they want for themselves. Interfering with the right of individuals to keep what they have earned through their own efforts does not strike them as fair.

They are reluctant as well to force wealthy individuals to help the poor. Almost all these Cityville youth see merit in the proposal that people who live in the suburbs and work in Boston should contribute to the tax base of the city; they believe that such people are "living off" the city without contributing anything to solve its problems. Yet they are loath to require such contributions, in part because of their aversion to forcing individuals to do things and in part because of their belief that the moral value of sharing with the needy comes from its voluntary nature. Well-to-do suburbanites, like the very rich, should *want* to help the poor.

Thus, despite the inequities they see in the American economic system, these young people do not easily lend their support to proposals for change. Since they do not count themselves among "the poor," they do not feel that they have been greatly hampered by the system. And they are committed to making their own way, without the opportunity to benefit from anyone else's labors. These Cityville youth believe that if they *do* succeed in getting what they want, they will have done so in their own terms and through their own efforts.

56

Townline in the 1970s

Working-class adolescents in Townline live in what is generally thought of as an upper-middle-class Jewish community, whose public schools have a national reputation for academic excellence. Actually Townline, an inner suburb of Boston, includes a broad spectrum of social classes and a substantial non-Jewish minority.

The 59,000 people of Townline live in 6.5 square miles in which neighborhoods, segregated by ethnicity and social class, contrast sharply in character. They range from very wealthy suburban areas with old mansions and elegant modern homes set back on large estates to declining urban sections with small business districts and housing projects for low-income families. An urban renewal project is "upgrading" one traditionally Irish working-class neighborhood, transforming its center into blocks of fashionable shops and high-rise apartments for Townline's growing number of young professionals. Another neighborhood has a history of mobility: families who move into Townline settle there, hoping to move up someday to a more prosperous part of the town or to some other suburb farther from Boston. Half of the adult workers who live in Townline are professionals and managers, many of whom work in Boston; 20 percent are blue-collar workers, some employed by the town.

One reason that people move to Townline is education: the schools, starting with neighborhood elementary schools and ending in the citywide high school, are innovative and progressive, nationally recognized for their excellence. High school graduation is almost universal, and 80 percent of the graduates of the high school go on to college.

The politics of Townline are controlled by liberals who use the town's revenues to maintain many parks, libraries, and other facilities, in addition to subsidizing a school budget based on one of the highest per pupil expenditure rates in the state.

3
TOWNLINE:
Struggling to Set One's Own Course

It was not hard to choose a single life-story, that of Joe Mendoza, to introduce the youth of Cityville: in his life are sketched in some form the central situations, hopes, and struggles experienced by almost all those who grow up working-class and promising in Cityville. In contrast, we cannot choose a single young person to portray the major themes in the lives of Townline youth and instead must choose two.

The reason lies in the experience of ethnicity within the two communities. Most of the young people of Cityville were Irish-, Italian-, or Portuguese-Americans, but they rarely discussed their ethnic backgrounds and never spoke of being treated differently because of them.

The situation is dramatically different in Townline. Here, although all these adolescents have in common a relatively high level of intellectual ability and a relatively low level of socioeconomic status, the consequences of growing up working-class, promising, and either Irish-Catholic or Jewish are profound. We begin therefore with portraits of two individuals, Peggy Daly and Danny Genzuk.

We mean Peggy and Danny to represent the different paths of the Irish-Catholic and Jewish working-class youth of Townline, rather than the differences between the experiences of young men and women there. These gender differences—as important as those in Cityville and more complex—are explicitly treated, as in the last chapter, throughout the text, although intimations of them are certainly present in the lives of Peggy and Danny.

Peggy Daly
"From the top of the bottom to the bottom of the top"

Have you ever done anything politically?
No.

Are you interested in politics?
I follow it. [Pause, then suddenly] I want to run for school committee, I do, really.

Do you think you will?
I don't know.

But this is a dream in the back of your mind?
It's more like an anger.

Now Peggy Daly thinks back on her high school years as a time of difficulty, anger, and pain. She remembers feeling "very confused" when she entered Townline High as a ninth grader:

> I had been to, like, the worst school in Townline, in the worst neighborhood. But you don't realize at the time how bad it is. I was at the top of that school, and when I came to the high school, they put me in all Honors courses and — I was — it was too much for me. I went down to Standard subjects. It was like going from the top of the bottom to the bottom of the top.

Top, bottom, high, low — now, four years later, Peggy has learned the rankings and distinctions that are made at the high school, and she sees how low her elementary school education ranks in comparison with that of young people from other parts of Townline: "It was like a dirty trick!" But as a freshman — and separated from friends from her neighborhood of "Rum Hill," an Irish-Catholic enclave of Townline — Peggy took her confusion and lack of knowledge as personal failings. "I had the feeling that people were picking on me deliberately. It made me feel inferior to everyone else. I figured I could have done extra work and stayed in Honors, but I didn't think that was fair, because everybody else had a head start." Over the next four years Peggy worked hard "all on my own," and was placed in some Honors courses.

Peggy believes there is a wide gap between Townline High's reputation for excellence and the realities faced by the students "placed back in lower courses." The school prides itself on its academic standards, the variety of classes it offers, and its attentiveness to individual students — for example, it allows students to choose classes from several levels of difficulty rather than from a single track. But Peggy believes that these advantages are disproportionately bestowed upon "straight" students, who achieve high class rankings because their grades in Honors or Advanced Placement courses carry more points than the same grades in Standard and Basic courses. The "straights" run the student committees and the school-based activities; Peggy and her friends "don't care that much about school," and although they really need help, they seldom get it. "The teachers *say* they're around, but when you need help and want to talk to someone, they're not really around. And some people won't ask for help. The teachers have to be more aware." Peggy herself has received little help — "I've had four different guidance counselors!" — and she remembers with anger her one attempt to talk to the administrator responsible for her. "The housemaster wouldn't talk to me. He kept me waiting for an hour and a half and then he came in and said, 'Okay, that's your detention. You can go.'"

Peggy believes that Townline High's program of flexible scheduling is equally hypocritical. Just before Peggy entered, the school installed an open campus system, allowing students to leave the school grounds when they are not in class, and created a small alternative school that allows its students to participate in governance and to meet informally with teachers. But for someone like Peggy, who worked in a supermarket until nine o'clock at night during her senior year, no options were available. Peggy had trouble waking up in time for her first-period Spanish class and could not reschedule it. "I missed a lot of Spanish and they started screaming that I wasn't going to graduate." But Peggy handed in all her homework, and her teacher "gave me a *B* because she had to, I knew everything." Peggy thinks the school administrators "should decide if they are going to be liberal or conservative. It looks liberal from the outside but from the inside it's really not."

Peggy's work experience has also been difficult, subject to the control of managers she considers uncaring and unfair: two weeks ago she walked out of the supermarket in anger. Just before high school graduation, she asked for more hours at her cashier's job so she could save money for a trip to Europe at the end of summer. Instead, she received the mixed blessing of a different job—wrapping meat. "They stuck me down there in the meat room, and I didn't like it much, but I was getting more money and more hours, so I stayed." But the situation soon got worse. "They got a new meat manager and he cut my hours down to 11. Then the next week they put me in another department for just 5 hours. This, after I'd asked for more hours in the *first* place!"

Peggy's two goals for her future both have to do with gaining some power. The first is her angry wish to become a member of the school committee. The second, discussed as a more serious possibility, is her desire to be put in charge of a supermarket someday. "What I expect to do is to move up in that kind of thing. I want to become the manager of a store." Being a manager would signify to Peggy that those in charge have judged her successful and capable:

> I want the responsibility of being able to run it
> and say, "This is my store." You know, they
> wouldn't let you do it unless they thought you
> could—watching your profits and saying, "Hey,
> you're doing a good job." You can't do that just
> wrapping meat or something.

Becoming a supermarket manager seems specific and practical compared with other "vague and idealistic" goals Peggy has had: "Like I wanted to write, and that's not really a job." Although there are now few women managers in supermarkets, Peggy believes that there will soon be many more. "Now, there are women head cashiers, which had always been men, so women are moving up in that sense." Peggy has a strategy for pursuing this aim: first she would work to save money for one year's tuition at a nearby university, and then she would enter its work-study program. After five years she would receive a degree in marketing.

Peggy speaks as if she believes that she can become a supermarket manager. "I'll just probably take it as it comes. From down here, it's something big, but moving up gradually, I don't think it will be that big a thing." Yet she is not certain that this is what she really wants and that she is ready to go to college. She says that college used to mean more to her than it does now. "I don't want to go. I don't feel a need for it. There's nothing there that I want. Like if I find something to major in, then I'll go. But right now I don't just want to jump into it." It was just before graduation that Peggy realized that her grades had slipped badly and "figured my marks weren't good enough to go to college right away." She found support for her decision to put off college from older friends at the supermarket who told her that they had appreciated college a lot more after a few years' break from school.

Peggy has become used to making decisions on her own, like postponing college. Asked to think back and say what has been the most important influence upon her, she pauses and then says, "I don't know, just myself mostly. Finding things to do myself that made me make decisions. No one influenced me." Although she is not completely satisfied with her development — she wishes she were less critical and less apt to "knock myself" — Peggy is proud of how independent she has become during her high school years. "Before, if I went and did something on my own, I'd feel really self-conscious, as if I wasn't supposed to — even if I had the feeling it was the right thing to do." She likes her straightforwardness, her lack of hypocrisy. "I won't lie, you know, like tell someone they have a nice dress when they look like a slob. I can't stand that."

Peggy mentions her parents only in response to direct questions, and she says, "I haven't been having that much to do with my family since the start of high school." Neither of her parents cares if she goes on to college, although her mother is supportive of whatever Peggy wants to do, "as long as it makes me happy." Peggy sometimes plays cards with her mother at night, but has scarcely anything to do with her father, who works as a heater repairman. She is critical of his indifference to the family and his habit of "walking away" whenever controversial topics are raised. When he does get involved, it is usually to make quick, thoughtless remarks, like his recent comment about a young man whom Peggy knows, who stole a car, got into a chase with the Townline police, and then was injured in the resulting crash: "My father doesn't think about what that's going to mean to the kid's family or his future or anything else. It's just that one incident at the moment, and he says, 'Good they caught the kid.' I take things more seriously."

Being thoughtful is an important value for Peggy; it enables her to take a long-range perspective on "the kid" who lost his chase with the cops. Being thoughtful has made it possible for her to plan ahead for a European vacation near the end of summer, and being thoughtful is the key to the independence that she treasures in herself. Peggy says the "high-tech picture" reminds her of astronauts and doubts that such a work setting has much to do with her own future. She would not want to marry a man who worked there: "I wouldn't think that much of him, 'cause I wouldn't think he'd be really using his mind. He'd get in a real rut." Peggy imagines that corporate life asks too little of workers. "They know what button to push, but that's not really knowing anything. It would be better if people had to think for themselves."

Being the only person from her group of friends in Rum Hill to take Honors courses at Townline High has allowed Peggy to see her friends from several points of view. She knows that they appear to teachers and administrators as indifferent students, unwilling to be helped, and to other students as freaks, "but they're not freaks—they're just kids with nothing to do." She still spends time "hanging around" with her neighborhood friends, particularly with two girls she has known from second grade who will accompany her to Europe. "We've known each other so long there's nothing new, so we fight just like sisters." Peggy thinks that she is more worldly and less naive than they are—"more quiet, philosophical in a sense. Maybe selfish in that sense too."

Moving through the various levels of courses at the high school, Peggy has concluded that students from wealthier parts of Townline have access to important connections, including political ones. "A kid I know whose father happens to be a judge, he gets away with murder. Other kids whose parents have money, they just get a good lawyer and they never get into trouble." Although Peggy's life has put her at some distance from her neighborhood friends, she feels herself to be most different from the young women at Townline High whose families are rich. "They all dress like fashion models, that's all they care about. Or that's how they seem — I've never known that much about them except what I've seen and the little bits of gossip here and there." Peggy imagines that these young women "will go to Radcliffe or something, and their mothers will introduce them to their second-cousin-once-removed's best friend's son who's good-looking and he's got an executive job — and that's their life."

In contrast to this image of easy achievement and affluence, Peggy's hopes for her own future are tenuous. She guesses that her chances of becoming a manager are "50–50," and the most important factor in her getting there will be whether she can earn and save the money for her first year's tuition. Given that Peggy is "counting the days" until she and her friends leave for Europe, it is clear that saving money for school is not her first priority. But from Peggy's point of view, her vacation is also an accomplishment — a sign that she has already become more active and in charge of her life than her parents have been of theirs. "They've never had the time or the money to do anything that they wanted to do. They wouldn't say, 'All right, we're going on a vacation.'"

What Peggy will do when she returns from Europe is unclear, and she is definite about only two elements of her future life: she will work hard and take her job seriously, and she wants to marry but not have children. Peggy wants marriage for the security she thinks it will bring her, but she believes that having children would interfere with her work and that she would never be "patient enough" to raise them.

Peggy is ambivalent about what she wants for her life. She is attracted to what she sees in the "kitchen picture": she would like to have "a really nice house with a kitchen like that" — she thinks everyone in America would — and if she thought "there was really a chance," she'd work hard to get it. But Peggy is determined not to want it so much that not

65

getting it would bother her a lot. She defines success as the feeling of satisfaction that people gain from their lives, rather than the worldly success they achieve, and she wishes that people could get away from the advertisements that urge them to buy expensive cars and to want more and more things: "Materialism, that's all they push."

Peggy says that she knows little about national and international issues, but she strongly opposes the American people's preoccupation with money and supported George McGovern's candidacy for president because he wanted to limit the power and income of the rich. She believes that "progress" has both positive and negative aspects: on the one hand, "it's making jobs and improving things," but on the other, "everything is too centered on that — progress is pushing people, wearing them out."

Being able to feel satisfied with what one has is a way out of the continual struggle. Peggy sees freedom in the individual's capacity to choose to be satisfied with fewer material things and with lower-status jobs — "If it's a lesser job, and if he *wants* to do it, his success depends on whether he'd be happy" — and this conviction makes her angry about the demands of blacks, especially those who choose to be bussed each day into Townline High from Boston and then complain that they are given racist treatment. "They're lucky to come here 'cause we have the best school in the whole area and they act like everybody owes them something. They can come here — I'm not against their coming here — but they should take it the way everyone else does." Because of the racism she sees in Americans, including herself, and because she thinks blacks are high-risk employees, Peggy thinks that they should learn to be less angry and more accepting. Blacks may not achieve equality, which Peggy considers "an idealistic thing," but instead each black person can be happy "in his own way doing what he was doing." It is tough for blacks to get economic toeholds in America, but Peggy believes that determined black individuals will find a place to start. And then "if he had the opportunity to start there and to continue there, he could keep progressing, if they thought he was worthy."

"If they thought he was worthy." Peggy's idea about

how blacks can gain acceptance parallels her belief that be-coming a supermarket manager would mean that she had gained the respect of the people in charge: "they wouldn't let you do it unless they thought you could." There have been many "they's" in Peggy's life so far; she has not gotten what she considers a fair deal from high school officials or super-market managers, and unlike the wealthy girls who will gain lives of easy affluence through family connections and elite educations, she feels that she cannot count on anyone other than herself. Peggy takes the risk of hoping that some day her ability will be recognized and rewarded by "them." And she protects her self-respect by insisting that what is most impor-tant is one's own sense of satisfaction, rather than how high one climbs in pursuit of false, materialistic goals.

Danny Genzuk
"I stopped just going through the motions"

Just before Danny Genzuk entered high school, his family was able to move from a shabby, dangerous section of Boston to Townline. "We finally got lucky," Danny says, and among the pleasures he anticipated was being part of a Jewish major-ity. "I'd always been a minority group in any school I'd gone to before. Like, most of the kids I knew were Irish-Catholic. They'd say, 'What's a synagogue?' And I came here and I thought, 'Oh, boy!' Here there were kids I could go to syna-gogue with, and it felt good at first."

But living in Townline brought unexpected difficulties:

> We had religion in common, but not so many
> other things. Like the games you play—in
> Townline you don't go down and make up games
> in a schoolyard or something. You have these
> tennis courts and these fields—nice this and nice
> that. I wasn't used to swimming pools. I just
> couldn't seem to fit in, because these kids had
> these fancy homes and I'd go in and say, "Now
> this is something!" You know, the way people
> talked. Let's say these kids are more cultured—

67

they've been brought up, you can't say *better*, but *differently*, much differently. They have more money.

Along with peers who were Jewish and wealthy came judgments about appearances. "No one where I lived before had *that* much money that they could afford to dress really well. You never had five pairs of shoes or something like that. But when I came to Townline I'd wear these brown shoes and they were tattered, whatever, and kids would say, 'I like your shoes, kid!' — you know, something very sarcastic." At first Danny was self-conscious and at times "very depressed." He longed to be accepted by the kids he met at the park near his house and by those at school. In his Honors-level courses he was afraid to speak. "I think I was in a level too high. Many times I'd be in a class where I thought the kids were always looking to pick at what I was saying and tear it apart, just for the sake of tearing it apart." A few of his old friends had also moved to Townline and agreed with him that in their old neighborhood "kids don't put on so many airs. It's easier to make friends. In Townline it seems like everybody's on their guard." Even among the not-so-rich Townline kids, "many of the groups are cliques. I met a few nice people, but on the whole I felt this kind of cold atmosphere."

For a while Danny felt stuck. He didn't want to deal with what he had found in Townline, but "I couldn't say, 'Well, this stinks. I'm going back to Boston and hang around the tracks.'" With time, Danny found himself caring less about whether he was accepted or criticized by the kids at school, and he became involved in two arenas that were new to him — the anti-war movement and friendships with black co-workers on his job.

Danny's political activity began with his immersion in "a whole scene, a whole culture of kids who had long hair and did drugs," who led student strikes at school against the war in Vietnam and joined in many anti-war activities in the greater Boston area. Danny found it hard at first to take part. "I rejected it because of my whole upbringing — my father says that it's wrong and everything. But then I started to get into these people and learned they were saying a lot of things that made sense to me even though they were so against what I had believed in about dope, let's say, or the world itself." From being politically ignorant — "I didn't understand what it was all about, 'What's this Vietnam? I never heard of it!'" — Danny believes that he has become realistic about the underlying nature of American politics. "It seems to me now that, no matter what, the government has lied. It seems impossible to me that their motives could be just helping the people. I think they have many unpure motives, making money and helping business."

For the last three years, Danny has worked after school in the mailroom of a Boston insurance company where his uncle knows the chairman of the board and was able to get Danny the job. Danny has become friends with his co-workers — mostly older black men — and with them engages in long political discussions. "We talk revolution and all." One man, Jack, has become a particularly supportive friend and Danny's guide to recognizing the subtler forms of racism and how powerless blacks are to combat the everyday inequities they face. Danny talks passionately about the talent that lies wasted in the black ghetto and the creativity used by blacks to survive in a racist society.

In the mailroom Danny feels more confident than anywhere else. "I don't feel like anybody's out to get me, everybody's willing to be my friend. I think it's mainly because the people are older. I feel comfortable there." He finds no guidance or comfort at home, where he lives with his father and younger brother and sister; his older sister lives and works in the home of another family while she goes to college. Danny's father, a postman, has raised his children alone ever since Danny's mother died, when he was seven, and Danny thinks that long before their move to Townline, his father had already failed him: "I think as a parent he cares, but he can't care enough to really do anything for me. Like he's never pushed me through school. When I was younger I'd come home with *E*s and *D*s and he'd say, 'Well, do better!' I think a good parent would have cared and tried to get me going."

Now their roles as father and son are reversed. "Many times he has a problem and he'll ask me. Which I don't mind — it's just the feeling that he's very immature for his age. So it bugs me. It bothers me that I have no one to go to. And I have to worry about *him!*" Danny rejects his father's passivity. "I don't have any respect for my father, and I don't have any respect for his life either. He's not going anywhere. He's totally apathetic. That's what bothers me—he doesn't care about anything!"

When his father has cared about something, he has failed. For a little while, Mr. Genzuk, a high school graduate, tried going to night school, but Danny says, "He couldn't hack it." And then Danny tells how his father struggled to regain his position as one of the top candlepin bowlers in the Boston area. "I learned a little about the game from what he taught me, and I used to try to help him get back to where he was. 'Cause he's like one of the fallen giants of the game. That was, like, a big goal of mine—help Daddy get back on the pedestal." Danny thinks about it differently now. "He's been trying for 10 years. Before, it was a goal of mine. Now it just seems kind of funny. It doesn't mean anything to me any more."

On social issues, Mr. Genzuk's closemindedness and inability to justify his positions anger Danny:

> My father considers himself openminded, but you
> know, maybe the view of a liberal has changed.
> Maybe he's a 19th-century liberal or something
> like that. I took my brother and sister—one's 13,
> one's 12—to see a R-rated movie and he was
> disgusted. He was so mad. I said, 'What's the
> matter? . . . Did anything happen that doesn't
> really happen? You're so ashamed that that's the
> way it really is?' He really didn't have any
> answers. That's the way it is usually between
> us—I ask the questions and he really doesn't
> have any answers.

Danny thinks of himself as having become completely different from his father—someone who cares about injustice, who seeks the truth, and who values "thinking things out." He distinguishes what is worth learning from the conventional subjects taught in school:

> You know, many kids went through high school
> and got fantastic grades and they just didn't learn
> anything. The kids who got the *best* deal weren't
> so straight — maybe they skipped some classes
> and they went somewhere and learned something.
> I'd never hesitate to skip class to go to some kind
> of protest rally, because I feel that's much more
> learning than you get in the classroom.

Danny feels different from the students who took school more seriously than anything else, and also from those "who can't seem to think about anything that's *really* important, like other than trivial matters around them, like who can beat up who and who's going to win a baseball game."

Danny believes that like these kids and his father, most Americans "let things go on around them without even looking at them closely." To him the "kitchen picture" expresses "the great American Dream. The middle class. 'Have a martini before dinner, have a couple of friends over for dinner!' That's a lot of what you see on TV. That's the kind of phoney life I wouldn't want to lead." Danny's greatest fear for his future is that his job might require him to "just go through the motions," that he would get "stuck in a rut" and end up without "anything of real value to look back on." Getting married and having a family seems to him like another way of becoming stuck — "it seems like a lot of bullshit."

Danny believes that until his junior year, he "really didn't care about what was going on. I was just going for grades and because high school is supposed to prepare you for college." Once he became politically active, though, "I started to do things on my own — to read and feel interested — I stopped just going through the motions." He respected some of his teachers, especially the woman who taught his sociology class. "She told me she thought I was much too bright not to say anything. Of course it was flattering, but I was too uptight in class to do anything about it." Through what he has learned in politics and some of his classes, Danny has come to value "knowledge" as the most important thing in his life and to believe that the most important influence on his future will be "how much I learn about myself. I have to know what I want." Now Danny is reading Freud.

He wants to become a person who is consistently thoughtful. "Right now I sometimes just don't think when I should. I just react and get lazy and lose total concentration." He wants to cultivate his ability to listen to those who don't agree with him, "to give people a chance," and he wants to deepen his understanding of social issues. Although Danny's political education began under the influence of radicals in the anti-war movement, he feels that he is more interested than they in hearing competing viewpoints. And he has come to doubt their sincerity. "I guess the kids from the richer areas put on a front. They can afford to wear better clothes, but they wear the tattered ones. They have the long hair. When you talk to them it seems they don't think so much."

Danny's view of himself as someone still learning makes him second-guess his social criticism. No matter how passionately he believes that the war in Vietnam is illegitimate, that the capitalist system rewards immoral people at the expense of the needy, that political candidates lie and take bribes, he feels that he may not yet know enough to criticize. "It seems like my opinions don't seem so valid, because I don't understand the political process as well as I should." For example, when he speaks of the distance between government and the people, Danny is careful to be tentative. "I think people should have more say, but maybe we have a whole lot more power than we think, and we just don't use it. So maybe it's the apathy in the country that's stopping things from being done. I'm not sure."

Similarly, Danny finds it hard to settle on solutions to the problems he sees. He criticizes capitalism for its inequities. "I talked to a girl from Yugoslavia who said that the ratio — highest wages to lowest wages — was something like six to one. Now over here, who knows what it is — a *billion* to one? And there's too many people on the bottom." Danny believes that financial success in America is gained only at the expense of human values. "Push, push, push! You've got to be thinking of it all the time. Get up there — for what? You have to lie, cheat, steal, kick people in the ass. Unless you were lucky and could inherit money or you could know somebody!" Yet

72

Danny is not sure whether moving toward socialism would make a fundamental difference. "It doesn't seem to me that many other systems are working either. It may be human nature, not the systems at all."

Danny also wonders whether, without being among the downtrodden in America, he can make a full evaluation. "I suppose I would have a lot more opinions on what I do and don't like if I was down on the bottom — especially on what I *don't* like. But when you're not being tested, when your life is fairly easy, it's very hard to think of just what's wrong and right." Danny's work in the mailroom has made him conscious of his privileges; not only did he get his job through his uncle's influence, but he saw his salary raised, after his first year of work, to a higher level than that of a black coworker with three years' seniority. Danny's view of the welfare system draws on his first-hand knowledge of how hard it is for blacks to get a fair deal. "I'd rather see people who need it get it and not worry about the people who're cheating on it."

Danny faces his own future with the same mixture of commitment and unsureness that he brings to his political views — and with a lot of nervousness as well. "I don't have any goals, I don't know what I want. I *can't* seem to find dedication toward anything, which *bothers* me. I'd like to get into something." In the fall, he plans to enter a state university two hours away from Townline, and he sees going to college as a way to continue learning: "I can't envision myself going to college to make money, but then sometimes" — and here Danny becomes characteristically self-doubting — "sometimes you don't really know your own motives." Danny also wonders how he will face the challenge of living away from home. "I worry about being on my own — how I can cope with responsibility, what I can and can't do. I don't know how I'm going to get along up there where it's totally different."

One of the few peers whom Danny admires and feels close to is a young man who works with him in the mailroom and is headed for a major in urban studies at an elite private university. Danny knows that such certainty is not possible for him now. "I can't get into something and say, 'I want to do this for the rest of my life.' I'm erratic, my feelings change. I'd like to change." Danny hopes that college will help him find his way through the process of transformation that he has begun. "Since I don't have any goals, I'd maybe like to get into that—just finding some sort of meaning which I don't understand now."

Confronting a Divided School and Town

Entering Townline High, bright, working-class youth discover the full range of wealth and status among young people from all over the town. Like Peggy, many are stunned to find that the high ranks and honors won in elementary school and the affection of their former teachers and principals have little bearing on how well they do at the high school. Like Danny, others find that being part of the Jewish majority does not necessarily bring acceptance or confidence.

By senior year Peggy and Danny have had four years to come to terms with their initial discoveries. Peggy is still angry about her plummet in status, but now she has a communal interpretation for it: she knows that her elementary school education did not prepare her for the higher academic standards of Townline High. Now Danny would not *want* to be connected to the wealthy Jewish kids who snubbed and insulted him when he moved to Townline: by his present standards, their values are false, their lives without meaning. But at first Peggy and Danny and other working-class adolescents experienced the shocks individually, as setbacks they must personally have done something to deserve. They blamed themselves for not having what it takes to be included in the top groups.

Through the names of the academic levels in which they are placed, promising working-class youth learn the judgments made by the school about the ability and fate of each student—Advanced Placement, Honors, Standard, and Basic. Although theoretically it is possible for one's courses to be drawn from different levels, most of these young people find that all or most of their courses fall into one, and they come to think of themselves and others as *in* Honors, or *in*

Standard. They learn that grades for the higher-level courses are given more weight in class rankings and that, as a consequence, students in the higher levels are being prepared for "the best colleges," and students in lower levels for the less selective ones.

Bright working-class youth make their own judgments about the character of students placed in each level, and Mary Condon's list is typical: "They put the average kids in the Standard courses, the uncommon ones in the Honors, and the AP course gets the elite, aggressive, and unique people. In the Basic you get the not-caring kids." Like Peggy, Danny, and many others, Mary was at first placed in upper-level courses and found it difficult to compete. In her Advanced-Placement freshman English class, she could hardly bring herself to speak:

> They were more aggressive because of their
> status. I was shy. They were repeating answers
> just to say something. I would think to myself,
> "That's right," but not say it. I *know* I have the
> English ability, I always have. But because they
> were aggressive, they came out with *A*s and *B*s. I
> got a *C* and had to drop out of Advanced Placement.

Dropping down a level or two during the first year is a common experience for these working-class youth, and some find their entire elementary school class "demoted." "There were kids so far ahead of us in French class," Suzanne Baer explains, "that the teacher moved them up and then she lowered our French class a level, from Standard to Basic. Because when we got there we hardly even knew the French alphabet!" Suzanne moved down on her own in other courses, with relief:

> You know in Honors algebra I felt It was just
> being *pushed* without knowing what I had passed.
> It was just no good. The kids in Honors seemed to
> be the snotty West Townline kids. They were all
> too high up to even bother if you need help. The
> kids in the Standard class were more free of
> inhibition — now, that's a classy way to put it!

Much less common is the attempt to move up; when the attempt is made, it is with the sense that one is struggling alone. When Robert Rezza came to Townline High, he was stunned to find that he had been placed in all Standard courses: "I was one of the best students in my grammar school, so I had to go to the principal and talk about what I wanted." Robert was told that if he did well, he would be rewarded with Honors courses. "I wanted to go out for sports and never had the time. I always studied. Then after school I worked in the hospital cafeteria from five o'clock to nine." Each year Robert was placed in one more Honors course until, as a senior, he had all Honors. Robert is still angry but also proud. "I showed them," he says.

Those students who seemed comfortable in the highest-level courses appear to most of these working-class youth to be very different from themselves. Tom McCusker contrasts the lives of the wealthy, Jewish, and extremely successful students with his own:

> They're in the Key Club and National Honor
> Society. They all stay together and don't really
> try to meet anybody else. They come from a
> better financial background than I do and
> probably want more money than I do. Like for
> them, more money would probably be three
> times the amount of money I'd see in my life.

Tom imagines that the Key Clubbers will go on "improving themselves" at the expense of family and friends and that they will have just a few children, maybe only a single child, in contrast to him and his friends, who come from large families and want to have large families themselves. When Tom was a top student in a parochial elementary school, he studied most of the time; as a high school freshman, he became part of a group of friends, with whom he enjoys spending most of his time. Tom believes that if not for his friends he would have remained isolated and studious and would now be headed for a prestigious private college, a fate he does not regret having forfeited.

Like their Catholic peers, many working-class Jewish students in higher-level courses feel at a disadvantage. But like Danny, some remain in Honors courses, dealing with their discomfort through silence. Others are more at ease in class; a few excel, like Rebecca Gross, who talks of a different sort of discomfort — being the object of determined generosity by wealthier students in her Advanced-Placement classes. Invited to use the piano in a classmate's house, Rebecca was able to take the piano lessons she had always wanted. But she never felt comfortable when she went there to practice and, after a while, stopped.

Part-time work also separates these working-class-youth from the wealthy students of Townline. Danny's experience in finding mentors and friends in the mailroom is unique; many have felt as isolated and unfairly treated at work as they have at school. Like Peggy, they have found it difficult to prove themselves to employers who neither know nor care about them. Many have little time left for the profusion of extra-curricular activities that the school offers. Keeping up with their academic workload is made more difficult by the demands of their jobs, some of which take from 20 to 30 hours a week. At best, juggling their activities gives them a concrete sense of themselves as young people who struggle now and will always have to work hard. Peggy Daly is more bitter than most at the contrast she imagines between her future and that of the girls whose family connections are likely to win them wealthy husbands. But none of these young people can take for granted the ease of life that their wealthy Jewish peers seem to enjoy. As Richard Auspitz says, "I won't get anything given to me. The feeling I have is that I'll get what I work for."

Like Tom McCusker, Andy Reilly admires the intellectuals at the top of Townline High:

> The smart kids who go to MIT, the brains who
> study a lot. They want things, like, to be written
> up in textbooks and have the glory of discovering
> something. They're self-motivated, to tell you the
> truth, and I'm not. It's just got to be there and I'll
> do it. I'm not going to go out and look for it.

But Andy is contemptuous of students who gain favor with school authorities not because they are intellectually gifted, but because their parents have money and influence. Andy is angry about the injustices he has seen and his answer to the question, "Who gets the best deal at Townline High?" is growled — "The kids with the big mouths, and their parents are just like them!" One such girl is in his class. "She's from West Townline, where the rich kids live — the snotty girls, the kids with the great cars — and she's got a rich, big mouth and the father can pull a few strings." When this girl was given a *D* in Andy's class, her father threatened the teacher with his influence, and, as Andy heard it, the teacher succumbed. "The teacher was scared stiff — it was his first year. He changed her grade to a *B*. I couldn't believe it!"

When Andy says that the girl with the "rich, big mouth" lives in West Townline, he is implying that she is Jewish, for that is where the wealthy Jews of Townline live, as these working-class youth see it. The central geography lesson they have learned is that Townline is divided by well-marked and seldom penetrated boundaries. Each section is filled with young people of a particular ethnic and social group, as Suzanne Baer explains:

> You've got so many different kinds of kids — I hate to classify them, I really do. But up in the west part of Townline, you've got the rich Jews. And down in the Village you've got your middle-class kids. And you've got your poor Catholic kids at the Hill, you know, Rum Hill — that's what it's called. Because it's the reputation they've got. People are hanging out of the windows swinging their beer bottles or whatever. And those are the major parts of Townline. Rum Hill is mostly Catholic, and Cabot Square is mostly Jewish.

At the high school, social life and extra-curricular interests are dominated, as these young people see it, by polarized cliques that have closed memberships and very limited contact with each other. When classes are not in session, certain areas of the school are occupied by each clique, particular tables in the cafeteria, particular rooms and entry-ways. Thus, the school and its grounds are perceived in terms of what might be called clique-geography — which group hangs out where. Andy explains:

> There's the freaks, the hippies — they're
> from everywhere. There's the open
> school, that's "hippie heaven." Then there's the
> Rum Hill kids — they're like the thugs more or
> less. Then there's the "fence" kids — they're the
> football kids, the big beeros who hang around
> near the fence in the playground.

Just as cliques at the school control certain pieces of turf, young people from each section of town make claim to certain areas of interest and excellence. As Suzanne explains, "Rum Hill and the Village kids win at sports and in the gym meets. They have so much in common that they're all against the West Townline kids, who come out ahead scholastically."

Janet Corrigan perceives a "constant war between higher and lower classes," a war that is "not spoken but to see who can outdo the other." A large number of "middle-class kids," in Janet's words, "gather toward the lower end" but are also "veering toward the higher classes." Janet adds that "everyone who's not Jewish hates the Jews," an attitude that she has been brought up to think of as a natural reaction to those who are in the majority and have the most financial power: "My mother says that when she was younger and lived in New Hampshire, everyone who wasn't French hated the French."

These working-class youth believe that the divisions among the people of Townline endure through the generations, a geography of life-chances. They perceive the academic levels at the high school as reflecting the socioeconomic levels of the neighborhoods in Townline: "the more aggressive kids from the best neighborhoods in town and the children of professional parents" end up in the upper levels of the high school; near or at the bottom are "the poor Irish kids from the worst neighborhoods who don't care about school and just sit back and let the teachers walk all over them."

Working-class youth believe that it is through the schools that the attitudes and social positions of parents are passed on to children. Diana Flynn explains:

A kid who has a father who's a mechanic hasn't really done so well in school because his father hasn't made him. So instead of going to the high school he signs up for the manual trade school. It's the same thing with someone whose father is a professor. He's not going to become an auto mechanic unless something has changed his mind.

The treatment of students in each level is believed to affect their view of what they can do; Mary Condon explains that students in the Basic level become used to having "a low opinion of themselves — 20 years later this affects you." Richard Auspitz's view of Townline is widely shared and, as we shall see, applied to society in general: "Wherever you come from, how much money your father makes is going to have something to do with how well you do there."

The Mixed Blessing of Living in Townline

Working-class adolescents remember the shock and disappointment they felt when they entered high school, and when they describe the system of socioeconomic status at work in their school and community, they are angry and fatalistic. Yet no matter how difficult their lives have been in Townline, these promising working-class youth believe that simply in living and going to school there, they are luckier than most young people. Robert Rezza, who "showed" the school authorities by adding one Honors course to his schedule each year, says, "We have everything in this school — it's hard to criticize the school." Even Peggy Daly, more bitter than anyone else about the indignities she has suffered at Townline High, wishes black students would appreciate that "we have the best school in the whole area."

It is because he lives in Townline that Bert Geller feels ashamed that his father is merely a house painter, yet Bert believes that growing up here has given him "unlimited possibilities." We see the same focus on gratitude rather than deprivation in Danny Genzuk's evaluation of his family's move from the dangerous streets of Boston to the status-conscious neighborhoods of Townline: "We finally got lucky," he says without irony.

Some of these young people are the children of immigrants to the United States, fortunate to have left their European villages before the war or to have survived the Holocaust; other parents, like Danny's, worked for years to be able to move into Townline "for the schools." Peggy's cousin from Boston will move into Peggy's house next year so she can go to Townline High. All these young people believe that, regardless of their grades and difficulties, their chances of getting into good colleges are better than those of students from other public schools.

They therefore tend to justify the same elements of high school life that they criticize. Thus, even though they are critical of how the school system discriminates against students at the bottom, they also believe that the different levels protect all students—saving upper-level students from boredom and sparing lower-level students from constant comparisons that would make them feel even more inferior.

During their careers at Townline High, many working-class students have received important help. Danny Genzuk's ability was recognized and encouraged by a sociology teacher; Andy Reilly believes that had it not been for his long after-school talks with his French teacher, he would not now be headed for college. Others praise guidance counselors. When she was a junior, Janet Corrigan's high school career hung in the balance. In her parochial grammar school, Janet had the highest grades and the affection of her teachers. "I was the best. I was a loner—I didn't need to fool around." Entering Townline High, she began "going downhill"; she became friendly with other teenagers in her neighborhood and with them "got into the drug scene." Janet's parents sent her out of Townline for the next summer and forbade her to see her friends. Her guidance counselor was the only person in whom she could confide:

> I was totally lost. I know it could happen to me
> again and that it happens to other people. That's
> one thing he helped with, 'cause I felt alone. No
> friends, and my parents were pushing me. He was

the only one I could talk to. He didn't act like a parent, he talked like an equal. He really made a big difference.

Mary Condon dropped out of Townline High as a sophomore because she had become pregnant and gotten married; her original ambition to be the first of her family's eight children to go to college — "I was going to be my mother's prodigy!" — seemed stalled. But the following year, embarked on family life with the help of her mother and mother-in-law, Mary was visited regularly at home by a tutor from the school, who not only taught Mary useful skills like sewing, but also helped her get back to school. "She was energetic; she taught me to go after what I wanted."

Robert Rezza, who believes that his political conservatism sets him apart from most other students, is enthusiastic about the progressive character of Townline. "In Townline we move faster than other places. We get a lot of things done." Although the general affluence of the city creates problems for its working-class youth, they are convinced that they are better off than they would be in other communities. Diana Flynn says: "The poor in Townline live in dingy apartments, but they don't have to worry about getting food. They go to a good school — not really *low*, but lower middle class. Maybe their father sweeps the streets, but they make enough money to get by."

Moving on the Edges

Making their way through high school is an unsettling experience for these working-class youth, exposing them to others' evaluations of their places in the geography of Townline and jolting their expectations about how the school would view their ability and who their friends would be. In the process they develop a sense of themselves as people with a special vantage point for judging life in Townline, the perspective of those who must question conventional judgments and stereotypes. They believe that they have become thoughtful, unable simply to fit in easily but needing instead to negotiate the various social arenas through which they move and to understand the conflicts among the groups they watch at Townline High.

These working-class youth have become critical of those who thoughtlessly accept the Townline stereotypes; their own journeys into worlds other than their own have made them feel more sophisticated than their friends who have never ventured beyond familiar territory, more acutely aware of how people like themselves are misjudged by authorities and by members of other groups. Peggy is furious that most adults in Townline, especially the police, categorize all young people from Rum Hill as losers and troublemakers, but she also feels that her friends there are naive and unschooled in the ways of the world. Danny disrespects his father for hating long-haired radicals but is also critical of his wealthy radical friends for their insularity: they cannot listen to the views of those who disagree with them and thus will never understand the majority of people, including Danny's father.

In a community where so many judgments are made on the basis of superficial appearances, it becomes important to look for what is real. "I can really understand other people," Janet Corrigan says. "I take people for what they are — rather than just see the outside part." Like many promising working-class adolescents in Townline, Janet has come to think of herself as a singular person, different from others in her family and from her friends: "I read books the way everybody else watches TV." After she became involved in drug use and was forbidden to see her friends, Janet realized that even unique people are vulnerable to influence and that she had become different from others in negative as well as positive ways.

High school has been a time for changing the role that friends play in the lives of these youth: the loosening of ties with early friends is part of the more general sense they have of themselves as individuals who are in the process of changing. For many, like Danny, the closeness of elementary school friendships is never repeated: there is no best friend, no steady circle to count on. "I had friends in elementary school," explains Bert Geller, "but never got in with any in the high school."

These young people become used to moving alone through the various arenas of their lives, finding individuals they can count on, making a friend here or there, moving away from a setting in which they felt rejected or uncomfortable into another. Danny's older friends in the mailroom make him feel at home there, and he no longer has to rely on peers at the high school. When Peggy went "from the top of the bottom to the bottom of the top," she gave up being a leader among her neighborhood friends. Now she draws on different friends for her separate needs: she takes advice about college from her co-workers in the supermarket and will travel to Europe with her neighborhood friends.

Often one's friends serve as points on a compass, showing where one has been and where one is heading; they become part of the individual's struggle to develop in certain directions. While Suzanne Baer was in elementary school, her father, an ice-cream peddler, abandoned the family and then defaulted on house payments; Suzanne's mother and her four children moved into an apartment and went on welfare. Around the time Suzanne entered high school, her mother went to computer training school and then found full-time work; Suzanne took on most of the responsibility for her two younger brothers and for housework and cooking; she also worked 20 hours a week for an answering service. At that time Suzanne suffered from shyness and the feeling that she had to act much older than her years: "I was very quiet, I never did *anything* wrong."

The direction of Suzanne's development during the next four years, fostered by an attentive guidance counselor, led her to become "more outgoing, more outspoken." Important to this growth has been a group of ten girls. Suzanne and these friends play sports after school and on weekends. They are carefree, constantly horsing around—"a relief from the home life. They helped me come out of my shell." Suzanne describes her friends as "very vivacious and outgoing and" — she pauses and laughs with pride — "rotten to the core, the type of people that get suspended from school three times a week."

Suzanne herself has never been a troublemaker, and

now, headed confidently for nursing school, she knows that she is "more intellectual and quieter" than her high school friends. She thinks of herself as also comfortable with other students she has come to know, "the more intellectual ones, the type who like to write." She is pleased that she has become a person "in the middle," someone who can be mischievous at some times and serious at others. The quality she values most in herself comes from spending time with people who are very different from each other. "I like best the understanding part of myself, you know, being able to comprehend other people's situations. Because I've been through most of them."

Some of these working-class adolescents have been led toward new directions and values by the friends they have made. Laura Goldberg began Townline High as part of a group of "straight, serious-minded" friends who had all been close in elementary school, who attended a Hebrew high school in the afternoon, and whose lives revolved around activities in Jewish youth organizations. At the beginning of her junior year, Laura met another group, more political, "into drugs and demonstrations. I guess they have a different outlook on life. They see it's important to do what you think is right, to stick to your guns and not just get pushed around in the crowd."

> My friends changed completely. I felt that I
> wanted to do something more, something better
> than doing the same things every day. I never
> used to read the newspapers or things like that.
> Then came Vietnam. I read about the
> demonstrations and went to meetings. I started
> taking sides on things.

As she moved from one group of friends to another, Laura also moved from one sort of Jewish emphasis — learning Hebrew and being observant — to one that stressed personal ethics more than tradition. In the process Laura feels that she has "kept lots of Jewish things," choosing aspects of Judaism that reflect her changing personal values.

Diana Flynn
Crossing Over as a Way of Breaking Loose

The most dramatic tale of how new friendships promote and reflect changes in the self was told by Diana Flynn, who has stepped across the lines that divide Townliners and gained an intimate knowledge of the lives of wealthier youth. Diana feels continually torn between her life as the daughter of an Irish-Catholic policeman — "a racist cop" — and her life as the friend of radical, wealthy Jews whose dreams are appealing but whose lives contain contradictions.

Diana's knowledge of people different from her family began in the fifth grade when she was placed in a special class for gifted children in a school in another neighborhood. "Most of the kids came from really weird backgrounds for me — their parents were doctors or psychiatrists, some were carpenters. Really different from being a businessman or a policeman." Classes "pointed the way toward discovery. I took care of gerbils." Diana's education at Sunday school was a contrast. "My mother made me study every Saturday night for Sunday school. I used to get slapped by the nuns. I used to tutor some of the kids in my Sunday school class, so I was always ahead. I always felt I was the smartest."

In her new class Diana found herself "being one of the lowest kids. There was so much competition. I respected those kids so much that I really started learning everything that they were learning. I've been competitive ever since then." In high school Diana faced harder work and more competition. She began to rebel against the pressure and "started doubting the whole thing." She managed to stay in the highest levels but took some of her classes in the alternative school, which let her do independent projects under more flexible deadlines and close faculty guidance. She began to study acting, putting much of her energy into school drama productions. She also worked 20 hours a week in a hospital cafeteria.

Her family has always thought of Diana, the youngest of four, as promising — "I was always told I was different from my sister and from everybody else in my family. I skipped first grade" — and they are proud of her academic accomplishments. But the other side of her life in high school — as political activist and friend of radical Jews — horrifies them. Diana sees her new interests and friends as helping her fulfill her most important goal: "breaking loose from my family." In her friends' homes she sees other ways to live. "My friends have much looser home lives than I. My best friend, Emma — her parents are really radical. She has no restrictions. In her house there's an idealism. He whole family is involved with the [political] trials. They keep people, illegally, who are being looked for. In contrast, in terms of my family, my life seems sort of barren. I don't have the intellectual stimulation she does."

Diana's parents hate Emma's clothes and the general unconventionality of her life. She once informed Diana's family that her sister's husband is black. "My father was polite," Diana remembers, "but after Emma left, he asked questions like, 'How many niggers does she have in her family?' All those dumb questions! My father is really a racist — and he's a cop. He's arrested people I'm in sympathy with." Diana feels that her parents are trying to "hold back on me" and are responsible for her many "irrational" fears of getting into new social situations, fears that her new friends help her overcome. Her parents forbade her to spend 18 dollars to go to an anti-war demonstration in Washington. "They said it was too much money, but it was just they didn't want me down there with all those roughnecks. My mother just didn't want me to be a hippie."

Diana wishes that her parents did not make her spend so much time at home, but she is not completely comfortable with her new friends, many of whom are actors as well as political activists. "A lot of what we do is make really funny jokes, use funny voices. Everybody's always trying to impress everybody else with their strengths and sometimes their weaknesses." Diana often withdraws into silence and listens to Emma, who she feels is more confident than she, more easy with personal revelations and expressions of anger about political injustice.

But Diana finds inconsistencies in the lives of many of the wealthy young people she has met, including Emma's boyfriend. "He's hypocritical in many ways. He wants to go to fancy restaurants, wear fine clothes, and be tactful all the time—and yet lots of times he's totally against all that. There's such conflict. He seems like he's going to break someday." Diana labels as cowards those students who criticize the political establishment but will not join in demonstrations lest they jeopardize their future admissions to medical or graduate school, and she is troubled by the hypocrisy of some political activists "who have blatantly made the decision to go into their fathers' businesses."

Diana's goal for her own future is to continue to experiment and change, a goal very different from the comfortable, well-defined lives she imagines many wealthy Townline "radical" youth look forward to:

> They've decided that they want to be liberals and
> that they want to have an artistic house. They
> want freedom. They want to have sort of an
> existence with somebody always playing the piano
> in the background and somebody always holding
> up a peace sign. No maids or anything. The father
> is an artist and the mother is an artist. This is a
> very equalized thing.

Diana intends to take risks, to keep learning about life and people. She wants to travel, to try living alone and with lots of people. "I'd like to have lots of boyfriends throughout my life. Maybe I'll have kids, but I'm not sure I want to get married." Next year she will study acting at a private university. Acting intrigues Diana because learning to portray other people is a means to understanding them. Being an actress gives her a reason now to listen to and observe her mother; as an actress she believes she will find the courage to learn about people who frighten her, "like really interesting professors, like big fat men that work in gas stations. I don't want to be afraid of meeting people I don't really understand. I want to not be afraid so that I can understand more." A second career choice, if acting falls through, is waitressing, which Diana views as another form of acting. "I really want to be the perfect waitress, to know how to act in front of each set of people differently, to know how to make people happy."

A life of continual discovery will protect Diana from one

of her worst fears: "I don't want to become what my parents are. They grew up under conventional circumstances. They really didn't have the opportunity to question anything. I would like to develop what I think is closer to the truth. I would like to discover what is actually meaningful."

Breaking the Generational Links

Diana's journey has been dramatic, but most of these promising working-class youth think of themselves as having faced the unexpected, raised their own questions about life, and drawn their own conclusions. They feel very different from those Townline youth who seem to fit comfortably into cliques and to accept things as they are, inheriting their parents' social status, assumptions, and behavior and heading for familiar lives.

Like Danny, Peggy, and Diana, these working-class youth feel singular, having already faced complexities that their parents do not understand and have not been able to help them through. Although, as we shall see, the young men who are Irish-Catholic still hope to continue the basic pattern of their parents' lives, the rest of these young people find little in their parents' lives to emulate. As Richard Auspitz puts it, "My parents — they live their own life. They're different from me. What they believe and what they're searching for is different from what I'm searching for."

These working-class youth see their parents as "stuck in a rut," bogged down by regrets and worries about money. Those who are Jewish have struggled with the discrepancy between the generally high financial status of Jews in Townline and what their own fathers have achieved. Bert Geller's father is "a house painter, in a hospital — it's really a lousy job." Yet Bert associates another value with his father's work:

> But it's a thing that saved his life. He was in
> Europe in a concentration camp. There they used
> to break lines up into two lines — people who
> worked and people that couldn't. Well, his friends
> told him, "Say you are a painter and they won't
> put you in the gas chamber." So he said he was a
> painter, and that saved his life.

Bert has struggled to come to terms with being the son of a painter in Townline. "He really didn't have a trade. He only went to sixth grade. And you know, if that's the thing that saved his life, I can't — I can't really be ashamed about it. I can't be ashamed and say, 'Oh, my father's only a painter and everybody's father is a doctor around here,' you know."

Susan Siporin used to feel shame when she thought of her father's failure to make use of the master's degree he earned from Harvard before the Second World War and his later failure to become the owner of his parents' thriving bakery. After the war, unable to find a teaching job, Mr. Siporin tried out other kinds of work and eventually returned to the bakery as an employee of the new owners. "It's sad for someone like that just to make it as a baker," Susan says. "He's very smart. He knows so many languages." Until she was 12, Susan felt that her father was "not at all successful. We weren't rich, and he was a baker." More affluent relatives ignored her family. But on a trip to California Susan and her father talked at length about his views on life; she found that she had underestimated him, that he was a man of great wisdom. "Then I said, 'What is success?' Now I really feel bad for him, that he couldn't have done something more that he might have liked better."

Fathers of Irish-Catholic youth are protrayed as close-minded, unwilling to listen to divergent points of view but all too willing to harangue their children with their racist opinions. Although most of these young people, like Peggy Daly, speak of their fathers' limitations with anger, they are sympathetic to their dilemmas. Janet Corrigan cannot discuss anything with her father, a policeman. "He and I have separate views. He believes you should obey the laws down the line. If you don't agree, he raises his voice to pound it into your head." Yet Janet also has pity for her father: "He was put down a lot. That's why he became cynical." Diana Flynn separates her anger at her parents' prejudices from her evaluation of them within their community of peers; she stresses that they are liked and respected by their friends and co-workers.

Although Townline youth believe that their fathers have been unable to find what they sought, they view their mothers' failings as the result of the conventional traps of their day — not seeking enough for themselves in the first place, allowing their lives to be narrowed by the men they married, and having too many children. Most of these adolescents get along better with their mothers than with their fathers, and they feel that their mothers care for and support them. Daughters heed their mothers' urgent warnings not to depend on their future husbands but instead to head toward careers.

Only Suzanne Baer regards her mother as a model. After her husband abandoned the family, Mrs. Baer trained as a computer programmer and went to work full-time. Suzanne became a virtual mother to her three younger siblings and is among all these working-class young women, the only one who hopes to get married and have children. She believes that she will be able to interrupt her career as a nurse and then resume it when her children go off to school.

Most of these working-class youth question whether they will ever want to become parents themselves, for they believe that being a good parent precludes living an interesting life. Richard Auspitz describes the father of his friend John, who gives John no guidance but insists that anything his son does is all right with him. "He's a lousy father," Richard says, "but he has great ideas. He wants his life to be non-materialistic, with no responsibilities. Being a father is one thing, and being a person I respect is another."

The young men who are Irish-Catholic are less critical of their parents than the rest of these working-class youth, and clearer about their own ambitions. Aside from work, these young men find their parents' lives satisfactory, and they see their fathers' closemindedness as appropriate for men of an older generation. They hope to create the kind of families they have grown up in, with their wives at home raising the kids, as they believe women should do. They imagine a future containing the same sorts of friendships they now enjoy, although they think they may want to move out to less populated suburbs than Townline.

These young men look ahead to lives that differ from their parents' only in their occupations: as Tom McCusker tells it, he will go to college and find a job less vulnerable to being "replaced by a machine" than his father's job as a pressman, a job he would otherwise not mind having. For Andy Reilly, whose father works as a security guard, the job must be a "desk job," something with a steady routine, paperwork, and some responsibility. Andy's friends "always want to fool around," and he is glad to be going out of state to a liberal arts college. But he worries how he will do there: "Everybody you talk to just about doesn't make it through." The other young men head for local colleges, and despite their being the first or only people in their families and friendship groups to go to college, they are optimistic that they will get what they want.

For the young women who are Irish-Catholic, the future is more uncertain and clouded with contradictions. Most want to work toward careers that are out of the ordinary and will bring them some prestige. Almost all these young women were singled out as the most promising children in their families; they are determined, as Mary Condon says, not to end up "suppressed" as their mothers were. Like Peggy Daly, almost all of them believe that they must go to college to fulfill their goals, but, except for Diana Flynn, none of them has applied to college or set about getting the money to go.

The ambitions of these young women seem like slogans of hope, ungrounded in realities. Peggy believes that she can become a manager, that she may become a manager, that she would suit the job and it her, and that, in becoming one, she would show *them* her mettle. Yet this goal coexists with her present reality: Peggy has made no plans to go to college, and after her vacation in Europe, she does not really know what she will do.

Even sharper is the contrast between Janet Corrigan's present life and visions of the future. Still feeling isolated from others and yet vulnerable to their influence, she has just gone from working part-time to working full-time in a department store at a job she hates. So far she has given little thought to college. But she says with conviction that she will go to night school to "look over a lot of fields" and then will go into "something to do with research in science," a field, she was recently pleased to discover, that does not necessarily require a lot of math. She is certain that she does not want to become a teacher. Mary Condon thinks ahead to a time when her husband will be finished with school and started in his own business. Then she will go to college, and although it would take many years of training, she would like to become a psychiatrist. "I'll sit there and I'll have the knowledge. People can come in with their problems, and I'll pick them apart." Her sister thinks her vision of life is "crazy," but Mary likes her ambition: "I like to think big."

It is power rather than money that these young women seek in the careers they envision, and the idea that they will have risen above the ordinary. As Janet says, "I'd like to accomplish *something* — I couldn't stand this day after day of nothing." Money is necessary — as Janet says, "I guess these days you have to have a lot of money to have peace." But they are not comfortable with the desire to be wealthy. "I don't worship money the way some people do," Janet says, but adds that "it would be nice to be able to do anything I'd like to do —" for example, to be able to "give away money and not have to worry about getting paid back."

The young women who are Jewish struggle to reconcile their conviction that their future must help bring about social change with their parents' advice that going to college is the next practical step for them to take. Laura Goldberg begins her discussion of what she will do after graduation with a weary laugh. "My parents said, 'You need a good education.' So I said, 'Yeah, you need a good education.'" As she thinks through the conflict between the world as she would like it to be and the world as it is, Laura finds some merit in confronting the dilemma on practical terms: "I guess in the sense that society isn't going to change, I have to change to meet the society. So that's important — a good education. Everybody gets a good education nowadays."

Like all the young women who are Jewish, Laura will go to college. She doesn't know what her career will be, but she hopes passionately that her life will be "very meaningful — doing something helping others." She maintains her belief that as far as possible she will work to change the way things are, and she has rejected social work, her sister's profession, because she believes that social workers only help people adjust to society: "Why do you have to change every person to conform to society — why not change the society a bit?"

Right now Laura's thoughts focus on college — "What will it be like? What will it offer me and will I take advantage of it?" She thinks about the future not in terms of concrete plans, but in terms of alternative life-styles, one of which echoes Janet Corrigan's vision:

> Sometimes I can envision myself — gee, it'd be nice to have a lot of money and live in this big house. You could help everyone and give money to everyone. But then I don't ever see myself getting that rich. And I can see myself living sort of plain and trying to make the best of what I have. If I can't change the world, I'll help the people around me on a small basis.

These young women feel that they must temper their idealism with pragmatism. Rebecca Gross analyzes her desire to become a doctor: "College applications ask why, and I said because I want to help people. I sometimes see myself as a crusade-type doctor." But this career is also a practical choice, from Rebecca's perspective:

> At this point there's sort of a limit to what a girl who has brains and does well at school and can compete on a level but doesn't want to have to constantly be shoved into proving herself can do. I don't want to be a teacher and I don't want to be something very small. So to me the only *alternative* is being a doctor.

Danny Genzuk is typical of the young men who are Jewish in believing that the pursuit of any conventional goal, especially that of making money, would interfere with the important explorations he wants to undertake. He is amused by the double meaning in the question "What is important in determining whether or not you get ahead?" He intends to concentrate on "getting a head" and will go to college in order to understand why people behave the way they do and discover some meaningful goal for himself. Most of these young men believe that they are going to college for their own reasons, not because their parents have urged them to. As Richard Auspitz says:

> My parents are not the single cause of why I'm going to college. They believe you have to go to college to get a better job and all that. Well, I believe them, it's true. But I'm going to college because I feel like learning something. If I have to die very shortly I want to take something with me.

For these Jewish working-class young men, the future offers the chance to keep learning and to keep moving. Bert Geller, who thinks that he might become a teacher, is quick to explain that as a teacher he will always be able to change jobs and scenes: "I see myself as a kind of wanderer." A few say they want to have steady relationships with mates, but all think that legal marriages and children would interfere with their lives. What they most want is to avoid being trapped in any conventional commitment that precludes further searching — "getting stuck in a rut where my job is my main concern," "trapping myself," "calling the shots too far in advance."

The Roots of Social Injustice

Proud of their ability to see the truths that underlie appearances, promising working-class youth in Townline scrutinize American society as they do the social structure of Townline. The political hubbub of the times has been part of their high school experience — manifested in demonstrations, discussions, curricula — and whether they have marched, signed petitions, or simply listened to their social studies teachers, they have become aware of the critiques of the war in Vietnam and of American politics. Some of these young people find points of disagreement with the "radicals," and many are suspicious of their sincerity. But almost all believe that their criticism of American society is near the mark.

As adolescents almost all these young people have longed for things they could not have — singing lessons, vacations, stylish clothes, tuition money for college — things that wealthier students take for granted. Learning to come to terms with the feeling of deprivation has been an important aspect of growing up for these working-class youth. They believe that they have learned to do without and in the process have discovered what really counts. After Mary Condon's tutor taught her to sew, she got compliments on the "outfits I had put together myself." She looks back on her longing for expensive clothes as childish.

These Townline youth believe that materialism is responsible for most of America's problems. As Bert Geller says, "People put more value in the type of house they own or the type of car they drive than they do in their own mind." Materialism is the motor that drives Americans to violence and hatred. These young people believe that the desire "to get up there" lies at the root of the struggle among the cliques in their high school and the stereotyping and distrust they have witnessed.

Dave Greenbaum's hatred of violence has personal as well as intellectual roots: Dave's family moved to Townline when he was a sophomore, just after he had been mugged for the third time on the streets of his Boston neighborhood. Dave points to his first anti-war rally on the Boston Common as critical to his political awakening; after that, he attended almost every demonstration, often working as a marshall to prevent violence. Dave believes that "people hate each other in America," and he hates racists. "The only good thing" he can evision for the future of America is "the changes that I *hope* will come about. If the change does come about, it will be because people will get sick of the way they are living, get sick of trying to grab another dollar or trying to step on someone to get above them."

It seems so obvious to Dave that life would be much better if people stopped hating each other that he "cannot understand why people can't see that!" Bert Geller also speaks to this common theme in the political views of Townline working-class youth: "In my mind, I can't picture anyone thinking different than me. I can't see how other people can hate another black person. It doesn't register in my mind." Yet Bert and Dave and other Townline youth must set the passion of their beliefs against the high school training that tells them, as Peggy Daly says, that "there are always two sides to a question." Moreover, they believe they must show respect for the opinions of others if they are not themselves to become bigots, but they find tolerance is hard. As Bert says, "I guess that's what this country is founded on — differences of opinion. But it just doesn't seem right. It seems that I'm right. I know what I'm talking about. In my mind, what I pick as a solution is right, nothing else is right."

These young people have become convinced that the rich control society: as Andy Reilly puts it, "If you've got money, you've got power; if you don't, you've got nothing." They have seen what money can buy in Townline: head starts into Honors tracks for peers who live in wealthier neighborhoods, the ability of wealthy parents to "tell teachers off" when their children are mistreated, the influence wielded by businessmen who talk judges into letting their kids off with warnings for escapades that land poorer kids in jail. These young people believe that money exerts the same influence at the state and national levels of government, that "big business" controls American politics.

They hold the wealthy and powerful responsible for promoting materialism among the common people. "The people" have become trapped into wanting what they are told to want and deluded into believing that they will be able to achieve the American Dream. Bert Geller sees the kitchen advertisment as a cruel tease directed at the American poor. "That's sort of the ideal life. When you think of all these poor people — they envision that one day they will be there, working and achieving all. It's not really the way it is, but it's the way business people want them to think. That could be one of the reasons for all these crimes."

The young people of Townline doubt that America's problems can ever be set right, because they are sure that nothing will change the hearts of big business men and that government will never be "more for the people." Nor do they see how "the people" can be made to understand how manipulated they are and where their best interests lie. Rebecca Gross responds to the question of who runs the country with a portrayal of the American masses with which most of these young people would agree:

> It either ranges between a small group of invisible elite or the masses. I think that any sort of mass can have a lot of power, but it can be guided. You may not be able to get anything done without the mass, but all you have to do is point it in the direction you want it to go and let it wreak havoc. The people are very easily what I call "blindfolded."

The image of the blindfolded, easily coerced masses haunts these young people because they view "the people" both as the source of democratic ideals and the betrayers of those ideals. Laura Goldberg struggles with this paradox when she is asked how the country might be changed. "It's very hard to change people's ideas, and that's the only way to change the country. We're supposed to have all these marvelous ideals, but we just don't live up to them." She interrupts herself to consider another point of view. "I don't even know if this kind of government is the right kind of government in the first place. Like America's aligned against Communism —right? Who's to say that Communism is wrong?" Laura concludes that any positive change is difficult to imagine: "It's probably impossible because who becomes President? The people elect the President and then this is the kind of President we have. So obviously if this is what the people wanted, then you're stuck with it. You can't have these kinds of changes. So I'm just contradicting myself."

Although they see the people as the pawns of the rich, these young people also cling to the possibility of a gradual, almost mystical awakening in which the people will come to recognize where the truth and their best interests lie. Bert Geller says, "I know that things have to change very slowly in this society. I know that you just can't change things overnight. I guess the attitudes of people have to change — just the basic attitudes towards other human beings, towards nature itself." His voice trails off. After a moment Bert continues in an even more hesitant tone: "I think if you let things happen the way they are, they will happen for the good. Things will tend toward the better. I think the good always wins over the evil. It takes a *long* time."

The possibility that people can be changed through education is one source of Bert's lingering hope. He believes that he was helped by several teachers to see beyond his early lessons and to develop a mind of his own. One reason Bert is considering becoming a teacher is that he thinks "the reason this country is so fouled up is the lack of education," and his sense of good fortune at having been educated in Townline coexists — as it does for most of these working-class youth — with his anger at the inequities he sees in Townline and the nation. We can hear the motifs of gratitude and anger when Rebecca Gross, whose parents survived the concentration camps of Europe, immigrated first to a declining section of Boston, and then — just before Rebecca entered high school — moved to Townline, considers how much credit America deserves for taking in her refugee parents. "I suppose America's been very good to my parents," she says. "Certainly after the war, it was just about the only place they could go and manage to raise themselves up." Rebecca then interrupts herself to qualify her endorsement. "It's not really the idea of raising themselves up, because at least my mother went to college in Europe and was close to middle-class. But people who had absolutely *nothing* after the war now had something." And then Rebecca goes on, "But on the other hand, I could say — had America done the right thing before the war, had Roosevelt not been too afraid to rile the Germans or rile the big business men, the war could have been stopped before these people . . . " Her voice trails off and she resumes quietly, "Our closest relatives could still be alive and that sort of thing."

The systematic inequality of opportunity in a society that promises justice is another of the radicals' concerns that speaks to the experiences of these working-class youth. A powerful inequity in their own lives has been the uneven quality of the elementary schools in Townline and the disadvantage they have experienced in comparison with students from wealthier neighborhoods. These youth see little sign that the situation in Townline will ever change, and they imagine the advantages being passed on with each generation. When Suzanne Baer speculates about how this disparity came to be, she wonders spontaneously whether wealthier people are naturally smarter:

> I don't know, you know, because it's really strange that the kids from up in West Townline are able to go faster. I don't know what it is. Maybe they're — you know, I've never heard anything like intellect being inherited — I don't know if it is or not — but that might have something to do with it, I don't know.

In trying to explain the lasting inequities in education and wealth in America, Rebecca Gross draws on her father's life in Europe:

> My father had four years of schooling in a *cheddah*, the little Jewish school you always read about in Sholom Aleichem. His schooling was interrupted by the German invasion of Poland during World War I. They established a rule making it mandatory for all children to go to German schools instead of the *cheddah.*
> The small, quaint *cheddah* provided the child with a lunch and the German regulation school did not provide lunch. In order to be able to eat lunch, my father had to earn enough money to buy it, and to earn that much money he could not go to school.
> So he used to let the truant officer deposit him at the door of the school and he used to disappear. By the end of the war he was too old to go back to school.

Rebecca easily draws parallels between her father's stunted education and the persistence of unequal opportunities in America from generation to generation:

> Look, a small example: if a poor man wants a job and has no schooling, the only job he can get is something that's on exactly the same level where

100

he already is. There's no way of advancing
himself. Maybe, or maybe not, he will make
enough money to send his kids to a higher school.
Okay, in that case the chain is broken. But it's
never really broken—unless you want to believe
in Horatio Alger or miracles, which I find it
rather hard to believe in!

Rebecca illustrates how poverty dooms a person from the start:

A poor man wants to get a job, and to get a job
you have to dress—not fancy, but nice enough so
you look clean and neat. But if you don't have
enough money, you can't borrow money from the
bank to buy a pair of clothes so you can go into
the employment agency so that you'll get a job.

However they explain the process, most working-class
youth in Townline believe that despite rhetoric to the con-
trary, the wealthy stay wealthy and powerful in America and
the poor stay poor. Inequities persist, and the hardest hit are
American blacks and other minorities. Blacks, as a group,
pose a challenge to the political ideologies of these young
people, for they consider themselves enlightened and liberal
on the question of race, advanced beyond the prejudices of
their parents. Yet they have, as students at Townline High
School, been confronted with the vocal and controversial
presence of the largest contingent of black adolescents to be
voluntarily bussed from Boston into the suburbs. Like Peggy
Daly, most of these working-class students feel hostility from
black students and consider them to be overly suspicious of
white students, ready to take offense at the slightest remark
or incident. And they object to the special "hands-off" treatment they believe blacks receive from school authorities.

Diana Flynn, one of the most radicalized of these young
people, struggles to reconcile her political commitment to
the legitimacy of black anger with her personal feelings of
being misunderstood by individual black students:

I think white people can very easily criticize what

101

black people do, and black people have no choice but to criticize what white people do.

The result is that when the black person thinks that things are racist that are not, the white person has the choice of telling the truth and having the black person suffer — or being overnice to them. It's so complicated!

Struggling with Cynicism and Idealism

Race relations are but one of many problems that have come to seem insoluble to radicalized working-class youth in Townline. They have become pretty certain that neither they nor anyone else is going to be able to change the world. Those who were politically active have become convinced, as Laura Goldberg says, that "demonstrations don't really help," and that only if people devote themselves to sustained political work will society be fundamentally altered. But Laura has been surprised at how easy it is for her to ignore the political scene. "I'm not really involved any more," explains Laura. "It sort of faded out. I'm like detached from it. You can go by and never know what's going on in the country. You could live your whole life and never read a newspaper and still get by. Sometimes I say, 'What's the good to know all this stuff if nothing's going to come of it?'" Another young person who became politically active, Lance Meyers, now focuses his energies on trying to become a serious writer. He does read the papers, feeling increasingly helpless and wondering whether he has become part of the system:

> I read the paper every day and it frightens me — that I'm sort of floating along through something that's so enormous and so ugly, and to think that it can smash down at any time when I'm not looking up around me enough to really see it coming and to do anything about it. That worries me.

> *That you're so helpless?*
> Not so much that but that I'm not making the choices I could make. I support the system I don't believe in.

102

Like Lance many of these youth struggle with the conflict between their idealism and their cynicism, and feel they have learned that they are susceptible to the apathy they criticized in others. They hold deep moral convictions, yet they doubt the possibility of positive social change, and they are suspicious of everyone's motives, including their own. Rebecca Gross wonders if her political activism was not motivated at least in part by a crush on one of the student strike leaders and subjects her vision of herself as a doctor to the same sort of critique: "I would like to think that I will not become a doctor who charges very high fees and gets a comfortable practice." But she immediately casts doubt on her motives by explaining, "First, I'm too lazy and it's too much of a problem to set up a separate practice, so I'll probably stick with a hospital or clinic." Her second reflection is less cynical—"And I'd like to think that I have at least enough convictions not to do it. I've often thought if someone gae you a million dollars, what would you do with it? And I used to immediately say, 'Oh, I'd keep enough for college and enough to buy my parents a house, and I'd give the rest away.' Now I think, 'Before I give it away, I'd like to buy a couple of little things to put around the house.' I like to think that I would go back to my original view."

Whether they will be able to live up to their best versions of themselves is an important issue for these Townline adolescents as they face the future. They have gained confidence from having been able, out of the difficulties of their high school years, to evolve ideals and standards in opposition to ones that they consider evil, stupid, and conventional. They think of themselves as standing pretty much alone, relying on their thoughtfulness, energy, and knowledge of the world to protect themselves from being duped into pursuing false ends. They hope to find others who share their convictions and to put the head start they believe they have gained by growing up in Townline to good use as they set out in search of new directions.

Milltown in the 1970s

The working-class adolescents of Milltown grow up in a small industrial town that is 25 miles away from Boston and almost surrounded by affluent suburbs. Most Milltown adults work at blue-collar jobs, many in the factory of the high-tech computer firm that dominates the town's economy.

Throughout most of its history, Milltown's fortunes were tied to the textile industry. The mills faltered during the Depression and finally closed down in 1950, but unlike many other small towns in New England, Milltown successfully recruited new industries to take over the abandoned mill buildings in the center of town.

Because of the spectacular success of the computer firm during the last decade, Milltown is now thriving: population and per capita income are rising, unemployment rates are much lower than in other comparable towns in the state, and the small downtown shopping area, while still shabby in appearance, is doing brisk business.

Beyond the crowded business district, the 9,700 residents of Milltown live in modest, neatly kept one- and two-family houses, each on a small plot of land. Family life is also thriving in Milltown: the divorce rate is extremely low, and the proportion of children living with both parents is correspondingly high. Many Milltown families have lived in the town for generations, and most inhabitants of the town were born in New England.

Milltown's 5.2 square miles make it the second-smallest incorporated town in the state, and its residents see it as "one big neighborhood." All the town's children attend the same schools, moving from one building to another every three years until they reach Milltown High, a focal point for local activity. Most youngsters graduate from high school — the dropout rate is 12 percent. Small but increasing numbers — 28 percent of the 18- and 19-year-olds — go on to some form of post-high school education.

Despite the town's history of dependence on external economic forces, Milltowners have a strong sense of local autonomy: they believe in home rule and guard their independence, voting down proposals for regionalization of town services whenever they appear on the ballot.

4
MILLTOWN:
Becoming a Responsible Achiever

Rob Murray
"There is no way you can be perfect all the time"

> When I was a freshman if I had flunked a test I'd be worried and think, "Gee, I'm going to flunk out," but now, I just take it for granted that I'm going to have bad days and I can always make up for it. Like pre-calculus — practically the whole class flunked the first test, and I flunked a few good ones myself. It just doesn't bother me that much anymore — one test isn't going to ruin a whole year. The way the school is set up, they realize you're not going to be perfect all the time. There is no way you can be perfect all the time.

When Rob entered Milltown High, he looked at the "big seniors" and had difficulty imagining that someday he would be in their shoes: "I thought, 'Gee, I'm going to be one of those one of these days, and how will it be!' But now, like I am a senior, it's just the same as any other year." Rob's high school years have been a time of gradual growth, with no dramatic developments, but steady progress toward his goal of going to college to prepare for a career as a wildlife biologist. "How much I've changed?" Rob hesitates before answering. "I don't know. It's just more confidence in how to adjust to a new situation. I don't think I've really changed that much except for learning more from the years.''

Rob spends a lot of time considering the range of possibilities and wishes he were not so "sensitive." He explains:

> I'm not a worry wart, but I try to get everything set in my mind — what I'm going to do and what's going to happen. I try to get a big plan of what I'm going to do when I get out of school and stuff like that. But I'm trying to learn to just take it as it comes, just not be thinking about it too much.

Striking the right balance between planning for every contingency and "taking things as they come," between striving for perfection and accepting the inevitability of bad days, is still difficult for Rob. The progress he has made toward learning how to worry less makes him fear that he may have become too relaxed:

> I've taken Latin for four years. I took it for vocabulary work and I couldn't care less about it now. It just seems to be that I don't want to bother with it. But I suppose I should have a better attitude toward it. It's still a subject. There's probably going to be courses in college that I have to take that I don't like. I think maybe I don't like that about myself. I keep telling myself, "You should be doing the work," but I just answer back, "It's too much work, I don't want to do it."

Rob is critical of himself for "letting up" too much and not stepping in when his classmates were harassing a new teacher. Not doing his best makes him uncomfortable. The student Rob most admires does more than he has to. "It's not that he's just naturally smart, but he really works at it and he really studies hard. If he didn't study at all, probably he could still pass because he's bright, but he still works to make himself get as good a mark as he can."

Generally speaking, Rob feels that he has "a good outlook on life," which he attributes to his parents. "I've got pretty good parents. They let me do pretty much what I want, but if I want to do something which they feel is not right or would be harmful to me, they at least explain to me why it shouldn't be done. They don't just come out and say, 'No!'" Rob accepts the limits his parents set as sensible and fundamentally in his best interests. Thus, although he would have liked to visit some out-of-state campuses with a friend, he gave up the idea when his parents said the trip was too far and would serve no useful purpose. "If I had been wanting to go to the college it might have been different, but I just wanted to go for the ride, just to see a different place. We had a little argument, but it wasn't really that important anyway." On the important issues, he and his parents are in complete agreement: "They want me to become something. They want me to be happy, do what I want and be successful, not get stuck in a rut and just become miserable."

His father eagerly supports Rob's plan to turn his love of the outdoors into a career, something Mr. Murray, who works as a machinist in a factory, would have liked to do himself. "I was talking to my father and saying, 'Haven't you ever wanted to do something else?' and he said, 'Well, I got into this and it was just a source of money.' He always thought he'd want to do what I'm thinking of doing—work outside." Stuck inside the factory, "doing the same job every day," Mr. Murray found an outlet in scouting, an activity to which he introduced his son as soon as Rob was old enough to join the Boy Scouts. Next to his parents, Rob singles out scouting as the most important influence in his life: "Being in scouts *has* to have done something." Recently Rob turned eighteen, making him eligible to join his father as an adult leader. He sees this as a turning-point:

> When you're in as a scout yourself, you come in
> as a Tenderfoot and you have to work through
> the ranks. The way they have it is, as you work to
> get the rank, you learn more—how to camp and
> hike and all that stuff. When you're working
> through the ranks you're all occupied with that,
> but now that you've become Eagle, there's not
> much left you can do advancement-wise. Then
> you turn to help the other kids come in and work
> up through.

107

Advancing through the ranks in scouting, getting good marks for college, making sure the track team has a good season this final spring of his senior year — "This will be our fourth undefeated season. . . . People can't say, when you were seniors you started to go downhill" — these are the important challenges Rob has taken on during his high school career. In each of these arenas, there is pressure to achieve and to behave responsibly. A "big senior" himself now, Rob takes pride in his class and feels a sense of responsibility to those who are following in his footsteps.

Rob finds it difficult to describe how Milltown youth differ from young people in other places. Aside from some guys he has met through scouting, he doesn't know any teenagers from other places, but he suspects that "being from a small town reflects on the kids." As far as he can see, Milltown "kids seem to be all just about like me. Of course they have different interests and stuff." Rob draws a distinction between "kids who want to become something and kids who are just sitting out school," but then hastens to add, "I guess if they want to do it, it's their choice — they're just different types of kids." Although Rob is reluctant to make judgments about his peers and believes that people have a right to do whatever they choose, he values his own sense of direction and spends his time with friends who share his goals: "We're all in the same boat — seniors going to college." In the same classes, in scouting, and on the track team together, Rob can think of only one way in which he is different from his friends. "Some of them, on the weekend, they might go to a party for recreation. If I had the choice between going on a camping trip and going to a party, I'd go on the camping trip. I'm that kind of person." Rob hasn't had a girlfriend yet, and doesn't like dances and parties much, particularly not the drinking. Although he has no objection to an occasional beer, he feels that some of his friends drink primarily to impress older guys. As far as Rob is concerned, "You don't have to get drunk on Saturday night to prove you're a man."

His friends may drink more than he thinks they should, but "they still don't get themselves bombed out of their minds," and they steer clear of drugs. Rob knows that drugs are available in Milltown, but he has "never really associated with people who are drug addicts." Rob believes that the drug problem is undermining the country and disagrees with people who argue that smoking marijuana is harmless: "It's still taking a foreign chemical into your body. No one really knows what drugs can do to a person." Rob's wariness about drugs makes him wonder about how he will fare at the state university, where he plans to live on campus, for he has seen a lot on television "about all the freaks and drugs up at college." Although Rob is "not really scared," he worries about living away from home but figures, "If I can get through that first year, I'll be okay."

Rob's main feelings about setting off for college are excitement and curiosity. College represents the first step toward doing what he wants, and he is pleased that becoming a wildlife biologist is so much "in harmony" with who he is: "I'd like to advance up to chief biologist in charge of a preserve." Rob anticipates that the most difficult hurdle will be taking the civil service examinations required for federal and state employment. "They're very competitive. I'm a little thinking about how if there are so many people going into this field now, it will be flooded. Ecology is the coming thing, so there might not be an opening for me to fit in."

Rob's vision of the future includes getting married and having a family, and he hopes to bring up his children as he has been raised. "I want to try to make them have the same ideas about society and living that my parents have instilled in me. They never forced me into doing something I didn't want to do. Like my parents, I'd want to give them as much exposure as possible and let them make their own decisions but give them the information they need to have a good life and to do what they want to do." Rob feels doubly fortunate to be living in the richest country in the world, where "so much is available to us," and to be growing up in Milltown, where "we have pretty much what we need."

One of the best things about America, in Rob's opinion, is its high standard of living, but he considers the uneven distribution of that wealth one of the country's worst and most perplexing features: "There's so much wealth in the country, you'd think they'd be able to somehow distribute it evenly." To explain the disparities in wealth, Rob draws on

109

what he has learned in his U.S. history course about the country's original settlement patterns. "It's not the people's fault this has happened. People in places farther away from jobs— Indians or in Appalachia—just couldn't get there. They weren't given the opportunity to find work." Rob thinks that it might be better to try to do something about the poverty and hunger in this country instead of providing so much aid to other countries. Poverty is a problem that he believes can be solved: "We have the money; it depends on where we want to spend it."

Rob believes that two other major problems in the society—the deterioration of the environment and drug traffic can be solved—"We have the know-how. It's just a question of whether we want to pay the money for it." Because of the progress during the past hundred years, Rob anticipates that there will be "a lot more technological advances we can't even imagine," and he predicts that "the environmental issue will be cleared up because people are awakening now to what's happening. I see a lot more young people like myself who want to change it." Rob hopes to help by educating people about the environment, helping them realize that "they're still part of nature, the biological earth, and that they can't fight it." Although he intends to be "out in the woods, removed from the city" and its poverty and pollution, he also imagines himself doing basic research, the results of which could be used by others to tackle problems "on the spot."

Rob believes in progress and in the basic health of American society; he likes to think that "the country will become better and solve all its problems." He wants to see a return to "basic values," for technology may be put to good or bad uses, and it is the people who have the ultimate power to determine the country's quality of life: "By the very nature of democracy, people still have a big say in what's going on by their vote." Government leaders *have* to care" about what the people want, for if they don't, they can always be thrown out in the next election, or recalled during their stay in office, which Rob knows has just happened to a Milltown selectman.

In his social studies classes, Rob has learned not only

about the virtues of American democracy but also about some of its problems. While doing research for class reports, he has discovered that some government officials abuse their power, but he sees these instances as exceptions, not the rule. Rob disapproves of the government's showing favoritism toward oil companies by letting them do off-shore drilling that pollutes the environment, and he believes that ranchers should not be allowed to graze their livestock cheaply on park land: "It gets so they think it's their land when actually it belongs to all of us." He was particularly upset to read in Rachel Carson's *Silent Spring* that in order to justify giving one company a contract to spray pesticide, the Department of Agriculture classified as dangerous a species of insect that was actually harmless: "So they just killed them all off, and they were also killing off birds and everything else." Episodes like these make Rob think that "sometimes the government's just in it for themselves." But when he looks at the total picture, he concludes that "on the whole" the government serves the people's interests. Rob points out that "the government also favors the working-class person. The person who works at a steady job gets benefits from the government —social security, medical aid." "It's not like favoritism," Rob explains, "but rewarding them for doing a good job." In a similar vein, he concludes that "the industries on the whole are all right, but just a few get too powerful. There are a lot of industries that are really working to help clean up their pollution, helping America."

Rob does not expect perfection any more, either from himself or from the world around him, but he is strongly committed to living by a set of "basic values": work hard, be prepared, plan ahead, respect nature and adults, live a "clean" outdoor life, take responsibility for yourself, be considerate of others, and pass on what you have learned to the next generation. He believes that if everyone lived by these values, America would be a better country, and he sees signs that more and more people are awakening to this realization. He wishes everyone were as fortunate as he in having had a "good upbringing" and the preparation to pursue his ambitions.

Growing Up in a Moral Community

Rob's life-story exemplifies the strength of the moral dimension of life in Milltown: not all promising working-class adolescents who grow up there adopt the town's values as enthusiastically as Rob has, but they are all very clear about what the town expects from high school students, and they judge themselves according to whether they have learned the difference between right and wrong and have thus earned the right to be treated as responsible adults.

For some of these young people, concentrating on school achievement has been more of a struggle than it has been for Rob, and a few still question whether they will actually go to college. But all have sent in their applications and believe that going to college is what they should do next. A few see themselves as having grown beyond the parochialism of life in Milltown and have come to question the prevailing consensus about the right way to live. But even the questioners agree with Rob that growing up there has given them a solid foundation upon which to build the rest of their lives.

Milltown youth believe that they live in a community that cares enough about young people to teach them the difference between right and wrong, a place where children are accepted and protected as they gradually move toward maturity. Growing up in Milltown makes them fortunate in comparison with youth who grow up in radically different circumstances—the "wild" teenagers in the affluent neighboring communities who are given too much money and not enough adult controls to develop into responsible adults, and deprived youth in city slums who receive too little nurturing to develop "a good outlook on life."

Martha Jamison has imagined how it might have been if she had grown up in the city and gone to a big city school: "How different would I be? I could have turned out to be some dope addict in some far-away city or, worse still, turned off the human race, built up a shell of defense." Although Martha thinks of herself as "a ding-a-ling, someone who can get really high on life," she knows she is also "very moody, someone who can be hurt easily." For her, Milltown High has been a place where "you're allowed to talk to people, to

112

reach out. They don't shut you out." She has gotten to know her teachers, whose acceptance and support have helped her to feel free to say what she thinks. Martha remembers the beginning of high school: "I used to be afraid of teachers. I used to think they were some superhuman race. I used to sit in the back of the class and say, 'Yes, ma'am,' 'No, ma'am.' It took a long time to learn that teachers are just people. Here, they treat you like a human being."

In contrast to Milltown, the city seems an alien place. Boston is "fascinating" to Barbara Natti, but it scares her:

> I went in to Boston the other day with my
> girlfriend. It was *beautiful*, but I couldn't live
> there. I would like to live in a small town where
> things are normal. Pollution scares me, and I'd
> like to stay as far away from it as I can. I like
> Milltown. It's friendly and it's small and I think
> the children — especially if you're going to have
> kids, I want them to have a good education.

Martha Jamison credits her parents with helping her become a person who takes other people's feelings into account. "They brought me up to have a little respect, say 'Please,' 'Thank you,' have a little consideration. I wouldn't do anything I thought would really upset them or offend them." When she thinks about how many "loud" and "inconsiderate" kids there are, she wonders if "I was brought up wrong for this society!" but she treasures her parents' concern for her, and the limits they set. "They're very interested in everything I do — I'm a little scared to go away to school. That may sound strange 'cause so many kids are anxious to get out, but in my family, everyone's great. It's going to hurt a little bit to leave." Like Rob's parents, Mr. and Mrs. Jamison balked when Martha planned a trip to Indiana and Ohio to look at colleges with her best friend. "I could understand why — it was a long way to go for just two kids, but it sort of bugged me. Other than that, my parents are great. I know my limitations — what I can and can't do."

Even those young people who chafed at their parents' restrictions now believe that parents who let their children do whatever they want are abdicating their responsibilities

113

and failing to act in their children's best interests. Barbara Natti says that when she was a freshman, "I couldn't stand school. I couldn't understand why they gave us tests on stupid, picayune questions that I could never answer correctly." Her parents insisted that she do her homework as soon as she got home from school. "I'd get so mad. They'd say, 'C'mon, let's go. You might not see the importance now, but let's do it. You're going to school to learn and not goof off!'" Barbara has come to appreciate their insistence: "I've learned so much since then. Just recently, I've got this burning desire to read about these things that I've always wondered about. It's coming to light what education is all about." In the same way, Barbara agrees with her mother "on certain discipline. You know, I think it's fair that she tells me to be in at a certain hour. I never *really* get upset about it. She always has a good reason to have me in. She says you can't do that, well, that's fine. They're not unreasonable."

Larry LeClaire and his friends are all football players. "We do stupid things together, like—we're too young to drink but we go drinking all the time." Larry's drinking has been the source of much conflict with his parents and teachers. He tells of many escapades, like the junior class trip when he got caught with a pint by a United Nations security guard and was suspended from school for five days right before Thanksgiving; Larry has listened to a good many lectures. "I took a lot of advice from my grandfather—he was unreal. He was hung up on respect, and sometimes he'd be cold to you for a while, but if I got in trouble with my parents, he'd give me a lot of advice, tell me to cool it. He'd talk to my father, but he was really hung up on respect." Larry has changed. "I guess I just realized. I used to take school as a game but now, I took my applications out for college. I take everything a little more seriously." Now Larry feels grateful that so many Milltown adults have cared enough about him to give him advice.

Only Hank Groblewski is sharply critical of his parents: he deeply resents their lack of interest in him and their failure to recognize that he has developed into a responsible young man. Because his parents neither attend to him nor provide him with a model of how to live, Hank has no respect for them.

He had trouble in junior high school: "I don't know why they passed me. I think I failed three subjects. The kids that I hung around with then are still troublemakers." Hank now attributes his behavior to the conflict in his home: "I was really letting it get to me. Now I got into high school and realized that I was close to going out on my own anyway, so I can stick it out." From his current vantage point, his parents' lives have nothing to recommend them. "My father works in a machine shop. He hates his job. I don't see my father during the week. Depending on whether it's one of his good nights or his bad nights, he doesn't come home till after I'm in bed or he's asleep when I get home." Hank's mother used to work nights as a waitress, and she spends all day cleaning house. "As long as I can remember, they haven't gotten along. It seems ridiculous to me. I just don't want any part of that type of thing."

Given the disarray in his parents' lives, Hank feels that they are in no position to make judgments; thus, he is particularly infuriated by their unwillingness to acknowledge that he has matured in high school and is doing well in school. "My parents don't treat me as an adult yet. They've come straight forth and *said* that — 'You don't think you're old enough to make that decision, do you!'" His parents almost kept Hank from participating in the new open campus program at Milltown High. "Now during free periods, the seniors can come and go as they please. You have to get two [parental] signatures for permission to do that. You wouldn't believe the hassles I went through to get those signatures!" Hank bitterly wonders what his parents were afraid he would do if he left campus. "I'd like to know what they think! If I don't stay in school to do homework, I might go downtown for breakfast! I don't know what they think I'm doing."

Feeling that he has missed something important in not having parents who trust him and whom he can respect, Hank has searched for other models for his life. One such person was his father's brother, whose sudden death last winter upset Hank deeply. "He was the only member of either of my parents' families that I was really close to. I saw him quite often — at least every other day. I talked to him a lot. In fact he treated me pretty much as an adult. So when I felt like I wanted to talk to my parents, I always talked to him." Hank

115

admired "his enthusiasm. He always got involved in things. He was constantly involved in politics, and he had this concern for people."

Hank also admires some of his classmates. "Some people are really ahead of most people my age as far as just being good people. They have things that I don't have. I have a short temper, and I have some prejudices whether I admit it or not, about other people. And there are kids that don't." For Hank, maturity involves becoming a good person who treats others with respect.

Maturity also means knowing what has to be done and being able to do it without adult supervision. Hank feels that he has earned the right to be treated as an adult, but he is not yet completely satisfied with his development. Although he works after school, six days a week, as a janitor in a machine shop, he thinks he is "incredibly lazy," meaning that he has to "push" himself to get his homework done: "I wish I could just sit down and do it — come home from school and go right to work without thinking about sweeping the floors." But Hank believes that fundamentally he is becoming a person he respects. "I said I was lazy, but I think my friends will tell you, if you get my curiosity stimulated, I go crazy. If I get interested in something, I follow it through."

Most Milltown youth believe, as Hank does, that they have earned the right to be treated as adults by their school as well as their parents. Like their parents, Milltown High is viewed as legitimately setting limits and lifting them only when young people have demonstrated their maturity. Making open campus a privilege for seniors satisfies this gradual approach to self-discipline, but the program remains controversial. Not everyone agrees that even seniors have reached the point where they can make good decisions about how to use their time productively, and some view with alarm the loosening of discipline that has accompanied the program, seeing it as a threat that may undermine the good education that Milltown High has always provided.

Barbara's parents would not sign the permission slip: "There's *very* few seniors who can't leave. And I'm one of them." Although her initial reaction was very similar to Hank's — "I was really upset. I said, 'Why don't you trust me?'"' — she has come around to their point of view. "'It's not a matter of trust,' they said. 'You don't need the time downtown.' It took a couple of months to prove it to me, but they were right." She sees her classmates "squandering" at McDonalds the time that she is putting to good use in study hall.

For Martha, on the other hand, open campus is making her senior year tolerable. She's one of the few who feel that they have outgrown Milltown High. Although she thinks that the school has helped her develop into someone who isn't afraid to say what she thinks, she's had enough. "School definitely turns me off. To have to be here at such and such a time — to have to stay here when I think I could be doing something else — I'm tired of just marking time here." Martha "wants out" but also appreciates her situation. "The way I look at it, around here, it's pretty free. If you have to be somewhere, Milltown's a good place to be — we have open campus, my father lets me have the car a lot, and I can leave during study." Martha feels that she deserves this freedom. As a freshman, she set her sights on the National Honor Society, worked very hard, and at the end of her junior year was admitted: "I knew I could do it and I have done it, so now it's okay." But Martha does not believe that open campus is right for everyone, and she worries that, unless the rules are enforced, students will suffer. If she were in charge, she would make sure that there was a quiet study area. "The cafeteria's a supervised study area, but kids play cards and fool around. It's pretty noisy, and the library isn't quiet." She would also monitor the open campus system closely. "If I ran this place, I'd take away the open campus privileges from the kids that were abusing them. Too many kids are getting away with things that they shouldn't be — underclassmen going downtown, and that's a senior privilege. They shouldn't be allowed to leave campus."

Most Milltown students have mixed feelings about the changes at the high school during their tenure there. When they were freshmen, they looked forward to the day when they would be seniors because of the greater status and freedom they would enjoy; now that day has arrived, and they see their privileges being usurped by underclassmen. They believe in discipline and worry that too much freedom, particularly when it is unearned, will destroy students' ability to develop their own sense of responsibility. Helena Hemp expresses a widely held conviction in saying, "All the freedom that you have, you don't know what to do with it when it's thrown at you."

"Everybody is everybody's friend"

"Mostly everybody's the big, sports-minded, average bunch of kids" is how Barbara Natti describes "the kids in Milltown." And she believes that her own friends are "not too much different from everyone else." The five or six senior girls in her group are "just like me, because I suppose that's the way you pick your friends anyway. We're not the type with rich parents, or supereducated parents. We're just all normal kids that don't think the greatest thing is to go out and get drunk. We just don't *care* to do that." A majorette, a student council member, the vice president of the senior class, and the yearbook editor, Barbara and her friends are "the bunch of kids who are right in the thick of things, getting things done. We've always worked together to make an organization work, or to try and pull something up, like a class." From her secure vantage point in the midst of the group that her parents consider the best in town, the differences among students at Milltown High are not of concern, except insofar as the apathy of the majority detracts from student leaders' ability to get things done. "I like student council — you learn an awful lot about how people don't care and how people do care. It kind of influenced the way I think about school because as much as people think that student councils don't do anything, my three years on the council proved that they can do an awful lot."

Barbara is similar to the other Milltown student leaders both in her pride in her ability to "make things happen" and in her insistence that she is not that different from anyone else. Tricia Parisi, another majorette and the senior prom queen, describes herself as friendly: "I try to get along with everybody. I could be with an entirely different group and fit in." This belief that one can simultaneously be "just a normal kid" and a class "star" seems tied to the general disapproval of "snobs" that is expressed over and over again. What makes Milltown kids "great" is that "everybody is everybody's friend," and no one is excluded.

Despite this widely endorsed claim, these Milltown young people do make distinctions among their classmates, and the labels they use frequently have an evaluative tone. No one identifies any "real troublemakers" in Milltown or any "wild" kids on "hard drugs"; instead, Milltown teenagers are described as ranging "from kids who study all the time to kids who study and have fun to kids who don't care about anything," or from "the ones who are real straight who wouldn't do anything wrong, to just average kids, and then there are wicked kids who do anything just for fun." Promising working-class youth see themselves as either in between the extremes — that is, as young people who meet their responsibilities and who also like to party — or, like Rob and Barbara, as young people who don't have to get drunk to have a good time. There is some resentment of the straight studiers and some disapproval of the excessive card-playing and fooling around at the high school, but the predominant view is that people have the right to have "different interests" and to do what they want to do.

"Different interests" also account for a student's placement in an academic program, according to these Milltown youth, all of whom are in the College program. Throughout most of their high school careers, students in one program were not allowed to take courses in another program; thus friends are almost invariably students in the same classes, who also turn out to be in the same activities: "A lot of the time class officers and student council are all College. Industrial arts and home ec majors never get to be on anything, 'cause College kids always get everything, but it's good if that's what they want to go into." These Milltown youth report that their friendships developed around school-sponsored activities; given the amount of time they spend on sports and other extra-curricular activities, they find it difficult to make time for friends who are not involved in the same activities or classes.

Most youth view the high school as a place where all students are basically alike and accepted. Doris O'Hare is rare in criticizing the tracking system for its focus on college-bound youth, the assumptions made about their moral superiority, and their separation from other students. Parted from her junior high school friends when she was placed as a freshman in the College track, Doris is angry at the system's inflexibility and at the effect on her friends of their assignments. "There was no way we could get together during the whole day. A lot of kids that were really outgoing, they took the home ec course and were in with a lot of kids they didn't know, and they really changed. It was hard for them to get to know other kids 'cause they were off by themselves."

Although most of these Milltown youth wanted to be in the College program, Doris did not know which program she wanted and discovered that she had no choice. "College – that's all they push. I come up here and the schedule's already made out and they say, 'Just sign here.' They assume that if you're in the top groups, you *have* to take the College course – they leave you no other opening."

Doris remains unconvinced that college is the best direction for her. She works afternoons at a gas station and is happier there than at school; recently, she has become friendly with her co-workers. "If you work there, a lot of the girls turn out to be your friends 'cause you're with them so much. If you spend six hours a day with someone, you gotta find something about them that you like." She has discovered that she had misjudged them. "There's a few girls at the gas station that before they worked there I really thought they were awful kids. I judged them before I knew them — I always thought they knocked everyone down all the time. I found that they're really nice kids — I like them better than half the kids I know."

Other dissatisfactions with life at Milltown High have emerged for a few students. The apathy of other students is one reason that Martha Jamison feels she needs open campus to help her endure senior year. Although she is "psyched" on Milltown and its "great kids," she likes being active and is depressed by how difficult it is to get Milltown students involved. "One of the most satisfying things" Martha has ever done was to attend a 10-day ecology work conference on Cape Cod during her junior year: "We didn't just sit around and talk. We got out and did things — seeded oyster beds, cleaned up the walk in Bourne, cleaned up the island." On their return, Martha and two close friends tried to start an Ecology Club at the high school in hopes of organizing a program for Earth Week. "Out of 600 kids, 10 will come to a meeting. It gets a little discouraging. You keep working, but after a while it gets to you. It bothers me that I let it get to me."

Tricia, the prom queen who tries to get along with everybody, has become tired of her visibility. "All they do is gossip. I can't wait to get away from all that. Anything you do people talk about. They look at you if you wear something different. So you just have to follow the custom, the tradition that everyone follows." She blames the size of the high school — "The kids here are more organized, more controlled than kids in other places because our school is so small" — and she is looking forward to moving out onto the broader stage of the state university, where she hopes to feel freer.

Although Tricia and Martha feel that they have outgrown Milltown High, on the whole they are very positive about their experiences there, as are most of their classmates. Only one young person is sharply critical of Milltown life. Ed Gilbert, a musician in a rock group that plays gigs in towns all over the area, feels more worldly than his Milltown classmates. "I've been a lot of places, done a lot of things, and you meet different types of people, instead of the people that you are with all your life and that you grew up with. You get a different viewpoint on things." Ed likes Milltown's "facilities and the fact that it is a small town, but the people in it sometimes drive me wild":

> A lot of them are apathetic, really apathetic.
> Milltown is an old town and they stress sports a
> lot, especially football. They're not very culturally
> inclined. In the high school itself, we don't have
> that many music appreciation courses or art
> courses. . . . The kids are easy-going. Most of
> them want to go to college, but they don't know
> why. They're going to it like it's an achievement.

121

They want to go so that they can get a good-paying job or to get the status. If it wasn't required to go and they could get the job that they would, if they went, they wouldn't go. A lot of them are plastic people. They go along with society. Most of them are conservative. They all live in their own little world in Milltown.

Ed's classmates would not disagree greatly with the substance of his description of the Milltown majority; where they differ is in their evaluation of these characteristics. For most Milltown youth, living "in their own little world" has been an advantage: they appreciate the familiarity and the shared values.

But, for Ed, contact with a wider world is of crucial importance: the difference between Milltown young people and those he has met elsewhere is that "a lot of kids in the other schools do travel around a lot." Their exposure to diversity, he suspects, sparks their interest in thinking for themselves and makes them more "liberal," which is the way Ed thinks of himself. He feels that he has developed from a "plastic person" — "I'd go along with everybody else, and try to do what everybody else was doing" — into someone who tries "to take everything into consideration before I make a judgment. I'm not influenced by what is so-called right or wrong. I have my own set of morals, and I go by them." Now Ed tries to spend as little time as possible in Milltown. "I have a lot of friends in school, but I don't like to hang around with too many of them, too long, too much." He heads for Boston on the weekends in search of good music and in the company of a few close friends, who, like him, "can't wait until they get out of high school."

Measuring Up to Standards

Ed is unique among these Milltown youth in seeing himself as generating his own goals and interests, in enjoying being different from his peers in Milltown. What he means by "liberal" is that instead of doing what others expect of him, he tries to do what he feels like doing—"what comes naturally." Ed is unique as well in seeking to go to the best college he can get into. He has applied to nine, including the most prestigious private universities. "There weren't too many kids that applied to so many, but I felt that I never want to look back and say, 'Well, maybe if I had applied to Georgetown, maybe I could've gotten in there.'"

But Ed is proud of measuring up to his parents' standards, and he appreciates their approval. Except for Hank Groblewski, who hopes that his future will be nothing like his parents' conflict-ridden existence, all these Milltown youth want their lives to be essentially similar to their parents' but with more satisfying work. Ed thinks that in deciding to become a lawyer he is taking the path originally sought by his father, who is now retired from his job as a foreman in a lumber yard: "My father wanted to become a lawyer. Then he met my mother and she blew the whole thing for him. I think he's very much interested in college. He's very intelligent. He's about 65, but for his age he's pretty bright." Ed's three older siblings are well-established in their careers, and his 28-year-old brother, an area manager for a life insurance company, has offered to pay for his education, "anywhere I go. He's all gung-ho about education and he wants me to go to Harvard." Ed applied but does not feel "really qualified" to go there and would prefer "a place where I feel comfortable," where "I figure the type of person that I am will be there." Although the very best may be beyond his reach, Ed has confidence in his ability to get where he wants to go: "Usually if I want something I'll work for it and get it."

Like Ed and Rob, most of the young men from Milltown are pleased at having met the standards set by their parents and school, and they feel prepared to start out in the directions they have chosen. Milltowners teach their children that they are responsible for their own lives and that if they work hard to measure up, they will achieve their goals. The young men of Milltown are convinced that this is true. "If I work hard enough for it, it should come along eventually."

"The Man That I Marry" and
Other Contingencies

The young women of Milltown, however, make their plans for the future with a stronger sense of life's unpredictability and the realization that a critical contingency — the character and prospects of the men they marry — is beyond their control. When Helena Hemp considers what she wants her life to be like, her first words are, "I don't know if I want to get married." She goes on to talk about an early wish to major in art, her desire to travel, and her current plan to major in foreign languages so that she can open a travel bureau, as have two women she has recently met. "People come in to talk to them about their travels — some don't speak English. That would be wicked perfect — to have your own office with nobody bossing you around." Then Helena interrupts herself: "I probably will get married and have kids eventually and never use my college for anything. You can't really predict it."

During high school Helena has found herself under more than the usual pressure to measure up to parental standards because her brother has failed to do so. Born in Germany, Helena came to America with her family when she was three because "this was the place of opportunity," and has never stopped hearing how important it is to her father, a baker, that his children do well in school and go to college. Her older brother "never really thought much about school." He was accepted by a state college but soon dropped out. Now he works at a gas station, has a girlfriend her father does not approve of, and spends his weekends away from home: "I can't understand how he lives the way he does." Helena's father is always complaining about her brother, but she has not found it hard to please her parents. "I never do anything that bothers them that much, and I just do my homework all the time." Helena knows that her plan to go to college is in part "for my father, because ever since I was little that was the thing to do." But those are not her only reasons. She is looking forward to learning about subjects she has never studied, like psychology, and asks rhetorically, "If I didn't go to college, what would I do for the rest of my life?"

Helena's prediction that she may end up never using her college education would support Doris O'Hare's judgment that her studious older sister may not be as clever as she thinks. Doris thinks of her sister — an engineering major at an out-of-state college — as very different from herself: "She studies all the time. She never thought of going out anyplace or going to a party." Imitating her sister, Doris assumes a mocking tone of voice: "I can't go to a party — there's school tomorrow." Doris's sister is very diligent: "After school she'd whip out a book and start reading and finish it after half an hour and say to me, 'Well, that's a good book. Why don't you read it?'" Next year Doris's sister will graduate, and Doris imagines that she will work for a year and then marry: "She'll never use her four years of schooling. After she's married and has kids, she can't work part-time as an engineer. She'll probably never use her knowledge." Doris believes that "a boy who studies all the time can really be somebody," but girls like her sister — "always one of the studiers" — may be wasting their time.

Not every Milltown young woman believes that marriage inevitably spells the end to career plans, but it is certainly viewed as complicating them. Martha Jamison has very definite plans for the future and knows that marrying too soon could jeopardize them. After college, she intends to go into social work. "Something like the Peace Corps or Vista sounds good right now 'cause I want to get out and do something. Eventually there's going to be that spot for Mr. Right 'cause he's going to come along and I really want to get married and have a family 'cause I think having kids, raising them and being proud of them — that's really something special." Martha doesn't know how things will turn out: "I have no idea. This is what I want, what I work for, but you have to take things as they come." Only having to go to work right away would prevent Martha from pursuing her plans. "If something happended to my father I'd have to, 'cause my mother's job doesn't pay enough to support her. Other than that, nothing's going to stop me! If I meet Mr. Right I'm going to say, if you're really Mr. Right you're going to wait a year or two for me." Martha hopes not to work while she raises her family. "Working just after you're married, that's okay, but as soon as

I had kids, I'd quit. I feel sorry for any kid that has a working mother." She hastens to add that her mother is "fabulous" and went to work only because she had no choice, taking a night job at the library when Martha was in junior high school to help pay for Martha's sister's college tuition and to contribute to Martha's next year. But it also means that her mother is "never home" and "we don't know each other as much as I'd like."

Barbara Natti is planning to go to a hospital nursing school next year to train to become a registered nurse. "I like to see things that are wrong or hurting, and make them better. I'd like to do a *service* occupation." Barbara always assumed that she would be a good nurse, but a recent nursing school interview has made her wonder: "They say you have to be a certain type of person to be a nurse." If she discovers that she is the wrong type of person, she will change her plans. "I don't want to just stick out the book-work, pass the boards, and be a rotten nurse and bring pain onto people around me who are sick. That's really injustice — that's not fair."

Nursing is a career that Barbara imagines can be easily combined with marriage and a family, after she is older and has "taken on a few worldly responsibilities." Barbara believes that hospital nurses have a fair degree of control over their time:

> They have good hours. As a new nurse you can't
> pick your own, but as you work there a few years
> you can. I'm sure that I'll work a couple of years
> after school, and who knows whether I'll get
> married or not. But if I do get married, I would
> never work and raise children at the same time.
> As soon as I had children I would stop working
> — give them the guidance they really, really
> needed before I ever went back to a job.

Just as discovering that she is the right type of person for nursing is necessary to confirm her career choice, marrying the right "type of person" is of critical importance: "a good caring person about the family that I'm going to raise, just like my dad." As long as she finds such a man, "even if you have to go through a little and even if everything doesn't work out in the beginning, things will work out."

Life has worked out well for Martha and Barbara so far, and they are fairly confident about the future, particularly if they exercise care in selecting their mates. Their career plans are important to them, but their children's needs will take first priority. Young women with less self-confidence and clarity of direction feel more at the mercy of happenstance. Still unconvinced that college is the right direction for her, Doris O'Hare has for the moment succumbed to the urgings of her parents and guidance counselor and applied to and been accepted by a two-year business college, where she plans to study accounting: "It's kind of an easy way out — an easy two years already planned for you." Doris thinks that accounting is a better line of work for a woman than her sister's choice of engineering. It is work that can be done on a part-time basis and has practical uses — "for making out taxes and stuff." Still, she expects the unexpected: "You never know what you're going to do!"

The Responsible Individual in a Troubled Society

> In Milltown, it's not like you have any
> government. I never think about the President or
> hear any news. Nothing ever happens. We don't
> have race riots or anything. I don't worry about
> any of those kinds of things, 'cause I don't have
> any reason to, really.

Doris O'Hare's sense of insulation from the world beyond Milltown is more complete than most of her classmates', but feeling distant from national politics and the trouble-spots of America is typical of these promising working-class youth. Instead, they believe that they are well situated to enjoy the advantages of life in America, and Martha Jamison voices the common view: "We have a lot of troubles — racism and poverty. America has a lot of problems, but it's still better than anywhere else I can think of. I may not be the type that goes around waving flags, but I really believe in America."

Milltown youth feel akin to the majority of decent, hard-working Americans "in the middle," whom they imagine to be like the people in their town. These adolescents think of themselves as individuals whose lives progress as a result of their own choices and actions and feel fortunate to be growing up in a community that nurtures responsibility and morality. They view the few Milltowners who do not live up to the community standard of hard work and responsible living as unfortunate people, overburdened by personal problems, or as youngsters who haven't yet matured. Similarly, these young people feel pity for those youth who, in their eyes, have had no chance to reach maturity: the suburban adolescents whose parents are so consumed by the pursuit of wealth and status that they fail to instill a sense of responsibility in their children, and youth growing up in the distant urban ghettos, whose parents are too overwhelmed by poverty to bring up their children properly.

In social studies projects during the past year, these young people have learned about societal problems that challenge their faith in America. Sally Virgilio has just finished a paper on riots and their causes and has discovered "unbelievable conditions — I don't know how people even live there, how they can survive." The overcrowding in American cities makes her worry about the future. "No one relies on anyone else now the way they used to," she says, and she finds it hard to imagine that "people will ever get back together again."

Larry LeClaire has also been disheartened by what he has learned about the relentless cycle of poverty. "If your parents are poor and you're the same way, you're going to stay that way. You have the opportunity to change it yourself, but it's almost impossible. It's sort of like — you can do it if you want but it's virtually impossible."

Barbara Natti finds the government's farm policies incomprehensible:

We talked about this one day in class. I couldn't believe it. They pay people to plow under their crops when people are starving right here! I think

128

that's stupid! I don't see why they can't give the
raw grain to those people down South. There are
a lot of poor people, and you can make bread
from raw grain. It was done years ago. They say it
will upset the economy. I think it's sickening.

Most of these young people believe that the government
has a moral obligation to eradicate these terrible conditions
but they cannot think of specific solutions. Except for their
experience of the environmental pollution in Milltown, these
adolescents do not feel affected by America's problems, and
when they seek to explain why the problems exist, they speak
with detachment and generality, invoking a combination of
moral factors and impersonal historical forces. To a certain
extent, they tend to see the society as a testing ground upon
which the forces of good and evil struggle to gain ascendancy.
As Barbara sums up her views on the future of the country,
"Sometimes it seems like man is going to bring about his own
downfall. But I'm hoping that the advances they're making in
science will turn things around. I think with the knowledge
and the technology that America has, and the ability which
the American people have to change things, I think they'll
straighten it out."

Barbara's optimism is shared by all these young people,
who view the national condition as a state of temporary, not
permanent, malaise. They believe that the American political
structure is fundamentally sound and can be remedied by the
restoration of higher standards of individual morality—for
example, by the entrance into the political field of unselfish
politicians who will resist being bought off by the wealthy,
greedy people who have usurped the democratic process.

The route to solving the country's problems lies, as they
see it, in a return to "basic values" and the life-style of former
times, when life was, in Barbara's words, "simple but sufficient." These young people speak with longing of an idyllic
past. Hank, for example, is "really disgusted" by people's
disregard of pollution. "Last week I read *Huckleberry Finn*,
and all I could think about was the description of the Missis-
sippi River and what it looks like now, and how it's never
going to look like that again. It just makes you want to cry, it
really does." His father used to swim in the river that runs

through Milltown, Hank says, but "I wouldn't put my hand in it now!"

Freedom to live one's life as one chooses is a central American value for these youth, but they believe that freedom is being abused now in ways that undermine the society. Their views on political responsibility and freedom parallel their thoughts on the interplay of these forces in life at Milltown High. They believe that crime and corruption result from giving people too much freedom and not enough supervision, for as Helena Hemp argues," People don't care what they do and just do whatever they feel like."

As these youth think about social change, stricter rules and more stringent enforcement of existing regulations seem as necessary as the restoration of basic values. Hank is angry that pollution control seems to have been just a "fad": he feels that adequate laws regulating waste disposal are on the books but are not being enforced. Helena has concluded from her project on prison reform that the only way to deter those criminals who are beyond rehabilitation is through capital punishment. "Just get rid of them! That sounds wicked cruel, but say you came home and found your father, and there was someone there with a knife, you wouldn't think of rehabilitation. The way it is now, nothing will happen to you if you kill someone." Most of these Milltown youth do not prescribe such drastic remedies, but they do believe that tighter monitoring of behavior is necessary to check the decline in individual morality.

These young people believe that people will take the easy way out if they are given the chance and thus consider it important to make sure that rewards are given only to those who have earned them through their own efforts. Although sympathetic toward the poor and distrustful of the rich, they reject proposals that would force the rich to give up what these young people believe is rightfully theirs. Instead, Milltown adolescents wish that fortunate individuals would give generously to charity, as they themselves hope to be in a position to do.

These young people want Americans to become more concerned about social problems, for they believe that without the participation of the nation's citizens, the moral decay that is undermining the social fabric will continue to grow. But they are somewhat embarrassed to acknowledge that they are likely to become members of the "silent majority." Instead of political participation, they imagine that their own contributions to America will come through leading decent lives and thus setting personal examples for others. Sally Virgilio imagines helping to bring about the changes she wants "just by getting along with people." Most of the young women of Milltown intend that their careers in the "helping professions" will enable them to help less fortunate people, and the young men, like Rob, view their work in science and technology as the vehicle through which they will help make the world a better place.

Martha, the social-worker-to-be, is one of the few Milltown youth to envision a more active political role. Last year, she worked hard canvassing in a reform candidate's congressional election campaign, and she expects to continue to be involved. "I think it's my duty to society if I see something that I can do to help, then I should work for it. We read in English class about the 'new hero.' He's the guy who's going to take the steps toward change even if he's the only one, and I agree." The concept of the individual as a moral force in society also appeals to Ed Gilbert, who imagines doing "something for the people" through his work as a lawyer. "You're always hearing people say how crooked the law is, and a lot of them are — they have so many loopholes. The law is bent so much it's almost broken. I feel that I want to do something that has to do with that."

To all these Milltown youth, America is a nation of individuals. By choosing to lead responsible lives, individual citizens can help set the country back on the right path. As long as they continue to live up to the standards they have chosen, these young people believe that they will be making a constructive contribution — both to their nation and to their own success.

5
The Evolution of Social Identity

These young people need no passports as they graduate from high school and start out for life beyond their communities. They are all American citizens, all white, working-class, and promising adolescents who have grown up at the same historical moment in the northeast region of their country.

But at this moment in their development, they are also inhabitants of very different communities. And from life in Cityville, Townline, and Milltown, these youth have drawn different conclusions about where they stand in the social universe. They have identified with certain people, rejected others, and decided what it is appropriate to hope for — personally and politically.

These basic conclusions, identifications, and decisions form the "social identities" of these adolescents, the primary understandings they have about themselves in relation to others. The central task of this chapter is to compare the social identities of the young people of Cityville, Milltown, and Townline, and to explore how such contrasting identities have evolved from life within each community.

Our focus, however, is not simply on each community as a separate, free-standing entity, nor on these young people as randomly chosen or typical adolescents. These youth are working-class in a society that distributes power and money unequally; their parents have low-level jobs and little access to capital. Each community is permeated to some extent by the governing realities and myths of the larger society, including the conventional judgments of working-class youth as deficient and their families as incapable of providing them with the advantages and values necessary for optimal development.

We referred to these judgments in the first chapter as stemming from the adherence of mainstream psychological literature to a developmental vision in which the dominant upper-middle-class values of self-contained individualism are masked in universality. Within this vision, traditional working-class attachments to family and friends are considered constraints on one's opportunities for separation and individual achievement. Mainstream developmental theory, in insisting that pursuing individual interests is a precondition for the highest forms of development, justifies the current distribution of money and power and legitimizes the status quo.

Rather than judging the adequacy of the development of the young people within each community, we want to focus on *how* their development occurs, with all its complexity, contradictions, and tensions. Looking at the evolution of social identity in each community allows us to see individuals making meaning from their actual experience of the way the world works and from the public meaning systems available to them in each place and at this particular time.[1]

The concept of social identity begins with a view of the self as socially constructed; "who I am" is always a product of interior musings in relation to "who others think I am and expect me to be" and "who is like and unlike me." In this view, individual identities are inseparable from group affiliations and interests.

Our use of the concept is based in Robert Lane's discussion:

> A person's identity tells him something about his self-interest and, because it includes group reference, his group interests as well. Further it tells him something about his proper role in political affairs, what he can and ought to do, what is appropriate for him. In some ways an identity gives information on what one "ought" to get from government, what one ought to give

to government (am I rich or poor?), what rules
are appropriate for "me." By its social reference,
an identity establishes fault lines in society—
indicating friends, allies, opponents, even
enemies. (1973, p. 110)

From Lane's terms we see concretely the role community plays in shaping the identities of its adolescents. As they move into the neighborhoods and schools of their community, young people encounter a cast of moral and political characters from whom they learn who has privilege and power and what kinds of behavior get rewarded. The social geography of a community depicts the "fault lines" that divide people one identifies with from those who seem different, and allies from enemies. From the universe of types of people in a community, young people draw conclusions about what sort of people they are, what society has in store for them, and what they can therefore hope for. From these assessments of their social location come adolescents' ideas about their future — definitions and questions about success, conceptions of maturity, and standards for judging their progress. Finally, the values and social interpretations of a specific community act as filters through which historical and political events take on particular meaning.

Here, then, is our analysis of the evolution of social identity within each community:

Cityville

The young people of Cityville focus not on the crowded density and bustling urban life of their community but on their lives in intimate arenas—their homes and the homes of grandparents, aunts, and uncles—and in neighborhoods that feel like home. These youth feel that they inhabit familiar territory, in contrast to Boston and Cambridge, which lie just a few miles away but which seem exotic.

Within this familiar territory, young people encounter problems: family strains and feuds, neighborhood bullies, floundering peers, the large and impersonal high school, dishonest local politicians. These difficulties, in the local sphere

135

of life, they can understand and cope with. In contrast they find alien the larger, more distant sphere outside Cityville, in which wealthier people live and the national jockeying for power takes place.

These youth identify themselves as Cityvilleans and claim a global kinship with "the people," ordinary, decent folk who care about other people and value relationships above individual achievement. Their sense of "I," of self, emerges from their sense of "we-ness," the encompassing identification they feel with all those who are unpretentious, able to respond to the needs of others and to enjoy life in the company of others.

The socioeconomic homogeneity of Cityville enables them to focus on their similarity to others: they translate their acquaintance with people on welfare into an appreciation that people can easily be overwhelmed by circumstances and believe that people in a fixed category of "the poor" live far away, in Appalachia and the urban ghettos. They believe that their group interests lie with those who must work hard because they have little savings or access to credit.

Most of their families are one generation removed from the traditional ethnic urban village and remain involved in extended family networks. But these youth feel based in their nuclear families and view ties to other relatives as problematic as well as nourishing. The peer-group society with its values of group solidarity is transmitted through neighborhood life, which is a primary arena for the young men. Neighborhood acceptance and maintaining credibility with friends are important, and neighborhood loyalty often survives moves to other parts of Cityville.

The impersonality of the high school and the perceived incompetence and indifference of most of its staff have made these youth and their parents distrust all but its credentialing function. It is through the caring of their parents — and sometimes other adults in the family and neighborhood — that these young people believe they have become ambitious, and thus fortunate in comparison with the majority of Cityville youth who have not been similarly nurtured and face empty futures. Neighborhood friendships are viewed as separate from considerations of the future, and these youth consider their close friends similar to them, whether or not they are similarly ambitious.

The young women want their future jobs, mostly as public school teachers, to be of intrinsic interest, separate from the roles they anticipate as wives and mothers. They perceive these jobs not so much as a source of income but as interesting work that can be left when children are young and then resumed, and as a reliable source of self-worth no matter what difficulties they find in marriage. The young men are uncertain exactly what jobs they want — blue- or white-collar — and thus do not know if they should go to college. They view future work primarily as the means to a good life in which the solidarity of life with friends and family can continue, and in which they as future fathers can provide for their families.

For all, wanting what is possible signifies taking the future seriously and caring about oneself and one's parents. And it signifies the commitment to remain oneself while becoming somebody, thus continuing to draw a sharp line between "us" and "them" and remaining among the "we."

The sphere inhabited and controlled by "them" exists at a large distance from Cityville. Although these youth are outraged at the dishonesty of local politicians, they locate the source of power at the national level, where it is controlled by the immensely wealthy. They are angered by exposés of corruption in Cityville because they believe corruption exists everywhere, covered up more easily by wealthier communities.

These young people believe that it is inevitable that the powerful will pursue their interests at the expense of the powerless. Americans might enjoy more freedom than citizens of other countries, but the nation's leaders are not different from rulers at other times and places. This conviction about human nature has been reinforced by their and their families' experience with authorities in the schools and local government.

These youth intend to control their own lives, achieving what they can within the perimeters of places like Cityville and with people like themselves, keeping out of realms controlled by "them." Although they feel vulnerable to the universal temptations of greed and laziness, they are confident that they will not take advantage of others and that they will work hard.

Their hopefulness finds support in their sense of belonging to a new generation, more tolerant and open to change because it did not experience the deprivations of the Great Depression. Although radical activists and countercultural hippies seem alien, their criticism of hypocrisy and injustice has some appeal. These youth draw hope for social change from the unwillingness of young people to accept the status quo. They do not intend to have their own freedom of expression limited by the demands of religion, bosses, or live-in parents or in-laws.

These young people are determined to accept the constraints they cannot change but intend to act whenever they can. The large inequalities in society are unjust and will never be corrected, but these youth believe that there is room enough for individuals who can work hard and gain the necessary education to succeed. They are sympathetic to blacks and other minorities, whose plight they have studied in Problems of Democracy classes, but they believe that they should devote their own energies to small, local efforts to bring about a more humane world.

Their pragmatism makes them think of social programs in practical as well as moral terms, believing both that the wealthy might have worked hard for some of their money and that forcing them to give to the poor will only make them more unjust. These youth appreciate the fragility of people's situations and how quickly bad luck or ill health can destroy a family's income. They define themselves as lucky, caring people who will help those who are less fortunate.

Townline

In contrast to Cityville youth, Townline youth feel that they inhabit alien territory. They see fault lines everywhere: sections of town and school are inhabited by different groups of people with distinct ethnic and economic interests, all vying for recognition and success. Where these young people stand in this divided landscape, what their interests are, and

138

whether they have any allies became questions when they entered high school.

It was a moment in their development when their expectations were unmet, and their sense of themselves and where they were headed was shaken. They faced a stunning discrepancy between their socioeconomic status and that of wealthier peers at the same time that their neighborhood ties were loosening and their worlds were becoming more complex than their parents could understand. Whatever uniqueness they had felt was intensified, and for all but the Irish-Catholic young men, there began a lasting feeling of being marginal to group life, of not belonging to anything larger than themselves.

Until they entered high school, these working-class youth never confronted the range of social differences in Townline. Irish-Catholic youth were high achievers at school, secure and valued participants in the life of their neighborhoods. Jewish youth lived in more transitory urban sections or moved into town from deteriorating sections of Boston. During high school, all came to think of themselves as disadvantaged members of an affluent community. Their "I" is linked to no "we," and "they" are everywhere — administrators who enforce the ranking system of the high school, elite, snobbish students, and unfair bosses. These youth see their parents as negative models, people who have achieved little satisfaction in life and are unable to understand the complex realities of their children's lives.

Townline youth came to perceive the task of growing up as one of figuring out their own goals and defining their own standards. This task was the product not only of their singularity but also of the dominant upper-middle-class culture of Townline and its high school. The value of acting authentically on the basis of one's own beliefs was expressed in the ideology of the student anti-war movement, which was supported by high school administrators and teachers. This task was a practical necessity as well, given the array of competing views these youth encountered about appropriate adolescent behavior, the validity of the American Dream, and the legitimacy of national leaders. In the process of making their own

139

judgments, they came to question the wisdom of simply going along with the majority or the conventional view.

In contrast to Cityville youth, they feel that they have little in common with others. Except for the Irish-Catholic young men, these young people feel different in some essential way from everyone else and marginal to all the groups of peers they see around them. Their marginality extends even to areas of life where they do find some companionship and support. Groups of friends they meet seem more comfortable and stable; leading political activists are wealthier and the risks they claim to take seem a pretence. These Townline youth move on the edges of groups, forming transitory attachments that change as their interests and commitments change.

They take pride in their lonely struggles to become thoughtful, to move beyond common habits of stereotyping and judging people on the basis of appearances. They feel that in doing so they have become different from the masses of people who accept what they are told and are duped by the wealthy and powerful into becoming materialists.

These youth draw mixed conclusions from the diversity offered by the town and high school. They feel more sophisticated, seasoned by their exposure to young people of different backgrounds; their cosmopolitanism gives them some confidence that they can handle complex situations, and they move easily on subways in and around Boston. But their experience of diversity is problematic. They are strangers in the sections of Townline where wealthy people live; although they view the diversity of ethnic groups at the high school — black, Jewish, Irish-Catholic — as interesting, it is the dominance of the wealthy Jews that has drawn their attention, and the favored treatment given to blacks. Bussing seems to them a positive social gesture, but the hostility of blacks has been hard to deal with. Similarly, they have been more impressed by the rigidity of the lines drawn among the many cliques than by the multiplicity of student interests. In contrast to Milltown and Cityville youth, they feel that the peers most different from them — either wealthy and Jewish or black and from the slums — are favored by school authorities.

At the same time, these youth believe that they are fortunate to live in a progressive, wealthy community like Townline, and especially to have the chance to go to a high school that has a national reputation as academically rigorous and enlightened. This sense of good fortune — coexisting with their anger and sense of injustice — has been nourished by the individual teachers and guidance counselors who have helped them through the difficulties of the high school years.

The Irish-Catholic young men have taken a more City-villean route. After the shock of entry into high school, they continued or renewed their ties with neighborhood friends and their sense of similarity to their parents. They maintain their anger at such inequities as the devaluation of their neighborhoods by the community and high school, while they aspire to recreate their parents' lives in their own future families, but with more secure and higher-paying jobs.

The rest of these youth see few models for the lives they hope to lead and feel that they have already moved beyond their parents' conventional views, routine lives, and histories of failure. They hope to use their singularity in creating positive futures, although they are uncertain how to do this. The Irish-Catholic young women want to find careers that will give them some power to manage or guide others, but they have made no specific plans to go on to college. The Jewish young men hope that college will introduce them to kindred spirits and a deeper understanding of politics and show them how to create lives that enact their ideals. The Jewish young women have bowed to their parents' pragmatism and are aiming at specific careers, yet their central purpose is to find some way to contribute to social change.

The materialism and conflicts they see in Townline seem to them the inevitable result of a political world ruled by profit and power. Greed and corruption govern national politics, and the masses do not know their own interests. These young people want to remain uncontaminated by the social system, yet the young women believe that they will have to negotiate it in order to have careers. The young men expect to stay outside it, wandering and searching. All these youth doubt that they will have children, fearing compromise and stagnation.

In contrast to their peers in Milltown and Cityville, they

141

have no sense of being better off and more motivated than many others around them as a consequence of their parents' concern. Instead, they have experienced the limits of their parents' ability to aid them, becoming vulnerable to others' judgments of their talents and status. Although they had ready explanations for the wide range of social strata in their town and could point to the ways in which money and status were passed on through the generations — modes of explaining that were consonant with an explicitly radical analysis — these understandings did not resolve their uncertainties about who was responsible for their own situations and whether they would be able to get what they wanted in the future.

These youth accept the inevitability of inequities in Townline and the larger society and find in the hostile attitudes of blacks bussed to the high school more evidence of the entrenchment of the system. But they are determined, through their understanding, caring, and vigilance, to search for ways to make the political system better. Although they doubt that the masses can awaken, they cannot give up hoping. If they can overcome their own doubts and confusion, they feel that they have a chance.

Milltown

Milltown youth believe they are fortunate to live in an island of decency in a society that has temporarily lost its moral bearings. Few notes of discord interrupt their perception that they live in a coherent, stable moral community where children grow into teenagers, and teenagers into adults, in a steady, continuous line. The tenor of the community is familiarity: as Milltown children grow up and move through the townwide elementary, junior high, and high schools, they are recognized and welcomed. They see few strangers or threats within the borders of Milltown, and no enemies; they view the great majority of Milltowners as sharing the same basic values and perspectives.

These youth see allies everywhere in Milltown — and in the majority of decent, hard-working Americans who have not fallen prey to the disorganization and materialism of modern society. The enemies of Milltowners live elsewhere, in places of declining morality where people have ceased to care enough about each other and the social order. These are the minority of Americans at the top and bottom levels of society who seem in different ways responsible for the nation's difficulties. At the top are the powerful and greedy people of great wealth, who have managed to gain control over many politicians; at the bottom are the poor, likely to remain so because they are denied the educational opportunities they need to move up in the world.

The "I" of these youth emerges from being part of a coherent small town of like-minded individuals, but unlike their counterparts in Cityville — where the "I" always draws its meaning from being part of the "we" — Milltown youth believe that adolescents should become independent. The end of high school is the time to move on, to say good-bye to childhood friends. They assume that individuals are ultimately responsible only for themselves and their immediate families; using all they have gained from growing up in Milltown, they head for individual rather than collective futures.

They are grateful to their parents and schools for having taught them the values of restraint, responsibility, and hard work. Having proved that they can measure up to their community's standards, they feel they are entitled to achieve their goals — to go on to college and to careers that offer interesting work and the chance to fulfill their potential. They believe that the political-economic system that offers such just desserts is fundamentally healthy, and that if they succeed, they will be doing what is right for America as well as for themselves.

The unity they perceive between the goals of the meritorious individual and of American society leads them to view the nation's problems as those of a basically sound system that has temporarily gone awry. From the perspective of these youth, if everyone recognized and lived according to simple, small town values, a general restoration of individual morality would cure the nation's ills. But these youth believe that only individuals in the middle class are likely to make moral choices, for they believe that young people in wealthy, drug-infested suburbs and urban ghettos alike have not been given sufficient guidance by their parents or communities to develop standards of individual morality.

Their optimism about their own possibilities draws on their success in having gradually given up childish ways, accepted the close monitoring of their behavior by well-meaning parents and teachers, and thus proved themselves worthy of respect. They have grown from uncertain high school freshmen into competent and confident seniors, and they expect to maintain this course. They hope to be able to meet the more rigorous academic demands of college, to endure financial hardship and the strangeness of being among people with diverse beliefs and habits, and finally to enter careers that give them financial security.

The young women are uncertain exactly how their plans will be affected by the men they marry, for they assume that they will tailor the shape of their future lives to fit their husbands' expectations. Yet they imagine that they will find men whose characters are like other Milltowners' and anticipate no major shifts.

These youth are more town-proud than the young people of Cityville and Townline. They see Milltown's economic prosperity and thriving downtown as evidence of the town's capacity to take care of itself and its own. They attribute a similar independence to the people of the town, who have chosen the good life of a small town and then have, through their hard work, maintained stable, close-knit families. These young people believe that they have been sheltered from the disorder and tension of the world outside, and though they feel ready to leave for college, they intend to remain basic Milltown folk all their lives and to raise their own children in similar small and wholesome places.

They also believe that they will remain insulated from national politics and admit that they are likely to become part of the "silent majority," whose apathy contributes to America's problems. But the strong link they make between individual morality and the larger political sphere gives them reason to believe in the importance of setting a personal example of good citizenship through leading an exemplary life. If everyone else tried as hard as they will to improve themselves and to behave generously to those who are less fortunate, the nation would flourish.

Demography Experienced

Certainly it is fruitless to ask which aspects of life in each community have been most significant in the evolving social identities of these youth. It is impossible to understand fully one element in isolation from the web of connections in which it is entwined. Our analysis suffers if anything from an overabundance of significance, but that could also be said of life.

We chose the communities of Cityville, Townline, and Milltown because they offered demographic contrasts that we thought might be influential in shaping the social worlds encountered by their promising working-class youth: the socioeconomic mix of the population, the size of the community, and its urban or rural status.

We have seen how these factors structure daily life: how they affect the range of privilege and power encountered in each place; the emotional supports, educational resources, and adult models available to youth; the degree of consensus or conflict in community messages about what young people should value and how they should behave; and the insularity or openness of each community.

And we have also seen how the social interpretations of youth in each community reflect the special character or ethos of that place, based in its particular ethnic, economic, and political history. These social and historical dimensions of community life are critical mediators of demographic facts as they are experienced.

For example, the smallness and the small town character of Milltown—in contrast to both Cityville and Townline—are certainly important to its working-class young people's perception of themselves as part of a place where people know each other. But their very positive sense of Milltown as a place where they are especially fortunate to have grown up draws both on the community's economic comeback after factory closings that depressed other mill towns and on its placement among wealthy suburbs whose youth appear decadent and neglected.

Similarly, the largeness of the high school populations in Cityville and Townline takes on different meanings from other aspects of life in each community. Working-class youth in both communities feel that their high school is too large, and its staff too indifferent, to recognize them for who they really are or to respond adequately to their needs. But the homes and neighborhoods of Cityville provide its youth with arenas where they feel known and valued, and they rely on the high school only for the credentials it offers them. Few positive neighborhood attachments continue for Townline's working-class youth after their freshman year, and they do not feel understood or supported in their families. They have little to buffer the pain of their high school experience and feel enormously grateful to those teachers and guidance counselors who helped them make their way through.

Neighborhood life mediates the density as well as the largeness of Cityville, whose young people feel that they are located in small, familiar arenas within a larger community. Although Cityville youth perceive the congestion and noise of their neighborhoods as negative features of city life, they focus on the sense of being at home. The smallness of Milltown leads its youth to experience the town as one large neighborhood, and the smallness of their high school offers them many extra-curricular roles to fill.[2] In such a small school and town, the patterns of life seem legible to youth: they feel an integral part of their community and gain confidence from feeling known and necessary.

We had imagined that being close to a major city and part of a heterogeneous community and high school would encourage Townline youth to become cosmopolitans, experiencing and enjoying diversity, whereas Cityville youth, surrounded by a more homogeneous population, would be less comfortable with different kinds of people. In fact, although Townline youth feel seasoned by having survived many kinds of experiences, they hold the diversity of their high school population responsible for the constant tension and strife in the school and their own feelings of marginality and devaluation. They leave high school longing to find people similar to themselves, in contrast to Cityville youth, who hope to encounter somewhat more diversity than they have known.

146

Closeness to or distance from an urban center also becomes meaningful in relation to other factors of daily life. The moral consensus in Milltown, 25 miles away from Boston, leads its youth to think of the modern city as a symbol for the alien, dangerous, and unknown.[3] Townline youth come to feel like urban people and go into Boston with ease, although they are strangers in the wealthier parts of Townline. Cityville youth also live close to Boston, but it is largely irrelevant to their lives, an exotic place to explore occasionally and to commute to when they enter college.

The social histories of each community, including the histories of its ethnic groups, play important parts in the evolution of the social identities of adolescents. The Irish- and Italian-American families of Cityville retain enough of the traditional extended family structure, to give their young people the sense of being included — whether they want to be or not — in larger family entities. Cityville youth never spontaneously refer to their ethnic origins, which, like the air they breathe, they take for granted. The young people of Milltown also find ethnic distinctions not worth mentioning, but for a very different reason: their ethic of individual responsibility minimizes the importance of group memberships. Although Milltown history records the important role of competing ethnic clubs in its social life in the 19th century, its current inhabitants see themselves as essentially alike, upholders of the fundamental American values exemplified in small town life.[4]

Ethnicity in Townline is a very different matter, enmeshed in all the socioeconomic distinctions that are salient to its youth. Working-class adolescents who are Jewish have to contend with their relatively low status in a community where Jews are generally perceived as wealthy and powerful. Working-class Jewish families in Townline are a small and declining minority, the tail-end of a migration wave. Whether adolescents experience their family's position as a result of powerful historical circumstances such as the Holocaust or of their fathers' personal failure, they still struggle not to feel ashamed of its low status. When wealthier relatives offer them financial help, they either resist it or accept with the fear that they are "taking advantage," like the more privileged peers they criticize. Many of their families are recent arrivals in Townline and lack the support of grandparents or other relatives; some have suffered the death or desertion of one parent. The marginality experienced by these youth in high school was compounded by their families' marginality in the community and the world.

Townline adolescents who are Irish-Catholic have to contend with both the stereotypical images of their neighborhoods and the lower status of their group in comparison with wealthier Jews, scarcely noticing the existence of Jews —young people or adults—whose economic situation is similar to their own. Confronted with a dramatic loss of status when they left their neighborhoods for the high school, the Irish-Catholic young men find refuge in group solidarity, while the young women, experiencing considerable personal isolation and academic failure, evolve dreams of power and influence.

The Contextualization of Class

Certainly the social identities of the adolescents of Cityville, Townline, and Milltown demonstrate how differently social class is experienced in various contexts. In the first chapter, we agreed with Connell's concept of class as a structuring process of power at work in particular places over time, rather than as a rigid system of power. In Connell's words, "as power is exercised and contested, social relations are organized" (1982, p. 180). From this perspective, differences in power frame and organize, but do not determine, people's thoughts and actions, and the meaning of social class evolves as individuals construct and reconstruct their social identities as they act in specific contexts.

Let us first examine the meaning of parents' work and status. In all three communities adolescents perceive their fathers' work as difficult—physically exhausting, insecure, low-paying, unfulfilling. Their mothers, when they work, are also confined to low-status jobs with limited possibilities. But the positioning of social classes in each place had important consequences for young people's evaluation of their parents'

148

standing. The working-class youth of Townline came to feel the need to defend or justify their parents' status in comparison with the middle- and upper-class careers of the parents of wealthier and more powerful peers. As they entered adolescence, these young people had to cope with their parents' inability to understand their dilemmas and give them support, their parents' sense of not having succeeded in various aspects of life, and the shock of their own academic inferiority at the high school. The devaluation felt by Townline youth during their high school years was a natural result of this triple blow, but it might have been less powerful if their parents had not admired the Townline schools so much and expected so much from them for their children. The judgments of the school could be criticized but not ignored.

In Cityville parents did not admire the schools and expected little of them. Consequently, their children were not as vulnerable to the indifference they perceived there or to the schools' negative judgments about them. They drew guidance and support from their parents' belief in their abilities and insistence that they become ambitious. Because they did not have to contend with a large middle- and upper-middle-class population in town or at school, their parents' jobs —no matter how unrewarding—were nothing to be ashamed of. They could respect their parents as workers, and in the homogeneous working-class world around them, they felt fortunate and confident.

In Townline and Cityville, working-class youth recognize differences in power as a crucial feature of class relations. This is not the case in Milltown, whose young people conceive of classes as defined primarily by income rather than power and give morality the starring role in the social class drama they construct. These youth place the rich and the poor at the extreme ends of the range of income distribution and identify with the large middle class. They wish that their parents earned more money and found more enjoyment in their jobs but see their parents as successful providers of the emotional and economic essentials for positive development. They see different rules operating for people in each class, believing that only people in the middle class can gain full satisfaction from their individual efforts—only there

149

does the possibility exist for individual mobility and thus individual responsibility. People at the bottom are trapped because they don't have the economic or emotional resources to change their situation, and people at the top, who have so much that they don't need to strive, are exempt from the consequences of their immorality. In this conception, conflicts of power between classes are barely recognized, and morality replaces politics as the dynamic of social change. Milltown youth believe that American society can be redeemed if people return to small town values and thus, as individuals, take responsibility for their fates.

Thus, the meaning of class for young people evolves from the structure of everyday life in particular places. This fact has relevance to the long-standing debate on the effect of "high-status" contexts on the development of ambition among working-class youth. Some social scientists argue that exposure to middle-class life and culture helps promising working-class youth by giving them the chance to rehearse the values and behavior of the class to which they aspire; with middle-class role models to imitate, it will be easier for them to learn the skills and attitudes necessary to undertake higher education (see Spady, 1976; Turner, 1964). Others argue that working-class youth may lose some of their confidence in their own prospects when they compare themselves with higher-status, high-achieving peers (see Alexander and Eckland, 1975; Nelson, 1972).

From our perspective, the consequences of high-, low-, or medium-status environments for the ambitions and self-esteem of working-class youth depend not on the dominance of one community factor over another but on what they learn from the entire constellation of their experience within a community — what meanings they give to hope, ambition, and class, and how, in the process of growing up, they reconcile competing messages, identify sources of support, and recover from setbacks to their self-confidence.

In addition, we conclude that researchers should not take it for granted that becoming upwardly mobile necessarily means the same thing to all working-class youth, for the meaning of ambition varies from place to place. Thus, although youth in all three communities came to think of them-

150

selves as strivers, young people who must plan and work for their own futures, striving means more than aiming for jobs that have higher status than the jobs of their parents: in Cityville, where the continuity of relationships takes priority, striving is viewed as the way to get the job one needs in order to support a family and have time left over to spend with friends; in Milltown, where being hard-working and responsible is a matter of character, striving is a sign of maturity, important in and of itself; in Townline, striving takes on the additional meaning of searching, of refusing to be satisfied with convention or routine.

How these young people feel about their progress is related — but not necessarily in a simple way — to their estimations of where they stand in relation to their peers. In the predominatly working-class community of Cityville, promising youth compare themselves with the majority of their peers whose parents have not helped them to take the future seriously. Ambitious youth feel well-off, convinced that they are strengthening their relationships with caring parents. Milltown youth, also growing up in a predominantly working-class community, prefer to downplay the differences between themselves and less serious students and draw pride from the community consensus that pursuing their individual ambitions signifies that they have become moral persons of strong character. They too feel confident about the future and, in addition, lucky to be starting out from Milltown.

In contrast, the working-class youth of Townline, with many upper-middle-class models, perceive them generally as examples of what *not* to aim toward. Their allegiance to many of the upper-middle-class values of their time and place — the desire for authenticity, a critical stance toward authority, belief in the importance of personal transformation — makes it harder to arrive at their own definitions of ambition. Further, although it is difficult to say whether these values were adopted as a means of emulating their higher-status peers or of defending themselves against them, observing these peers certainly contributes to their confusion about what is worth aiming for and their conviction that material success contaminates those who pursue it. The social identities of Townline youth represent both an incorporation and a rejection of the

151

dominant standard in their community as they struggle to take pride in their situation as lonely searchers and to build up confidence in their ability to endure and overcome difficulties.

History and Community: Activism, Freedom of Expression, Feminism

All these working-class youth grew up during the same historical time: their earliest political memory is being sent home early from elementary school the day that President John F. Kennedy was shot. Between then and their graduation from high school, several other national leaders were assassinated and political movements burgeoned—to end the war in Vietnam, to ensure the extension of civil rights to blacks and other minorities, and to change the status and values of women. It was a time of social tumult, with college-educated youth in the vanguard. Traditional social and political mores were challenged by a counter culture that asserted the validity of experimenting with drugs, music, and life-styles.

To activists and to most non-activists, there seemed to be more than enough food, jobs, and status in America to go around. The image of the United States as a land of plenty still dominated the public imagination, although there were intimations that the number of jobs was being outstripped by the huge increase in the number of available young people and that resources were being depleted.[5] Education still seemed to promise mobility, and questions about the American Dream centered on whether it had ever included the oppressed and whether it led to personal satisfaction—not whether it could still be achieved.

As Elder's work shows, the impact of historical events is rarely uniform among all the members of the same age group: "class, ethnic, and residential variations" influence how "sub-groups 'work up' historically relevant experience" (1981, p. 8). By the early seventies, even as the media and many commentators portrayed the nation's youth as full of "fiery vehemence" (Marin, 1972), some pointed out that only a relatively small proportion of young people were active (see Adelson, 1970). Some predicted that working-class youth were likely to be part of the "backlash" against social protest and innovation (see Berger and Berger, 1971), and Keniston (1970) imagined that working-class youth who entered college would feel too "tenuously included" in the middle-class system to risk challenging the status quo.

Our work reveals important community differences in both the exposure to and the interpretations drawn from historical events and shows, moreover, that going to college does not necessarily mean wanting to enter the established system. Commonalities among the young people from all three communities seem to be based in what they perceive as their group interests in terms of both class and age.

As they leave high school, the promising working-class adolescents of Cityville, Townline, and Milltown see themselves not as rebels, but rather as part of a new generation that has enjoyed the relative plenty of the decades after the Great Depression. They anticipate being able to express themselves more freely than their parents did, to find better jobs, and to choose where they will live, and they believe that going on to college will provide access to the work they want.

In addition, the young people of Cityville and Townline claim as part of their legacy the option of using marijuana, wearing their clothes and hair as they wish, listening to loud, irreverent music, and enjoying sex that does not necessarily produce children. Those whose parents are religious, and who were so themselves when they were younger, feel that they have moved away from conventional religion and can choose to keep some beliefs and practices and abandon others. Milltown youth have also begun to question rigid adherence to religion but disapprove of what they see as the excesses of more open life-styles. They blame the confusion and disorder of contemporary life and its celebration of hedonism for the disappearance of decent living and consideration for others. They are attracted to the "simple but sufficient" life-styles of earlier times.[6]

In Milltown and Cityville, the sense of being part of a youthful and more expressive generation is not experienced as rebellion against parents, as a commitment to experimental life-styles, or as part of a political stance of opposition to the status quo. These young people simply feel that they are accepting the role of youth at their time in history, a time when young people are less restrained by economic scarcity and able to go on to college. They have concluded that the nation is in difficulty, but, as we have seen, Cityville youth see social and political problems as part of the human condition, and Milltown youth believe that the nation's problems can be solved with a return to traditional American values and behavior.

Although Boston is a center of activism, few demonstrations or marches have taken place in Cityville. Most of these Cityville youth think of the activists they read about in newspapers and watch on television as asking the right questions but tilting at windmills. Cityville youth believe that it is in the nature of government to represent the interests of the powerful, and although they sympathize with the plight of oppressed minorities, they have never expected a just society. Cityville youth and their parents have joined local actions: forming neighborhood groups to protest against the building of an interstate highway through the town, petitioning the school committee to retract the firing of a popular radical teacher, trying to get a new bus for the high school band. But these young people do not connect such actions with the national unrest; they see them as interpersonal rather than systemic attempts to improve their own and their neighbors' conditions. These youth headed for college with little desire to become accepted in upper-middle-class society; they hope instead to achieve their career goals without changing either their characters or their life-styles.

In contrast, working-class youth in Townline have experienced an oppositional movement, seen and joined demonstrations led by students and supported by the high school staff, and found much of the movement's analysis and rhetoric appealing. Their rejection of materialism draws on radical questions about the worth of the American Dream, as well as their own antipathy toward the wealthier people of Townline, and they feel that they have a role to play in redressing injustices done to the oppressed. But by the time of high school graduation, those who were politically active no longer have much hope that the political and economic sys-

154

tem can be moved. In addition, they have become cynical about the sincerity of the wealthy leaders of the student radical movement, and they question their own motives in their political involvements as in all that they do. Far from wanting to be included in a system they see as corrupt, they intend in college to remain searchers, hoping to escape contamination.

As is true of all adolescents, relationships with the opposite sex concern these working-class youth. Few have had serious relationships, but they hope to in the future, and they have thought about the impact of those relationships on their future lives. Coming of age at a time when traditional gender roles are being challenged by the feminist movement, they feel little sympathy for those whom the media portrays as bra-burners, but all — male as well as female — agree that women should have equal access to careers and equal pay.

The young women of all three communities want careers for themselves, in contrast to their mothers, who have either remained homemakers or have taken jobs when their families needed more money or when they found themselves unexpectedly responsible for supporting their children. To the young women of Cityville, careers mean that their lives will be interesting and not confined to the home. Many intend to be public school teachers so that they can leave their work when their children are young. They have no doubt that they will marry, in contrast to Townline young women, who are preparing to go it alone and do not see what they would gain from having children or husbands. In Milltown young women prepare for college and careers but feel that their lives, including work, will largely depend upon the men they marry.

At this point in their lives these young women have no concept of sexual politics; they have not, even in Townline, drawn systemic conclusions about the dominance of male power in society. Milltown young women do not pursue the contradictions they perceive in their future plans. Men are not a political category for the young women in the three communities; fathers who are seen as having let their wives and children down are judged deficient individuals, examples of what to avoid in choosing their own future husbands.

The young men of all three communities recognize that if they ever do have families — and, except in Townline, all intend to — there will be substantial sharing in the relationship between husband and wife. This is perceived less as a response to feminism than as a natural result of belonging to a youthful generation in which they as parents will spend more time with their children and depend less on authority and tradition than their parents did.

Moving into the Future

The promising working-class youth of all three communities think of themselves as starting out toward futures they have prepared for. Looking back at their development from children to teenagers, from high school freshmen to graduating seniors, they all feel that they have become competent in important ways, learned to speak up for themselves, started to distinguish what they deem important from what is valued by the crowd, and begun to redefine their relationship with parents away from dependency and toward self-reliance.

Becoming young people who can think for themselves has different meanings in each community. Becoming your own person in Cityville means developing a character with enough consistency and depth that you cannot be taken in or over by false standards. No matter what you face, you remain true to who you really are, which corresponds to what you are like with the important people in your life. In Milltown, it means that you have developed beyond the need for external controls into a person with an internalized set of standards. You have achieved self-discipline and can be trusted to know what is right. For Townline youth, being able to think for yourself means that you have become committed to a continuing effort to understand yourself and your own motives, to avoid false appearances, and to value only what is authentic.

These interpretations of what they have become as individuals coexist with their shared sense of themselves as children of fathers with manual or low-level white-collar jobs and as young people who have been told that they are capable of moving up the socioeconomic ladder. They cannot take their futures for granted; for many, exactly what to strive for has been an issue, and whether they can achieve their goals has been a question. Few can look forward to financial help as they make their way; instead, most have held part-time jobs and full-time summer jobs for years and are used to earning their own money for clothing and entertainment; in college they expect to pay for their tuition and books. They think of themselves as young people who must struggle and scrimp if they are going to get where they want to go.

But no matter what difficulties they foresee and no matter how fixed the system of social inequities appears to them, these young people are hopeful about the future. And they believe in a central tenet of the developmental vision and the American Dream: that they confront the future as individuals and that their own efforts will largely determine their fate.

Even in Townline, where socioeconomic strata are clearly visible, and working-class youth see status being passed from generation to generation, they do not see their own future chances as seriously threatened by their working-class status. They feel that they are freely defining their own terms for success, searching for goals that reject materialism and reflect the importance of being different from mass society. In a similar way, the goals of Cityville youth reconcile the systemic inequities they see and their pessimism about the long-term fate of society with their personal hopefulness. These youth focus on what they can achieve within the perimeters they have drawn to define what is practical and moral for people like themselves to aspire to. Milltown youth, perceiving few inequities that seem relevant to their lives, see plenty of room in American society for individuals like themselves, worthy through having become responsible.

As these young people graduate from high school and move into arenas of life outside their communities, their hopes for the future rest upon their belief in their individual efficacy. Is this belief — and the contradiction it embodies between what they know of systemic inequities and what they assume about their own possibilities — best considered a vulnerability or a strength in their lives? We raise this question here as a prelude to portraying their lives during the next four years, and will, in the final chapter, discuss the many issues it raises.

6
Confronting the Worlds Beyond Community

Cityville: Moving Out and Staying In

The promising working-class youth of Cityville set out from high school to pursue their twofold goal: to become "somebodies" who were serious about the future while remaining themselves, the same sort of decent, unpretentious people as their families and less ambitious friends. Four years later, they look back with pride at the progress they have made and their struggles to overcome difficulties they did not foresee. As these young people had hoped, there have been many continuities in their lives: most continue to live at home with their parents, leaving each morning for school and work, and spending their evenings and weekends with the friends and mates they knew in high school. Their pride and confidence in themselves are drawn in part from the respect they have gained and the independence they have won within relationships that endure, and from their belief that they have taken major steps into adulthood during these years.

Like Joe Mendoza, most of these young people imagined careers for themselves that were straightforward and within reach. The difficulties they foresaw seemed significant but resolvable. Many of the young men wondered whether they should go on to college because they were not sure whether they wanted white-collar work. But they thought that the options they considered were practical and the way toward them would become clear. Now, four years later, Joe's life and thinking are not as representative of the Cityville sample, but he is still typical in two respects: first, in his having been taken by surprise by many events of the intervening years and discovering that getting to the career he wants will take a lot longer than he thought; and second, in his continuing to believe that if he perseveres, he will eventually succeed.

Joe began his studies in electronics the September after high school graduation, but by the time he earned his associate's degree two years later, he had learned that given the shortage of work for electricians, he could not expect to earn much more money than he did from his job as a stock boy in a supermarket warehouse. Joe bought a car, planning to commute 40 miles a day to a technical institute that trains electrical engineers; almost immediately he was laid off from the supermarket and was forced to borrow the money for his tuition as well as his car. In Joe's family also, unexpected problems have required his energy and resourcefulness. After his mother's almost fatal heart attack, he helped her get to physical therapy and later supervised her exercises at home. He considers it his duty to encourage his younger brother to do his homework and tries to keep up the spirits of his father, who has been unemployed for some time. Joe worries about his family and about his own future: he fears that he may not be able to find a job close to Cityville and even that he may be forced to move out of the state in order to work as an electrical engineer.

Family illness and strain, the prospect of not finding work in their chosen careers, difficulties with part-time jobs —these elements have been common in the lives of the promising working-class youth of Cityville during the past four years. But now Joe is exceptional in his insistence that he will work in electronics even if he has to move; most of these young people believe that they will change their careers if necessary in response to the tightness of the job markets they will enter. And Joe's view of college as simply the means to the ends he seeks has now become rare as well. Few others now believe that their college degrees will necessarily help them advance their careers, but they value their college experience for its non-vocational benefits: they believe that going to college has diversified their experience and given

160

them confidence that they can deal with worlds beyond City-ville.

John Coutermarsh's evaluation of college is typical. John no longer wants to be a lawyer, partly because he hasn't liked any of the lawyers among the faculty at the private com-muters' college he attends in Boston. And although he would like to become a counselor for adolescents, he doubts that he could get into graduate school in psychology. Four years ago, he says, he would have laughed at the idea of becoming a postman; now he would feel lucky to get such a job, even though it doesn't require the bachelor's degree he'll get next summer. But he treasures what he has learned in his years at college: "You don't have to take a humanities course to be culturally improved by college. It's a chance to see different people from different places. You do more growing up in college than in any six years before."

College has given many of these young people the chance to find out how good their minds are. Two weeks before her marriage to her high school sweetheart, Tina Stel-luto talks with pride about her studies in classics at the urban state university and her anger that her part-time job as an office manager — 30 hours a week — made it impossible for her to do the extra work she would have needed to graduate with honors. Yet Tina is glad that she could pay for her own tuition and expenses: her job bought her the chance to prove her independence from her parents, who had wanted her to go to nursing school rather than a liberal arts college. Tina doubts that she will be able to find a teaching job in her field or that her degree will be helpful in her life with Jim, who has since high school worked at a series of clerical jobs he dis-likes. As a high school senior, Tina thought becoming a high school teacher was a more practical goal than her other interest — opening a dance studio and giving lessons; now she imagines that she will help to support her new family through teaching dance and performing. Yet she does not regret having gone to college and believes that dealing with people like her professors — very different from the people she knows in Cityville — has helped her become more worldly.

Tina and John, like most college-going youth from City-

161

ville, spend the time they have left after studying and working with family and friends who know nothing of the worlds they experience in college, and they feel the pressure not to seem superior to or different from the others. Almost every young woman is involved with a man who was in high school less ambitious than she and who did not want to go to college, and like Tina, these young women worry about whether their future mates will find stable jobs they enjoy. Tina works hard not to seem to be "putting on airs" when she is with Jim's friends and is proud that she has been able to change their first impressions of her as a snob. Although their college- and non-college-going friends mingle easily, most of these Cityville youth remain on guard. John is the only person in his neighborhood to have gone to college, and he is glad that his group of friends now includes young people from a nearby neighborhood where there is also one young man in college. Not only is John unique in being in college, but he has had a fellowship, loans, and — until last summer — a social security allotment added to his aged parents' check, so that he has not had to work his way through. From the point of view of his friends, John says, "that makes three strikes against me."

> It's not something that somebody would come out
> and say, but it's there. It's something you can
> feel. I have two lives, you know — keeping the
> relationships and trying to go to college. My
> friends are having a hard time — some of them
> made three or four attempts at night school and
> dropped out. I have friends that never finished
> high school, or who finished and are custodians
> there.

John believes that all the young people he knows should "aim upward" toward college and not simply "go from job to job trying to get as much money as possible." He has caught "missionary zeal" and constantly encourages his nephews and the children of his neighborhood to go to college for the cultural broadening he believes they will find there. But he worries that he is becoming "as pushy as the Christians when they tried to Christianize the heathens. It's a hostile field, and

162

they don't trust somebody that's too smart." Yet John is encouraged because his friends often come to him for advice, a sign that he is still rooted in his neighborhood.

Tim Johnson also advises and helps his friends and works hard to defuse their envy of his success. Tim — like many of the promising young men in Cityville — wondered in high school whether he wanted to do manual or white-collar work and is now no longer in school. He graduated from a two-year college with an associate's degree in accounting, found a job in a bank, and bought a wardrobe of expensive suits and shirts; only two weeks after he started, Tim decided that he would never be happy behind a desk and returned to the window-washing job he had done part-time in high school. Soon he began his own cleaning business and has now made enough money to buy his own home and truck and support his wife and baby daughter. From Tim's point of view, college was critical: it gave him perspective — "how to keep up with things" — and taught him how to do his own books and to understand how trends in the general economy affect his business. In contrast, many of his friends have become overwhelmed by their jobs and children since they left high school: "They thought it was a joke when I went to college." Now they take night courses when they can afford to.

Just as Tina and John work to balance their lives at college and in the neighborhood, Tim juggles the demands of his ambition with his ties to his friends, most of whom he has known since childhood. Tim married his high school girlfriend when he left college, and he and his wife and their infant daughter moved into a two-family house — a traditional first investment for Cityville couples — that was advertised as a "handyman's special" in a town 12 miles from Cityville and was much cheaper than anything available there. But Tim's life is still focused on Cityville: his cleaning jobs take him there at least four days a week, and he is likely to leave his wife and daughter with his mother or her parents while he is working. He hires his friends and his younger brother, and when he and his wife go out for dinner, it is with their Cityville friends. He helps his friends with loans as well as advice, and when his wife calls him a "sucker" — because they often do not pay him back or help him out as they promise—he smiles and agrees. "I'm a sucker," he says, "but I enjoy it," adding that his life in Cityville taught him the importance of helping others, whereas his wife grew up with fewer close friends. But he wishes that his friends understood that although his credit is good and he can co-sign their loans, he is not rich, that he struggles to pay the bills for his business and house, that he cannot always stand drinks for them. He tries to persuade them not to spend their money on winter vacations: "I wait for my suntan till July."

As he did four years ago, Tim has a long-range plan for the future: he wants to have more children and work hard until he is around 40, when he imagines that his children, as adolescents, will need him to spend more time with them. By then he hopes to leave the actual cleaning of houses, businesses, and hospitals to those who work for him, to sell his house and buy a better one—preferably in Cityville—and to spend most of his time with his family. In his life so far, he has had the constant support of his mother, who insisted that he go to college, encouraged him to marry, and remains his most trusted advisor on business matters. Another central person in Cityville is Bobby, his first employer, who became a second father when Tim's father died and who refused to hire Tim after high school because he wanted him to go to college. Bobby has helped Tim get started in his own cleaning business and admires his ambitiousness. When Tim graduated from college, Bobby sent him a card with some cash and a note: "For the kid from the Point who made it."

Tim has made it in the manner most prized among Cityville youth: he has succeeded on his own terms at work while remaining deeply involved in his relationships. No one else in the sample feels quite as clear as he about the future, nor has anyone else become as financially successful; but almost all feel that they have made progress in their work lives and become more responsible and caring in their lives as friends and family members. They look back at obstacles they worked to overcome and at options they have helped create in their struggles. As a high school senior, Bob O'Neil was afraid that he would be overwhelmed by the largeness and anonymity of the technical institute where he planned to study draughting, as he had been at Cityville High when he came there after years of parochial school. But Bob found himself less troubled by school than by his status as an impoverished student in an uncertain job market. Waiting for the bus in the morning while his non-college-going peers drove by was galling, and, after his freshman year, when he learned that cancellation of government contracts threatened the draughting career of his older brother, Bob decided not to return to school. He worked briefly as a roofer, and, learning that a slight heart murmur made it impossible for him to join the marines and thus become eligible for a subsidized education later, he decided to work at roofing full-time. The unsteadiness of work in one company led Bob to another, where the boss was overbearing and dishonest, encouraging the workers to create new problems in roofs while repairing the old ones. Bob decided to start his own roofing business and is successful enough now to have his own truck and to pay rent to his mother. He considers himself fortunate among his friends, some of whom remain in college — "we call them the professional students" — and still lack the money to buy what they want. Bob tries to get them part-time work on his roofing projects but finds himself having to redo much of their work. Other friends have tired of the jobs they have held since high school and envy the fact that Bob is his own boss.

His business success parallels the development Bob sees in his relationship with his family. Still respectful of his mother, Bob has become "free to do what I want" because he pays his own way and also contributes to his mother's "big bills." His mother and older sister now come to him for advice, and since his father's death, Bob believes that he has taken on enough responsibility to be considered "the man of the house." His father's long fight against cancer led to major changes in his relationship with Bob, and Bob feels that it is his father's death that "changed me the most." Four years ago Bob focused on his father's alcoholism and stinginess; now he tells of the positive qualities he found in his father when he took his brothers' advice and gave his father a chance:

> Before, I never asked him for anything, but my
> brothers said, "Go ahead, try it. Just ask him for

something — for five bucks if you need it." So I
did. And he never turned me down. He liked that
and we got closer. We'd go out and have a few
beers and my father would say, "Don't drink — I
don't want you to turn out like I did." But as I got
along, he just saw that drinking wasn't as big a
part of everybody else's life as it was his.

Now Bob tries to find a physical reason for his father's faults:
he wonders if Mr. O'Neil's cancer might have been present
long before it was diagnosed and been the cause of his alcoholism. "He wasn't one that went to doctors all the time. He'd
take an aspirin and go to bed. My father never missed work."
Bob feels accepted now as an equal by his older brothers, for
he was able to join them in helping their mother financially
during the nine months it took to transfer their father's social
security payments to her name.

    Like Bob, most Cityville youth believe that although
they have stayed at or close to home, they have also taken
important steps into adulthood during the past four years and
that their relationships with their parents have undergone
significant changes. In becoming financially responsible for
themselves and in contributing to the support of their parents, these young people feel that they have earned the right
to make their own decisions and their own mistakes. The
independence they feel they have won rests not on physical
separateness but on the respect, and often the gratitude, they
have gained from their parents. Joe Mendoza's mother and
Bob O'Neil's father are typical of the many Cityville parents
who have become seriously ill during these years and have
depended upon their children's help, financially and emotionally.

    As they nurture their parents, Cityville youth gain new
perspectives on them as individuals and as forebears. They
feel that they now see their parents more accurately than
they did when they were younger, speaking of the difficulties
their parents faced because of the times in which they grew
up and because of the limitations of their personalities. Like
Bob, most of these young people have revised the negative
images they held of their parents and now feel more identifi-

166

cation with them. Tim Johnson, who was trying as a high school senior to judge his dead father less harshly, now focuses on what he knows of his father's personality when he was Tim's age — before he became alcoholic, diabetic, and abusive to members of his family. "He was like me," Tim says. "He was everybody's friend."

Most of these Cityville youth have gained new respect from their parents and, as in Bob O'Neil's case, from older siblings, without moving out of their homes. But a few have had to struggle to get curfews lifted and to convince their parents that they must not try to manage their children's lives any more: one young woman tells of moving into a girlfriend's house for a few days, until her parents agreed that she could stay out as late as she wished; she then came home bearing gifts and flowers and was welcomed back.

More rare is the experience of those who feel that they must leave home to live as they wish. Barbara Lockhart, who feels that she was overprotected as a child, left her grandmother's and mother's home to share an apartment a few blocks away with her boyfriend, who reminds them too much of her alcoholic, deadbeat father. The move deeply shocked her family. They keep her room exactly as it was, pretending to neighbors — as well as social workers who monitor social security payments for dependents — that she still lives with them. Still, they have begun to accept her independence, and on her frequent visits they talk to her as a woman rather than a little girl. She in turn values them more than she did before, finding links between her own emerging strength of character and her grandmother's "domineeringness" and also her mother's courage in learning a new job even though she is deaf and has difficulty speaking.

As these Cityville youth become launched into wider worlds that test them as individuals, they feel their parents becoming part of the supportive background against which they lead their own increasingly independent lives. They still view their parents' early concern as critical in their having become "somebodies," and even when they must struggle against them, these young people view their parents' protectiveness as appropriate: another young woman talks with pride of her parents' sadness that she has decided to move

167

next year into an apartment with friends. Finding positive legacies for themselves in their parents' characters is part of the process by which these young people become increasingly separate from their parents; as one young man puts it, "Now it's all inside me, so that they don't really have that much influence. It's all up to me."

The working-class youth of Cityville are simultaneously moving out from and staying part of their families, and in the process are finding mates with whom they hope someday to create families of their own: many are involved in steady relationships with members of the opposite sex, whom they hope to marry when circumstances are right, and two are already married. Mates, to whom these young people turn now with their most personal problems, are perceived as critical to their future success. Mates provide support and advice as well as affection, and, as in the case of Tommy, Barbara Lockhart's boyfriend, role models: "Tommy speaks back to his bosses, he never lets himself get pushed around. I learn from that. I spoke up for my raise this year." Tim Johnson, who married much earlier than he had planned and who relies on his mother for business advice, talks playfully of using his wife's advice as a foil to react against. "She tells me what *not* to do" — not to start his own business so young, not to work so hard — "and then I go ahead and do it." The young women of Cityville who have chosen partners less ambitious than they and more confused about the future actively encourage their men to think about jobs and ways to save money.

In most cases, relationships with mates consolidate rather than challenge older ties, becoming part of the constellation of existing relationships with family and friends. Their mates are usually welcomed into these young people's homes and become part of their circle of friends; several youth who have become alienated from their own families feel that they have been adopted by the parents of their mates. Except for Tim, who already has a daughter, these young people talk less now than they did as high school seniors about the children they expect to have. Instead, having realized that achieving their goals will take longer than they had once thought, they focus on the process of getting where they hope to go and the mates whom they expect to come with them.

These Cityville youth have found their lives as workers more difficult than their relationships, and they have come to think of themselves as strugglers—people who must work one or two part-time jobs that are seldom intrinsically satisfying, who must endure work situations that are often unfair as well as unpleasant, who must continually overcome obstacles and find new paths to take toward their long-range goals. Although they find points of identification with their parents' difficulties on the job, these young people think of themselves as still learning and changing, and thus not consigned to their current jobs for a lifetime. Just as they perceive college as valuable whether or not it leads directly to material rewards, they value their work as an opportunity to learn how the world works and how best to respond: they have learned how unfair bosses can be and how to stand up for themselves; they have learned about their own limitations and capabilities and revised their long-term plans accordingly; they have learned that they can act on issues they deem important—like one young woman who joined the picket line of the full-time workers in the store where she works part-time, against the wishes of her parents and boyfriend.

As strugglers, these young people think of themselves as willing to work hard at whatever they are doing, to endure difficult situations, and to remain flexible enough to create end runs around the obstacles they find. Their belief in the importance of trying hard rather than achieving high goals leads them to think that they can be satisfied with a variety of different forms of work, as long as they have enough time and energy after work to spend with their family and friends. The high value they place on relationships makes them feel certain that they will be able to maintain their integrity. Like Bob O'Neil's boss, who trained his workers to create more holes in the roofs they were being paid to fix, the employers of many of these young workers have become examples of what not to become. These Cityville youth believe that they will treat their co-workers and their own employees honestly and fairly.

Before they left high school, these young people

thought that Cityville had been a good place in which to grow up, despite their criticisms of unresponsive teachers and administrators and the general overcrowding, dirt, and noise, and their awareness that Cityville politics were widely regarded as corrupt. During the past four years, they have spent considerable time outside Cityville and have had the new experience of being responded to as Cityvilleans by their teachers, fellow students, co-workers, and employers. They have been stunned to discover how negatively Cityville is regarded by outsiders. It was hard, John Coutermarsh recalls, to sit in his pre-law class in college and hear a convict, brought from his jail cell for the occasion, tell how his early life in Cityville — the easy access to the underworld, the pervasive petty crime and car thefts — prepared him for a life of crime. One young woman explains the reactions of her classmates at the state university: "People look at me and say, 'You're from Cityville?' Now I grew up there and it hasn't been that bad for me, you know. But people tend to look at you like you're a derelict or bum."

When, in high school, these youth read the newspaper exposé of Cityville politics, they were convinced that other communities were also corrupt but had the money to cover up their crimes. They still think so. They know that Cityville is not as bad as its image, and they are wryly amused at the naiveté of outsiders who are deceived by such stereotypes. As they look back, they are still grateful for the lively, informal, and unpretentious life of Cityville neighborhoods, for the values they formed there and the friendships they made, and for the start they got in becoming serious about the future. Yet they have more doubts than before about whether they will want to settle there.

They imagine that places outside the city, with "better homes and schools and more land," give children a chance to grow up more slowly and with less need to become defensive. One young woman imagines growing up in the suburbs:

> It's a slower place. You get to be a little bit more
> naive about things than people in the city. We're
> born and told, "Well, this is the way it is, honey,
> people will screw you left and right." We're

hanging around street corners when we're nine
years old, and things go a lot faster. You feel
certain things. You learn that no one's going to
give you a break, and you fight tooth and nail for
what you want.

To another young woman it seems that life outside places like
Cityville gives young people more chance to feel good about
themselves:

I think of a place where there's not too many
people and where somebody can grow up
thinking they're important. Let them have some
sort of strength from thinking that in *some* place
they are important, and then let them go out into
the world and see what happens.

Yet many of these Cityville youth wonder whether they could
be happy in a more rural place — "just the birds are twitter-
ing; that's the only action you see" — and they imagine that
suburban people would be snobbish: "they don't like working-class people in Annandale." Leaving Cityville is not a step
these young people would take lightly, and if they do leave,
they plan to maintain their relationships with family members
and friends who remain.

Four years ago several of these youth held higher ambitions than most of their peers and felt at odds with the majority in Cityville. For the two young men, whose lives have
centered on the private, primarily residential universities
that they attend, Cityville has now become merely a place to
sleep in their parents' houses at night: they feel severed from
former relationships with Cityville peers and from connections with the community. Greg Hynes had foresworn his
ambitions as a political activist at the time of his first interview
and decided to prepare for a life as a well-to-do dentist based
in a country "chalet." Except for summer jobs working in
Cityville playgrounds, Greg now feels that he has finally
escaped Cityville and the tensions of living among Cityville
peers. "Now I can use the English language as it should be
used," he explains, and says that he has found a group of
friends, all based in the commuter house at the university he

attends, just up the hill from his parents' home. Greg spends his time in classes and studying and hanging out in the commuter house: late at night he returns home to sleep. He feels relieved from the pressure to pretend to be like the tougher kids in his neighborhood, and he laughs at the unexpected admiration his fellow students feel for his having survived the streets of Cityville: "They think I'm some Humphrey Bogart character!" Greg is applying to dental and law schools and has not yet decided which career to pursue.

Tony Sambataro had a hard time avoiding the bullies in his neighborhood, but by the time he was a high school senior he felt that he had found good friends in Cityville, although he had no time to spend with them. Now he never mentions those friends and regards Cityville only as the place where his family lives and where he returns each night, after his classes, his job, and partying with his girlfriend and other fellow students. "I've learned that Cityville's a real dump," Tony explains. "Now that I'm getting older, I see all the slime coming to the surface. It has the highest population of hoods in the country." No longer certain he will return to Italy with his family when he becomes a physician and his father retires, Tony—like Greg—feels that his future depends upon the profession he follows and the college friends he has made.

The other young person who aimed high has not turned away from Cityville, and remaining loyal to her relationships has played a part in the lowering of her ambition. Barbara Lockhart was the only young woman who had high aspirations, hoping, against her family's wishes, to become a doctor. Barbara did very well as a chemistry major and enjoyed being part of a group of compatible, respected pre-meds at the urban state university while she continued to work 20 hours a week at the sales job she had held in high school and held a half-time job as a lab technician at a city hospital. She moved, as we have seen, into an apartment with her boyfriend, proving her independence while continuing to visit her family regularly. In her junior year, Barbara's grandfather became ill, and she spent a large part of one semester taking care of him, working her two jobs but failing to write up lab reports at school. After his death, she faced a sharp drop in her grades and decided to switch to a major in biology and to train to become a nurse.

Barbara interprets this shift as a personal failure. "I guess I didn't have what it takes," she explains. "I guess I just got lazy." She makes no reference to the conflicts she faced between the pressure for achievement, which requires that personal relationships be subordinated to the demands of school, and the values of Cityville, which elevate relationships above all. Nor does she link her difficulties to her need to work two jobs in order to go to school, although she is aware that life is easier for wealthier pre-meds at Harvard, where she took a summer school chemistry course. Barbara's interpretation of her dilemma, at least at this point in her life, is characteristic of the social interpretation of all these promising Cityville youth: despite their identification with "the people," "the little man," the "lower-middle class," or "the workers," despite their perception of themselves as part of a social group whose members start off behind many others, these young people think of themselves primarily as individuals and feel individually responsible for their futures.

Both their sense of being part of a relatively disadvantaged group and their commitment to their own individual responsibility intensified in the four years after high school. Originally Cityville youth made a sharp distinction between the world they inhabited along with other ordinary, decent people and the world inhabited by the rich and powerful. The problems in American society resulted from the greed and corruption of "they's" who cared little about people and were willing to trample over others in pursuit of their own selfish interests. These young people saw this division as universal because they believed that power inevitably corrupts. Four years after high school, they have had more personal experience of being treated unfairly by bosses, and they are even angrier about the unfairness of political life. In addition, they have discovered that the economy is more precarious than they once thought and that job opportunities are more constricted. As high school seniors just starting out, they believed that getting a higher education would be the critical factor in achieving their goals; now, they see few clear links between their degrees and their future jobs. "I used to think that if you graduated from college, no matter what degree you got, it was a golden opportunity the moment you graduated. You had a degree! That was it! But degrees don't mean much now."

Yet these young people believe that as individuals they will find a way to overcome the barriers they encounter and that despite what they have learned of social inequalities, they will personally reach the modest goals they have set. This belief underlies their hope about the future, as one young woman explains. She found herself intrigued by her college sociology course and by the assigned readings that attempted to expose the false promises of the American Dream by demonstrating that "no matter where you start out on the social ladder, no matter how hard you try, you are essentially trapped in whatever social strata you started out in." This young woman was angered by the implications of what she read, believing that society was indeed class-bound but unable to accept these same constraints on her own future:

> I had always believed in the Yes-America-is-the-land-of-opportunity myth. Some of the things they described said—well, if I took it to heart, I'd believe that the rich are doing everything they can to stomp on the poor!

But you don't really want to believe it?

> Well, if I believed it completely I'd be shutting off my future. So, I think maybe they're not entirely right and occasionally there is a chance.

As high school seniors, these youth drew a political distinction between themselves and their parents: they felt that they belonged to a more liberal generation, more sympathetic to the rights of minorities, and they believed that they, unlike their parents, would not simply complain about political injustices but instead would act. This distinction has diminished during the intervening years, and the working-class youth of Cityville look back on many of their former assertions as naive: "I thought all blacks lived in the slums; I never

174

knew they could go to college." Now they feel susceptible to political alienation and inactivity, and accept these limitations in themselves as well as their parents, just as they have come to accept the limited possibility of change in American society. Many of them feel guilty for not voting, yet they feel that they cannot "keep up" with the issues and that politics is complicated and overwhelming. "A vote seems so small, so *little*, you wonder if it matters," one young man explains. They have seen their social commitments waver before their own needs: as high school seniors their concern for stemming environmental pollution led them to favor the widespread use of public transportation; now automobiles have become critical to their way of life and sense of freedom, and they have come to believe that not only the greed and stupidity of automobile manufacturers are responsible for pollution but also the unwillingness of people like themselves to accept limits on how much they drive.

Four years ago these young people felt privileged in comparison with blacks, whose struggle for civil rights seemed just and long overdue. But in college they have seen black students being given priority through affirmative action programs and special scholarship funds, at a moment when these young people were discovering that their own struggles would be much harder than they had imagined. Now attempts to compensate black students for past injustices seem to these white working-class youth to discriminate against people like themselves, who had nothing to do with slavery and segregation, and who are themselves starting out all on their own with no help from anyone. Their acceptance of their own individual responsibility for their fate influences their attitude: they believe that compensatory programs deprive individual blacks of the need for initiative and thus the opportunity to feel proud of their achievements.

These Cityville youth have staked their lives on becoming serious about the future, and this means becoming practical and accepting what cannot be changed. Thus, while they believe that the ideal society would start everyone off equally, they have no illusions that it ever will, and they consider it their task — and the task of everyone else — to do the best they can within the existing system. They have seen few people willing to subordinate their own self-interest to the common good, and they do not imagine that human nature will ever change. They were not surprised by the Watergate scandals, for they expected little better from politicians, and they have serious doubts about whether it is possible to be right about an issue and to pursue it in public arenas without being corrupted: the career of Ralph Nader, whom they admire, makes them suspicious; they wonder how he can be succeeding unless he has sacrificed his integrity.

Because they believe that individuals can, through hard work, influence their life-chances, these young people hesitate to recommend large-scale measures to reduce existing inequities. Thus, although they decry the huge gaps between the wealthy in America and the poor, and wish that the rich would give more to those in need, they still do not favor measures to reduce the assets of the wealthy, such as stricter limits on inheritance.

Accepting the givens of society, their own social position, their own limitations, is part of the process through which these young people commit themselves to struggling toward their goals. They have relinquished hopes for social change and the belief that their generation might be motivated by social concerns as well as self-interest. Altruism has now become a suspect motivation for them, and the would-be teachers and physicians talk now about the pleasure they seek through their work rather than their desire to help others.

In a society that is complex, usually unfair, and generally indifferent to people like them, these working-class youth believe that their focus on achieving what they can is a mature stance, a sign that they value themselves and their parents. What counts most in the years ahead is knowing that they have worked hard to do what they can within the constraints of their lives. Individual effort will give meaning to their lives, whether or not they can achieve what they want. Hoping to enter medical school next year, Tony Sambataro has aimed higher than almost everyone else. Yet for him, too,

> Success doesn't have to mean doing and being
> what you always wanted to do and be. What's
> most important is that you *try* to do that, *try* to be

176

that way, *try* to obtain that. If you don't try, then
you regret that, and I think the worst thing you
can ever do with your life is to regret a single day.

In this vision of success, as long as they remain caring people,
the youth of Cityville believe that they will gain a place of
honor.

Townline: Struggling Alone

If we think of the promising working-class youth of Cityville
and Townline as young voyagers starting out, we can easily
contrast what they sought in the four years after high school.
The young people of Cityville looked forward to voyages that
followed a familiar shoreline and stayed close to home. They
expected to be tested and matured by their journeys but not
fundamentally changed. They hoped that — after hard work
and serious training — they would be recognized among
their friends and families as having earned the rights of adulthood and welcomed back to steady lives among the relationships they valued. In contrast, most Townline youth felt that
they had already launched themselves into the future before
they left high school, their faces turned hopefully toward
what was to come. They set out alone, feeling unique and
proud of the thoughtfulness they had developed as they
coped with the loneliness and marginality of high school life.
They hoped to find in college understanding allies and fellow
travelers and meaningful directions for their lives. Most
wanted to set courses that would take them away from the
competitive race toward conventional goals that they had
experienced in high school; they wanted to create authentic
lives. Some headed for open seas, hoping never to settle into
routines that inhibited their freedom to move and change.
    The way through the next four years turned out to be
more tortuous and obscure than these Townline youth —
both Catholic and Jewish — had anticipated. They lived
these years intensely, and now high school seems to have
happened in another epoch. Some began college as residential students at the state university a hundred miles from

Townline, a few at smaller and more expensive private universities in or close to Boston. After four years, only a few were prepared to graduate, the rest having taken time off to figure out a direction for their studies and lives, or to make the money necessary to continue at college — or both. During these intervals, these working-class youth moved in and out of dormitories and apartments, often living in their parents' homes, or those of grandparents or siblings, in order to save money; from there they went each day to their jobs as waitresses, factory workers, bank tellers, and clerical staff. Some transferred from private universities to cheaper state schools and continued to work their way through. The few who were just about to graduate from private colleges had taken out loans, been given some scholarship aid, and worked summer and part-time jobs. Most of the young Catholic women had never begun college but had worked at a series of jobs.

For many of the Jewish working-class youth of Townline, whose primary goal had been to set their own meaningful agenda for their lives, the way was especially hard. In high school, Danny Genzuk had been representative, hoping to meet people like himself in college and to answer his questions about how to work toward changing the social order while living within it. Danny's struggles during the past four years, still unresolved, illuminate the issues faced by all these young people. Now he is working as an assistant trimmer in a Boston garment factory and living in his father's house in Townline; at the end of the previous summer, he decided to extend a semester's leave of absence from the state university into a year away. Danny has taken each leave (this is his second) not primarily because he needs money, but because he has found no answers to his questions.

At first Danny enjoyed being at college. His dorm was filled with students who, like himself, had been active in the movement against the war in Vietnam and who created, through their music, their friendliness, and their marijuana, a sense of community that he treasured. But early in his sophomore year, Danny realized that he had used up all his savings and was no closer to knowing what he was going to do with his life than he had been in high school. He took the next semester off, hoping to work through the issues on his own, but found himself settling instead into a routine of working in the insurance company mailroom where he had worked part-time in high school, and then watching television in his father's house at night. "Nothing came up — there wasn't any change," so Danny decided to return to school the next year and to major in history as a prelude to law school; but the next two years left him less sure than ever that he should be in college. Many professors wanted students to confine their ideas to the material presented in lectures and textbooks; Danny's grades went down when he wrote essays that conveyed his own perspective and opinions. He perceived most of his teachers as impersonal and glib: "Their lectures were like the Johnny Carson show."

An exceptional professor was a self-styled radical who first lambasted his students with criticism of their bourgeois lives and then predicted that they would never do anything different from what their parents had done. This man invited students to write letters to him about their readings instead of papers and examinations, and Danny became deeply involved in the course. He was upset to be given a grade of 40 on one of his letters and to read that the professor thought Danny's opinions were racist. "Of course we're all racists," Danny explains, "because we all grow up in a racist society. But I was being sarcastic in the letter because I thought we had a personal relationship. But he didn't understand that." Although Danny generally found it difficult to approach his professors, fearing to waste their time, he made an appointment to see this professor, worried about being criticized for "bourgeois slips" in conversation. "But he was nice, he was okay," Danny found. The professor accepted Danny's explanation of the meaning of his letter and withdrew his criticism but refused to change the grade because it reflected his judgment that Danny had not made reference to enough readings in his letter.

The social analysis taught in the course gave Danny some hope that he would find a method of social change, but as the semester progressed he began to dispair:

At first I'd analyze something and think that you

had to first figure out what's wrong and then you
could decide on your political objectives. But
then after a while I thought, "Hey, it's not like
that!" It started to hit me, "Hey, this situation is
part of my life and it's affecting me and it stinks."
But I still don't know what I can do about it.

Danny learned to identify with people who were apolitical: "I
finally understood those kids who were so apathetic — and
how frightened you can get."

He became increasingly critical of any paths he could
imagine taking, in work as well as politics. A new generation
of students appeared at the university, more formal, politically conservative, and headed for safe professions, and
Danny began to think of his commitment to studying law as
conventional. He also began to worry that he might graduate,
as so many liberal arts majors did, deep in debt and unable to
find a job. He thought he'd enjoy working with troubled
adolescents but knew that to become a professional psychologist he would need to go to graduate school and felt that he
could not survive the competition. As he had at the end of
high school, Danny came to doubt that going to school was
the best way to become educated, and he had lost confidence
that college would enable him to find a vocation in which he
could help himself or the world. Danny decided to leave
school for a semester, and has not gone back.

Feeling the staleness of his job in the insurance company, be began looking for work. One morning he showed up
to apply for a job that had been advertised in the paper and
found over a hundred people lined up before him. Finally a
friend's father interceded, and Danny was hired to cut cloth
in a clothing factory in a rundown section of Boston. There he
is part of "an ethnic business" — a shop filled with older
Jews, some Arabs, and a few young men who are recent immigrants from Puerto Rico. The shop is noisy with the sound of
machines and constant arguing. Danny believes that the old
men criticize and pick fights because of their "nervous tension," built up from the frustration of their dead-end lives.
And he compares their situation with his own:

I don't feel great about working there, but I'm

not stuck there and they are. I have some
opportunities, but I don't know what I'm going to
do. They always knew what they were going to
do — it stunk, but they always knew for security
what they were doing. Either way, it's frustrating.

Danny feels unstable and depressed — "bummed out."
"I don't have any title: I'm not a student, and I certainly can't
relate to being a factory worker." He misses being in school,
yet cannot think of a good reason to return. Although studying law seems a good way to become educated about how
society works, Danny cannot imagine spending the money
just to become better informed and doubts that practicing
law would be interesting enough — unless he became a trial
lawyer, which seems too competitive a speciality. Danny
enjoys helping the Puerto Rican workers with their English
and thinks of taking a night course in Spanish so that he can
help them more. As a result of this involvement he imagines
working as a lawyer to help underprivileged people, but as
with all the options he imagines, Danny thinks that it
wouldn't work out. He is scared about the future he sees
before him:

It's hard to find a job, especially a meaningful
one — that's the crux of it. It's that and then
seeing how your parents' marriage turned out —
most of the time, marriage isn't that great. There's
nothing you can step into, no shoes that you can
fit into. You're just left in limbo somewhere.

Like Danny, most of the Jewish working-class youth of
Townline who left high school as serious questioners of the
social order have discovered few answers to guide their lives,
and now feel alienated from the political arena. No one feels
as much in limbo as Danny, but most have faltered in college,
struggling to find a reason, and the money, to continue. In
sophomore year Bert Geller had no money for the spring
semester at the state university and felt lost: "I thought, 'This
is how confusing life can get if you let it — this is how bad it
can get.'" Bert came home for a term and then returned to
school, deciding to major in communications; now, as a stu-

dent intern, he is producing a program on dying for cable television. Although he doubts that he can succeed in the competitive world of professional television, Bert is glad to have found an interest that will get him through college. He keeps "on guard" against letting his questions overwhelm him, trying to take them one at a time.

Those few young people who have gone straight through college are more clearly focused about the future but no more certain that they are making the right choices. Rebecca Gross has spent all four years at an elite private university and considered herself pre-med from the start; now she waits to hear from the seventeen medical schools she has applied to. Yet she feels that she still doesn't know what she really wants to do and that she has merely postponed facing herself:

> Seeds of the uncertainty were there in high school, but being here in a system where you had to keep on going has kept me from thinking about it too much. I may be using medical school as just another way to delay the confrontation. It's the classic question — "What am I going to do and what's it all for?" Last year I came across a term — *anomie.* Suddenly I said, 'That's it! That's what I've got!'

Rebecca judges her years at college as interesting but also lonely and unhappy, and she wishes that she had taken a leave of absence, as many of her classmates did. But her tuition costs increased each year, raising the amount of money not covered by her scholarships and loans; Rebecca felt that she had to graduate on time and to forgo courses that did not lead to security. "If I don't get into medical school, I'll have a better chance for a job with a biological background, but I can't help thinking sometimes that I'd rather be starving and have a degree in English." Yet Rebecca continues to value her doubts and questions. "I'd rather be floundering like this than come to answers just for the sake of peace."

The struggles and issues have been somewhat different for most of the promising working-class youth from Townline who are Catholic and who, rather than searching for the meaning of life, sought to make something of themselves and

create lives that reflected their own priorities. In their journeys during the past four years, the need to make money —
which none of them had anticipated as a major concern — has
led them to take longer, more circuitous routes than they had
planned, and in the process they have begun to set new terms
by which they want to live. As she left high school, Peggy
Daly looked forward to a summer vacation in Europe with
friends, after which she planned to work her way through
college toward a job in management; after the humiliation
she had experienced as a student in Townline High and a
part-time worker in a local supermarket, she wanted a chance
to prove that she could run things the way she wanted. But
Peggy found it impossible, even working two full-time jobs,
to save enough money for tuition while paying her share of
expenses for the apartment she shared with roommates. So
she joined the army, which promised to pay for 36 months of
college after she had served for three years, and began training to become an air traffic controller. But poor eyesight
disqualified her, and now she works as a file clerk on an army
base in Georgia. Peggy resents the constant harassment of
enlisted women by male officers, but, with the help of a
woman colonel whom she admires, she has learned to deal
with unfair authorities in a new, more productive way: "I
weigh it all inside my head, but I don't let them know what
I'm thinking." As a high school senior, Peggy felt that she was
too impatient a person ever to want children; now she feels
differently. Her goal is to go to college after she has completed her stint in the army and to train to be a teacher of
children with special needs. She hopes someday to have a
family of her own. In the meantime Peggy is fighting to gain a
promotion that she has, in her view, earned but for which she
is not yet due, and she thinks she may sign up for ROTC as a
college student so that she can be an officer. Echoing her
earlier feelings, Peggy explains, "I don't like being a peon. I'd
rather be up there."

Lack of money led Bob Richards, like many others, to
transfer from a private university to a state college. In high
school Bob had been the only Catholic besides Diana Flynn to
spend time with Jewish students; Bob's friends were a group
of wealthy Jewish young people who counted on inheriting

places in their fathers' businesses, had expensive tastes and habits, and cared little about school. Bob's own father had gone from one promising but ultimately unsuccessful "deal" to another, and Bob characterized himself as "a rich man's son without a rich father," hoping to graduate from college and find a career that would be as lucrative as his father's fantasies. It was after his sophomore year that Bob decided he had taken out too many loans already and switched from the private university, which he believed was populated by "a lot of rich kids who were going to do all right anyhow," to a state college "where the kids were there to make something better of themselves."

After a semester there, Bob decided to leave. "It's not the most prestigious place, you know. It has a really gloomy atmosphere — old buildings, a lot of the students are veterans, policemen, and firemen coming to take a course or two." He took time off to make money, working as a taxi driver, a night teller at a bank, and then a bartender, living first with a girlfriend in an apartment, then with his grandparents, and now in an apartment he shares with his brother and a friend. Injured and unable to work for a while, Bob hated not having more than his disability check to spend, and he plans to keep two part-time jobs next semester when he enrolls at the urban branch of the state university, which recently moved into a modern campus. "It's brand new. There's a nice library, lounges, and classrooms. No creepy old desks and creaking old floors."

In the bar where he works, Bob listens to many customers who never fulfilled their dreams, and having become disillusioned with his father in the past few years, Bob is not surprised to see him sitting at the bar telling his own tall tales. Bob feels that he has overcome his previous naiveté — "I thought school would be more of my life than it is, and existence is more of my life than school" — but he carefully distinguishes himself from those on the other side of the bar. "They're old and going nowhere, and I think I'm young and headed somewhere." But he has changed his goals. Now Bob hopes to make it into the upper-middle-class, to become successful without "selling myself out": he has come to think of his openmindedness as an important quality and of his desire to be honest in his relationships with other people as an important goal.

The development of these new priorities in Bob's life is typical of the changes in the values of Irish-Catholic young men: they believe that they have become more open to different viewpoints, less susceptible to pressures to think traditionally and to want what their peers and parents wanted for them. Andy Reilly left high school planning to go to a small out-of-state private college; he saw himself then as part of a large group of young people very much like himself, and felt that if he did not leave town, he would fall "off the track" and give up his ambition to go to college and begin a business career. Now Andy looks back on his earlier vision of the future with scorn: "It was like the Dick van Dyck show — a house in the suburbs, a wife, two cars, and the kids and the dog." In high school he felt most different from "the smart kids who go to MIT," but now he thinks of himself as similar to them and different from the other Irish-Catholic young men he used to be friends with, who never left Townline, never went to college, and have not changed at all. "I don't even like running into them now — I don't like seeing them. To be polite I'll stand there and talk to them and ask them what they're doing, because I don't want to seem like a jerk who just changed completely overnight."

Andy attributes the changes in himself to going away to college, making new friends, and redefining his goals. He didn't like his business courses and became a liberal arts major, taking a special interest in questions raised by his philosophy course that challenged the traditional Catholic perspective with which he was raised. His friends were asking questions about life and politics, and Andy found himself trying to be consistent in applying what he believed — about ecological issues, for example — to his personal life. He decided to major in science but was disappointed by his courses —"the work was at a high school level." At the end of his junior year, he decided to leave school and return home to Townline, work to pay off his debts, and save enough money to get into a better school.

As a high school senior, Andy never mentioned that his father was an alcoholic, a fact that he now says greatly in-

185

fluenced his life. His mother tried to ensure that her children would not suffer as a consequence:

> I've always thought my mother just shouldn't have married my father — she got a bum deal marrying him. He was basically low class though he came from an upper-class family — that was his problem, he always had everything given to him. He brought himself down. My mother always kept herself up as well as she could. She couldn't do much with the house, because he'd just ruin it. But she kept us pretty together as far as leaving the house with clean clothes. We were always clean.

From Andy's point of view, leaving home in the morning looking presentable helped him escape the stigma of having an alcoholic father. His mother is a central influence. "She always said, 'You're going to college.' She always wanted me to rise above that." Living in a mostly Jewish area of Townline also helped:

> I grew up as a Gentile among the Jews — it was weird when I was very young to be one of the only kids in class on the Jewish holidays! In this neighborhood your house could be a dump and rat-infested, but if you say you live here, people would think you're okay. That's where it's at in Townline. With an alcoholic father, if I lived in the Rum Hill area, where all the Townies live — all the men who work in the garbage-collecting department, the park and recreation department — if I lived there it would have led to a lot of bad things. Living here gave me an edge. I didn't have *that* to overcome.

Andy's high school friends were Irish-Catholic, and his best friend lived in Rum Hill. "It didn't bother me, you know, his parents were great and his family was good." But Andy thinks that the reason his friend has now left Townline completely is

186

that he had to get a fresh start. "It's hard to go anywhere from the Hill."

Living at home again, Andy finds himself in a different situation. His mother divorced his father, got a job as a legal secretary, and is now involved in a new relationship. Andy has found a job as a bank teller and is taking night courses in a local state college, finding them inferior and hoping that he'll be able to get into a better school. His doubts increase about what he wants to do; feeling attracted again to a business career, he also wants to graduate with a degree in science. His close friends live out-of-state, and talking with them on the phone helps him sustain his sense of who he has become, but at night Andy walks by himself around his neighborhood, wondering if he'll be able to get himself back into college and which path he should take:

> At this point all I really want to do is find an
> avenue. I've thought I've found the road so many
> times, and then it ends. You know, there's a fork
> in the road and which road do I take? There are
> more and more forks every day! That's life.
> Decisions you have to make—to take the right or
> the left, the high road or the low road—I just
> have to decide. Sometimes I wish it was decided
> for me, but you know that's not going to happen.

Like Andy, few of these working-class youth, Catholic or Jewish, have kept up their relationships with the friends they had in Townline, and although many of them have had to live at home to save money, they live alongside their parents, thinking of themselves as separate from their families and leading lives that have little to do with Townline. While she works and goes to school, Diana Flynn has created an area of her own on an upper floor of her parents' house, where she tries to stay out of their way. "I'm building my strength for my next departure," she explains. Yet the legacy of having grown up working-class in Townline remains part of these young people's struggles. The ethnic and class conflicts they experienced, the educations they received, and the reputation of Townline in the wider world influence their perceptions of themselves and their life-chances.

187

Most of them have mixed feelings about being from Townline: on the one hand they have a sense of good fortune at having grown up in a progressive and affluent community, where there is public access to fine parks, swimming pools, and libraries, and where "the streets are always kept up and the money's not spared"; on the other, they have a sense of irony, mixed with some bitterness, at not having been on the top economically or scholastically. Just as Bob Richards gains confidence from reminding himself that his future will be different from the lives of the customers at the bar, he differentiates himself from people in the working-class area of Boston where he now shares an apartment with his brother and a friend:

> Coming from Townline gives me a positive
> attitude. I've noticed that the dogs around here
> have their tails between their legs — their ears
> are down, and they are looking at the ground.
> The people in this neighborhood are mostly the
> defeated people, and they walk around with their
> heads down. The dogs are barking in a coyote
> kind of way, out of fear as much as anything else.
> In Townline it's not like that — the people feel
> they have beat life, they have the upper hand.
> The dogs there look alert — their tails are up,
> their ears are up. They are barking at you because
> they mean to bark at you because they want you
> to stay away.

Now, four years after high school graduation, most of these working-class youth focus on the excellence of their education rather than on the deprivation they felt in relation to wealthier students. Wealthy peers are no longer part of the worlds these working-class youth move through; the state universities that most of them attend draw working-class students from all over the greater Boston area, and Townline youth have found their college classes boring in comparison with the classes they took at Townline High. Robert Rezza, who was furious at having been placed in the General track as a high school freshman and worked his way up into all-Honors classes by his senior year, feels that he has learned a great deal about foreign languages at the urban state university but also that the college is "a step down" from Townline High. He can scarcely bear to imagine what he would know if he had actually gone to an elite private college in another state which specializes in foreign languages.

Townline working-class youth are also glad that they do not speak with the typical Boston accent, which sounds to their ears uneducated and bigoted. Their fellow students assume at first that because they are from Townline, they must be wealthy, and these young people must continually set the record straight. A thousand miles away, on the army base in Georgia, Peggy Daly faced a similar problem when her roommates read an article in *Cosmopolitan* that described "the certain kind of people you could expect to find in Townline, U.S.A.": "I said 'Oh wow!' I think it's a big joke. Because a lot of it is big lawns and swimming pools, but then there's the other side to it."

The bitterness Peggy felt when she entered high school and discovered that she had moved "from the top of the bottom to the bottom of the top" is still alive. Although she values her army training and believes that having to work for the money to go to college will give her the maturity to succeed there, she still hates "the fashion plates" at Townline High, the girls who, she imagines, were sent straight through four years of college by their parents. When she looks back at her high school years, she feels that she lost her pride in herself and her motivation to do well, and she proposes that the inequities in Townline would be less damaging if there were two separate high schools, one for students from affluent neighborhoods and one for those like herself.

The pain of having been judged inferior to wealthier peers is not as sharp for most of these Townline youth, but many still struggle with their early sense of inferiority. Bert Geller, born in Israel to concentration camp survivors, moved when he was 10 from a rundown neighborhood in the city, where, as he thinks about it now, life was a lot easier than in his "sheltered middle- to upper-middle-class neighborhood in Townline." Bert remembers other kids sneering whenever he said that his father was a house painter, and he felt constantly under attack for not being affluent enough to be considered an American. Once a girl who lived across the street taunted him because his family rented out the first floor of their house, and Bert provoked her to rush at him, moving out of her way and watching her fall and break her collarbone. "Her family tried to sue us for $5,000!" Bert looks back on those years as the origin of his questions about what to do with his life. This search is not yet resolved, but it no longer centers on the approval of others:

> I'm just very slowly realizing all this: what was all that worry about — that endless thinking about people, thinking that you're not as good as they are? Was it justified — that kind of thinking? It's finally making sense. I don't have to prove myself to anybody, don't have to make excuses for the way I am.

When they were leaving high school, the working-class youth of Townline vowed to develop their own standards, to create selves to which they could be true. Most of the young people who were Jewish felt a strong sense of uniqueness, which, although it contributed to their social marginality and personal loneliness, seemed to them also a sign of worth. In the past four years, the Catholic youth have also come to value having their own opinions and choosing unconventional and unfamiliar paths. Although they are no longer in daily contact with their affluent Townline peers, these young people are still painfully aware that their lives would be easier if they had financial backing and did not have to struggle so hard. Their disappointment in their college courses has given them a sense that had they attended more prestigious colleges, their minds would have been challenged and their careers might now be off to stronger starts. Many of the young women from Townline have become waitresses to pay for tuition and have taken jobs in the grills and cafes around Harvard University, where they wait on students who appear to be living easier and more productive lives.

Diana Flynn is one of those young women. The only Irish-Catholic and working-class member of a group of Townline high school students who were devoted to political activism and drama, Diana has, during the past four years, perceived a deep division between the world of workers and the world of students. Now, from the refuge of her parents' upper floor, she struggles alone to figure out how to live her life. Her jobs as a waitress have played a key role in her development. At first she waitressed in restaurants near the private university where she spent two years majoring in drama, and her part-time waitressing jobs at that point felt like additional performances. "I wanted to be an actress. It was not a plan but a fantasy — there was a sort of gauze there and my name was in it somewhere." Diana shared an apartment with her radical friend from high school, who developed anorexia and began cutting her wrists, and eventually moved back to her parents' home in Townline. Diana lived with another roommate, a potter whose boyfriend had a steady job and could take her out for fancy dinners. Diana enjoyed an active social life among artists and students, but as she began to waitress long hours at night and to endure layoffs and scrimping, she began to perceive the contradictions in her life. "At school you're sort of being taught that someday you'll grow up and wear pretty dresses and be successful, and at work people say, 'Oh, you go to school? Oh, you want to be above this?' I see that people have the fake idea that they are going to be apart from workers, from people who suffer."

When her college scholarships were withdrawn after sophomore year, Diana left school and began waitressing full-time; fired suddenly, she was shocked to discover that because she had saved no money, she could scarcely buy food. At the same time a relationship with a man she had come to depend on ended, and she impulsively moved back to her parents' home. She was startled at how luxurious it seemed and how relieved she felt not to be completely responsible for her own needs. Now she has a waitressing job in a neighborhood restaurant and has begun night courses at the state university.

Diana feels that she has entered a new stage of her life, trying to turn away from her need to be noticed and her tendency to be influenced, and to see beyond fantasy and phoniness. Her first priority is to be alone and, without trying to make major decisions, to draw together the lessons of her courses and her life. Her classes in economics have raised some questions. Diana wonders how she can continue to study and head for a career and thus turn away from the suffering of workers. Her interest in anthropology makes her think about going to graduate school: as an anthropologist she could observe and analyze without being part of society, without feeling that she has to take sides. And yet Diana feels that eventually she will have to decide:

> You have to make a decision. Even if I go to graduate school, I'll just be postponing the decision of whether I'm going to work to feed the restaurant owner or the ice cream company owner. If I go into restaurants — not that I ever will, and it's not because I'm compassionate, it's just that I'm angry about all of it — I would like to *kill* some of the customers. I can't believe they could be so stupid as to expect something for the dime they leave. The way we run back and forth on feet that they don't even think about. On real feet, human feet. I feel like saying, "I have feet that hurt."

Work that appears to be helpful seems to Diana to deny the reality of exploitation. "Even if I did become something like a clinical psychologist, so I could help people, what would I be helping? If somebody has a big problem that is in their mind, there are so many others that have problems with their feet!"

When she thinks about growing up as a policeman's daughter among wealthier peers — Diana sees the seeds of the pretenses she now struggles to discard. "When you're on the edge of a class — you're not really white-collar, but you don't wear a blue collar — you can sort of pretend, by wearing clothes that are nice, that you're part of this great class." Not having a Boston accent, she is able to feel "far from the ignorant masses," and from this advantage she draws some hope for her own personal journey. "If I'm climbing, I don't feel I have as far to climb. At least there's a façade of some kind of standard of living." While Diana is committed to living without façades and is searching for her own truths, the more she thinks through her options, the more futility she feels: she strives toward an ideal, but she no longer believes in ideals:

> I can decide that I'm going to be a great
> psychotherapist or I'm going to be a John
> Maynard Keynes and revise economic theory so
> that everybody will have a lot of food to eat, but
> I'm really pretty skeptical of that for anybody.
> There are really brilliant people, but everybody
> sort of blurs together. The only people I can
> think of who really made an impact on the world
> are Christ and Hitler, and they sort of balance
> each other out in a way!

Diana's doubts are matched by her sense of the futility of conventional politics. "As soon as someone shows me a petition, I get sick. I start thinking about how insignificant one name is, and I hate that. I guess politics makes me feel small." Like many of these working-class youth, Diana's experience with the anti-war movement at Townline High left her distrustful of idealists who, although they seemed selfless and wise, were as egocentric and helpless as everyone else. But all these young people thought of themselves as interested in politics when they left high school: if they believed, as Diana and Danny did, that they did not yet know enough to propose workable solutions, they were committed to continuing their questioning and reading; if they were simply critical of American society, its materialism, militarism, and inequities, as Peggy was, they expected to remain interested. Nothing these Townline youth have experienced in the past four years has softened their criticisms; their personal struggles to survive economically are further evidence of how difficult life can be for people in the richest country in the world, and they feel more sophisticated in recognizing how business manipulates the masses through advertising. But although these young people have become angrier, they have also become more silent. They have moved far beyond disillusionment to a state of hopelessness in which they can imagine few issues that would rouse them to political action.

In part this development grows out of their relentless

questioning. As Rebecca Gross explains, "I've stopped being political. Once you've decided that everything is suspect, that everything can be criticized, there's no place else to go. I think I gave up. I've suddenly come to this realization that no matter how much you care, things just seem to go on and on." This sense of the insignificance of personal action reflects these young people's new fatalism, their belief that groups will always be in conflict, exploitation will flourish, people and society will not change. Continuing to care about politics not only wastes time but also undermines the sense of personal efficacy that these young people are struggling to maintain.

The young women of Townline now seem angrier than the men. In the past four years they have discovered that they live "in a man's world" and are continually vulnerable to the influence of men. "Who has too much power?" Mary Condon's answer is immediate and vehement — "Men!" Mary became pregnant when she was a high school sophomore and after graduation moved with her husband and child to the university town where the main campus of the state university is located. Her husband planned to take a two-year course, and she planned to go to college when he was finished. But her life took an unexpected course: Mary found herself wanting to be more active, not just "the homemaker —baking bread, taking care of the kid," and took a job in a large cinema house, soon being promoted to manager. Now she looks at her ex-husband as a traditional male, a younger version of her father — "I think he invented male chauvinism." When her husband finished school and wanted to move back to Townline, Mary decided that their values and aspirations were too different. She stayed on in the university town.

Finding life as a single parent lonely and hard, Mary eventually came back to Townline herself, living first with the family of her sister, who had offered to provide childcare at half the going rate, then with a childhood friend in a Townline apartment, and now in a new apartment in a government project. She looks back on her struggles to become a responsible parent and to support her child with pride — "I feel as a woman that's an accomplishment" — and some anger. The men in her life have limited her choices; she is "Mary-

194

mother" and, since finding a job in a local bank, "Mary-banker," and she has had to postpone her dream of going to college: "I kind of foresee the kid hitting eighteen and me going off in the red, white, and blue — glory! freedom!" Mary thinks that if she could find a man who allowed her equal influence in their relationship — "I haven't met any of them yet!" — she might marry again, but she would never have another child. She imagines that men do not face such responsibilities: "If I were a man I would be living in a very small studio apartment that would be set up so great. I would be keeping any hours I cared to keep, and I certainly wouldn't be tying myself down. I'd be going to pick up my kid on Sunday." Mary's boss at the bank provides another example of male power. Asked to take on another job in addition to her own, she decided to use the opportunity to demonstrate her competence. She mastered the new work, doing what two workers used to do, and decided to ask her boss for a raise. He reminded her that her work anniversary was coming up the next month and said that she could not expect to get two raises in one year.

Many of these young women tell similar stories of demeaning work situations where male bosses and customers harass and humiliate them. Most are as wary as they were in high school of the possible influence of mates and husbands, and only Mary considers marriage a possibility: several have been disappointed by boyfriends they had come to depend on, and all vow to be more independent in the relationships they hope will come at some much later time. Getting involved now, as Susan Siporin explains, "would screw up my life. I have goals, and it makes things tough." Their own struggles leave these young women no extra energy to fight back when men are domineering, and so they postpone relationships.

Their anger at the power men wield makes these young women want more power for themselves; thus, Peggy Daly imagines becoming an officer in ROTC when she gets to college. Yet these young women, like Townline young men, are not comfortable with the idea of having power: on the one hand they imagine that they would use it only for good purposes; on the other, they believe that they know how corrupting power can be, and they have hated the powerful people in their community and in national politics.

They experience a contradiction between their desire to succeed and their criticism of materialism. They now know much more than they did about how difficult it is to survive economically and how easy it is to become preoccupied with making money. When Mary Condon talks about her vision of success, she downplays the role of money:

> What is usually considered successful I don't — a stodgy banker, bank president, suits and ties, big gut in the middle. Never see them crack a smile. That's not success to me. If you have a goal and work toward it and attain it and be happy that you've attained it — whether it's to be an organ grinder with the little monkeys on the street or king of something or other — that's a person to be admired.

Mary says she would be happy to be "just comfortable — not filthy rich." Yet she admits that "money is a big part of success to me. I don't believe in just rejecting things your parents wanted." She describes an image of herself in the year 2001, an image that originated in a glimpse she had, as a child of five, of a woman who was "driving a really nice car. Her hair was bouncing, she had super sunglasses, and she was smoking a cigarette driving along. That hair! Terrific. She was great." Mary can imagine herself as "this chick that's got it made, not being hassled. Surrounded by classy people. A house full of fresh flowers all the time, nice soft rugs, big old comfortable chairs. Luxury. That's what I want. I'd like to be spoiled! But to talk about it like this, it sounds really dumb."

What Mary wants most is enough money not to have to struggle so hard, enough power not to be hassled. Yet she is susceptible to images of classiness and style, and like all these young people, attempts not to succumb while she strives to make her way. This endeavor is complicated still further, for Townline youth, by their growing awareness of how difficult it is to know their own motives. Dedicated to the search for self-knowledge, these youth are at the same time fiercely self-critical and fervently hopeful that they will make their own choices not only out of self-interest but also for altruistic motives. Yet they have learned how powerful their own socialization has been, and they wonder whether the belief that they can escape their early conditioning is not yet another illusion. They remain focused on their effort to think for themselves, to avoid being seduced or manipulated by "the people who really have the power and who impose their sense of reality on other people," as Bert Geller puts it.

Despite their deep political alienation, they maintain some of their idealism. In their hard-won ability to think for themselves they find a thread of optimism. Bert explains, "The key is individual consciousness. People who have the power don't want you to realize certain things. Raising consciousness might get people away from hating each other. That's such an idealistic thing, but I'm at that stage. I can't stop thinking of the ideal, of how good it can be and how you can move toward that." And Danny Genzuk thinks about whether politics is worth the time and effort. "It's a strange thing. Even if you know it's not going to work, there's nothing else to do. You have to do it, you just have to try."

Like Bert and Danny, Townline working-class youth left high school hoping to find allies, people like themselves with whom they could feel comfortable. Four years later, their sense of themselves as isolated individuals has intensified. Despite their longing for companionship, they find comfort in their belief that the free-standing individual is exemplary, free of the influence of others and not subject to their demands. Having grown up without heroes, they believe that remaining outside society allows them to see the truths behind façades and to remain impervious to the tricks played upon "the people" by the powerful. These young people still recognize the validity of the demands of blacks for redress of historical inequities, and they believe that the collective history of blacks is a legitimate basis for favored treatment. They hope that if they find themselves in a position to make choices they will support those who have been most discriminated against rather than advance their self-interest.

Danny's attempt to help his Spanish-speaking co-workers is an example of such personal action to help those who are oppressed. Another Townline youth who has suc-

197

ceeded in acting upon social concerns is Suzanne Baer. Although she worried about how her struggling family would fare without her, Suzanne decided to attend a residential nursing school that was 40 miles away from home. After completing her training, she stayed on as a registered nurse at the hospital associated with her school. Living by herself in an apartment close to the hospital, she speaks with pride of her success at work and in managing on her own.

In high school Suzanne participated in social studies class discussions and demonstrated a few times against the Vietnam War; she held strong convictions about social inequities and expected to become more politically involved in the future. She now describes herself as an apathetic citizen. She has never voted, wants nothing to do with politics, and turns off her television when the news comes on. Her answers to questions about political issues are perfunctory. When she is asked to think about whether there should be any limits on the amount of money people can earn—a possibility that seemed pertinent to her views on inequality—Suzanne takes a deep breath and is silent. "How do you feel about the question?" she is then asked.

I think it's a half-assed question—if you'll pardon the expression—'cause it's unreal.

Do you mean that it's not worth thinking about since it's never going to happen?

Right!

So working for something like that to happen is half-assed?

Yes. If they want to do it, fine!

Is that because you have a sense that the way things are is pretty set?

I think it's going to take a hell of a lot to change things, I don't know what. Maybe when they finally do push that little red button or when this era comes to an end and God descends on the earth.

Although she feels that efforts to reform the political system are pointless, Suzanne makes a critical distinction be-

198

tween the world of conventional politics, which she avoids, and the world of her hospital, which is deeply involving to her and her present friends. "Most of them are hospital-oriented, and I also am very hospital-oriented. Things like 'Who are you going to vote for?'—I could care!" About the distance between her ideals of social equality and the way things actually are, Suzanne says, "I do get agitated and upset. And then I do what I can within my own realm of reality. Instead of giving this person hassles—this person being black, Puerto Rican, Chinese, or whatever—I try to make it for him just as it would be for anybody else."

Suzanne goes on to describe her efforts to combat inequity and prejudice, often taking substantial personal risks to bring about changes she considers right and moral. For example, she has demanded that the hospital authorities provide equal treatment—in this case round-the-clock nursing care —for an indigent, minority patient with the same serious illness as a wealthy patient who had special duty nurses. The success of her effort has strengthened Suzanne's belief in being outspoken at work, and her professional identity as a nurse includes being vigilant on behalf of her patients' moral as well as legal rights.

Suzanne is unusual in already being launched in a career that gives her the chance to work toward her social ideals. The majority of these Townline youth share her view of what is worth doing, but are still searching for their "own realms of reality."

Milltown: Moving On Course

As high school seniors, Milltown working-class youth thought of themselves as preparing to leave safe harbor, setting out for the exciting but also frightening world of college. The voyage out was circumscribed by the time it would take them to qualify for the careers they sought. As the promising young people of a small town, they carried the expectations of teachers and parents that, having become responsible persons, they would do their best to succeed. They knew their destinations—lives as successful professionals and responsible parents, essentially similar to their own parents' lives.

199

The actual voyage out of Milltown was more complex and circuitous than these youth who left for college had imagined. They confronted ways of living that initially seemed repugnant and academic pressures that seemed overwhelming. Having survived these difficulties, they began to feel at home in the world of college life. They have come to see themselves as individuals involved in a long process of growth and change. Now they make a sharp distinction between themselves and those high school classmates who remained in Milltown, and they feel themselves gradually moving away from Milltown and a way of life that now seems stagnant and at odds with their own momentum. Yet they and those who did not leave continue to view their development as progress toward the careers they seek, and achieving and being good at the work they want to do remains of central importance to them. Growing up in Milltown and learning its standards of hard work and individual responsibility have, they all believe, helped them develop into persons of character.

Rob Murray's story continues to exemplify central themes in their lives. As a senior, he anticipated that his biggest challenge would be to survive his first year in college, and he was right. When he entered the state university to prepare for, a career as a wildlife biologist, the jolt of being completely on his own and confronted by an array of very different students and standards of morality caused him even more difficulty than he had imagined. The most immediate problem was his roommate, "a real freaky type — he smoked dope, and to me that was just really shocking. At college you can just sit around the campus and smoke — and in classes too — but in Milltown it was really a crime." After a couple of weeks, Rob "really couldn't hack it at all" and went to the head of residences. He was surprised to be moved immediately to a different building and assigned another roommate. Rob found himself becoming less "alienated" and by the end of the first semester felt "pretty stabilized," thinking for the first time about how people's backgrounds affected their character and outlook on life. Rob decided that "the only thing I should worry about is just myself and not what other people are doing," and as the years passed, he found that "when you get to know kids and get into the swing of things and get to know your way around, the college is a pretty nice place."

Yet academic life proved more difficult. Rob disliked the huge introductory courses and found himself unable to concentrate and organize his time as well as he would have liked. "Unlike high school, you never had teachers harping on you to study. It's just that the professor gives you the lecture — he just says, 'Here it is,' and if you don't study it, you take the exams and you flunk." Rob set himself the goal of achieving a *B* average but finally abandoned that dream his senior year. Still, he believes he has demonstrated that he can handle both the academic demands of college and his part-time job, filling Coke machines on campus.

In his junior year Rob decided that the wildlife biology major was too academic for his tastes and goals and designed an independent major in natural resources, arranging for an internship at an observatory, where he did a bird census. The unexpected news that his report has been accepted for publication gives him some hope that he will be able to find a job. Believing that the observatory will not be hiring, he is sending out his resume to environmental consulting agencies, taking a number of civil service examinations and also the graduate record examination, so that if he decides to seek the master's degree in ecology his professors tell him he will need, he will have a score on file. For now, Rob will accept any good job in natural resources management that is also near Milltown, so that he can "get some experience" and pay off his college debts.

Rob's most important relationship began in his sophomore year. His girlfriend, Susan, was a year behind him in school, majoring in special education. Susan grew up in a wealthy Boston suburb and meeting her has introduced Rob to intimacy and added to his understanding of the influence of different upbringings. Susan was "more on her own" at an earlier age, and she believes that Milltown adolescents obey their parents more than do young people from her town. Without mentioning the socioeconomic differences between the two communities, Rob speculates that Susan may have had greater exposure to the world because of the larger size of her town or its proximity to Boston. Rob is realistic about the risks graduation poses to their relationship: "I don't know where she and I will be a year from now." Although they "got very close to one another," their careers take precedence for both of them, and Susan imagines that she will have go go out-of-state to pursue hers.

Rob's parents' lives have been difficult during the last few years, and Rob feels guilty about not attending to them as much as he should have. During Rob's sophomore year, Mr. Murray's back pain became unbearable, and he finally decided to have the spinal fusion operation that he had been putting off. During the long recuperation period, he lost his job, and his unemployment and disability payments were not sufficient to support the family. Rob's mother began working full-time, and his parents worried about how much money he was spending at school. Now, although Rob's father has ulcers, he is back at work; his mother is still working full-time, and things have eased somewhat.

What Rob likes most about himself is having "become more independent and in control of my own life." On the other hand:

> Maybe I like least that I'm getting farther away
> from home. Sometimes when I'm up at school, I'm
> up there in my own little world. Probably I
> should try to remember people back home that
> have helped me pay for half of school and have
> gotten me where I am now — it's really easy to
> forget sometimes that you haven't done
> everything all by yourself!

Rob respects his parents' opinions and feels that they still influence him but "if I felt strongly enough about something, I would do what I thought." He also has a new perspective on his parents. "They're really confined in their own existence. Well, they never did have the opportunity to go to any school outside of high school, and they're probably set in their ways." Rob's contact, through Susan, with the women's movement on campus opened his eyes and led to his re-evaluation of his parents' lives. "My mother comes home from work, and she still has to cook and clean and everything, and she's always complaining about how much work she has to do.

202

I never really noticed it that much before." Rob contrasts his mother's situation with Susan's plans to pursue her own career. "I don't know if she'd be classified as a liberated woman, but she really knows what she wants to do. She came from a family of six, and she's the only one that didn't get married immediately—she's the only one that left home and is making a career for herself."

Now Rob identifies his high school classmates who are still "hanging around" downtown Milltown "with their motorcycles and stuff" as the young people he feels most different from. He suspects that they will stay in Milltown for the rest of their lives, whereas he wants "to get away from it and try to get a little different exposure." Although Rob still tries not to make judgments—"I'm not saying they're wrong either, 'cause everybody knows what's the best for them, so I have no right to condemn anybody just because they're different"—being from Milltown is no longer a positive identity for him. "At school you're always asked where you're from, and I'd say 'Milltown,' and they'd say, 'Where? Where?' Nobody has ever heard of it. It was just the stigma of being a hayseed from a small town." Rob is very definite now about not wanting to settle permanently in Milltown. "I don't want to completely sever family ties; I just want to get off on my own and make a place for myself." He would like to live in a rural place, "not too crowded," and "definitely away from the city."

Rob still sees himself as a "basic middle-class" person, a status that he views as a "nice, middle-of-the-road thing—you're not poor and you're not rich." He continues to be thankful that he grew up with opportunities and to see America as a fundamentally good society where an individual citizen can do "practically anything he wants. I've never been in a situation living in a ghetto, but I think it is possible that if a person wants something bad enough that they can get it." Rob still believes that society's problems can be solved, for "the technology is there" and "if you have enough money you can do just about anything." He cites his own successful battle with a large chain store about a defective refrigerator as evidence that individuals have some power. Rob complained to the consumer protection division of the attorney general's office and eventually got his money back. "Maybe it just seems to a person that he has too little power against all these big companies," Rob suggests. "I think it would be more the idea of a person realizing that if you just take a little bit of time to contact different companies and tell them how you feel, then you get some power." Rob's optimism about the future has been sustained. "I think it's going to be that government and big corporations are going to come to control things less, because people have seen that a change can be made if everybody wants it."

Rob is fairly confident that he will get what he wants by continuing on his set course. In addition to being successful in the field he has been "aiming toward all my life," his definition of a successful life now includes "being loved by somebody and loving back," and he also knows that "learning new things" and "finding new ideas" will always be important to him. Although he remains focused on his career goals, he has expanded his sights and come to embrace personal growth and exploration as significant goals; he doesn't want to be "confined by set ways."

Rob feels that he has matured during his college years and now defines maturity as becoming "more cynical" about the ways of the world. Surviving in a big university, he believes, is good preparation for later life, for one learns what to expect from people and how to roll with the punches. At the same time, he has maintained his basic stance as someone who is working hard, planning carefully, and taking control of his own life in order to ensure that he will achieve his goals.

Rob is gradually loosening his family ties and preparing to take off. Now more comfortable on campus than at home, he feels allied with the generation of students like himself who are headed somewhere. Although the major outlines of his personal and political beliefs remain unchanged, he has begun to question conventional sex role definitions and opposition to abortion and thinks that he has become more open to diverse life-styles and points of view. He defines himself as in a transitional preparatory phase of his life and envisions himself becoming more politically involved "once I get through with my education and am able to actually put to use things that I've learned."

Like Rob, most of the Milltown youth who continued in school stayed on the career tracks they chose for themselves in high school. The primary reason for their being in school was and still is to prepare for these occupations, and their titles are important elements in their identities — often the way they first describe themselves: "I'm a nurse"; "I'm going to be a pharmacist," "an engineer," "a physical therapist." Although Barbara Natti felt lonely, lost, and under enormous pressure during her first year at nursing school, she soon hit her stride, began to shine academically, got outstanding clinical reports on her work with patients, and dismissed her earlier worry that she might be the wrong type of person to be a nurse. She discovered that she can establish relationships with people from different social and racial backgrounds.

But nursing has not turned out to be as glamorous as she had anticipated:

> There is no glory involved. Any kid going to nursing school can think of the white cap, and it's inevitable that you think, wow, that's professional, that's really nice, but when you get right down to nursing, you're *still* doing the bedpans and you're still doing baths, which any person could do mechanically.

Yet Barbara feels that she really makes a difference in patients' lives, and she finds her work both rewarding and broadening: "I think I've seen more than I believe any other kids that are just going to college have seen. You face death, you face life, you face sickness that really wasn't a part of your world before." Asked how she sees herself, Barbara responds, "Number 1 — I'm a nurse! Number 2 — I'm more me than I ever was. I've kind of asserted myself more."

Interested in obtaining as much practical experience as possible in the fields they hope to enter, these Milltown youth are sometimes impatient with the academic requirements of their programs. Like Rob, they look for ways to add field experience to their studies, and doing well in these apprenticeships confirms that they are headed in the right direction. Larry LeClaire decided to commute to a large private university in Boston because it has a work-study program as well as a good pharmacy department. Larry's academic program has been as difficult as he feared. Despite his hard work, he failed organic chemistry his sophomore year: "I really worked for it. I had a C going into the final, and then I bombed the exam and he failed me." With no choice but to "buckle down and hit the books every night," he tried again and passed. Larry dislikes Boston and hates commuting. He'd like to "pick up the whole university and move it to the country."

But Larry feels that it has all been worth it because of the work experience. He was first placed in the pharmaceutical department of a large city hospital: "There I learned the basics because I didn't know anything." He is pleased about his next placement, in a suburban hospital near Milltown, because he enjoys working close to home:

> I like my job — it's very good experience. It's
> really what I want to do. You need 2,000 hours'
> work in a pharmacy before you can take the state
> boards, and I'm getting the hours. I'm learning all
> the drugs — the trade names and the generic
> names. That's a big asset because you have to
> know them.

The first steps in the long-term plan Larry outlined in high school are proceeding according to schedule, and the details of the road ahead are becoming clearer. After college he will work at a hospital until he has paid off his debts and built up enough capital to move out on his own. Then he will relocate in the country, in a less competitive area where there are fewer pharmacies. The lengthy preparatory period will pay off in the end. Larry has changed since high school. There, he points out, he used to spend his time figuring out how not to get caught by the authorities. Those playful days are over. "I think I've matured a lot — in respect to what everything is, the reality question. I know where I stand."

In the lives of two young women, we see not only a rejection of the general emphasis on vocational preparation in Milltown but also the awakening of feminist concerns common among the young women from Milltown who went to college, and a new belief that their development is important in its own right. Helena Hemp and Martha Jamison have given up their initial career directions and have not yet decided on alternatives; rather than viewing college as a place for career training, they have come to see it as an opportunity for personal exploration and growth. They have also changed their original belief that the shape of their lives will depend upon the men they eventually marry.

As a high school senior, Helena was less certain about a career choice than other Milltown youth; her most concrete plan was to make use of her fluency in German and major in languages so that someday she might open a travel agency. Finding the foreign language courses at the state college "really boring," she abandoned this idea in her freshman year. Fascinated by her first psychology course, she decided to major in psychology even though she viewed it as an impractical subject.

As they left high school, the young women of Milltown assumed that their plans for the future were contingent on the wishes and character of the men they would marry. Even Helena, who wondered whether she wanted to get married, imagined that she would. Now she links her assessment of the purpose of college with her anger at traditional expectations about women's lives:

> If there's one thing I can't stand, it's people who
> say you get out of high school, you go to college
> for four years, then you get married and then you
> have kids and then you can fall back on whatever
> it is that you're studying for. I can't see going to
> college to get a good job. I just like to go to
> school. As long as it's interesting to me, I like to go.

Figuring out where she stands and what she believes has become very important to Helena. "I spend a wicked lot of time thinking about stuff—I don't really know exactly what I think about a lot of things, and there's no way I'm going to know unless I read about them or hear about them or talk about them." Determined to pursue the ideas that interest her, Helena has difficulty finding anyone to talk with in Milltown, where she lives at home, commutes to school, and works 30 hours a week at a department store during the academic year and at two jobs during the summer. Her closest

207

friends did not go on to college, and she feels increasingly distant from them. "I probably think about a lot of things that they don't think about. When I go over to their houses, we don't talk about stuff that's going on. We just do a lot of reminiscing."

At college too Helena finds few people interested in ideas. "It's a real apathetic school—a lot of kids are just willing to sit in the class and take the notes and don't ask any questions. I can just sit there and carry on a conversation with the professor." Despite the pressure she feels to train for a career she can "fall back on" and the absence of people in her life who are supportive of her intellectual interests, Helena refuses to view college as vocational training: "Who wants to go to college for four years and be bored! I like it—that's the only reason I'm really there."

Many of Helena's girlfriends are married. As she thinks about their lives, she concludes that in marriage too she would want more than they have been willing to settle for:

> They're always complaining about this and that; it seems like if that's what it's all about, then I don't want it. Everyone's always saying, "I had to make him dinner, make him breakfast." If I ever get married, I'd want to do it. After I'm married for about three months, I'd probably say, "Make your own breakfast, wash your own clothes." I wouldn't call myself a woman's liberationist, but I'm really anti–domestic work.

Helena wants to go on to graduate school — "the only thing that would stop me would be money." She is thinking about joining the Peace Corps and would also like to work in Germany for a few years. Her dream is to get a doctorate in psychology.

In high school Martha Jamison was much more definite than Helena about her choice of social work as a career and her conviction that someday "Mr. Right" would come along. Life since then has changed both of these certainties. Disappointed at finding academic work at the state university much like high school, "almost a waste of time," and sociology, her initial major, "a lot of bullshit," the last straw for Martha was to find the sociology department unsympathetic to field work: "They think you should do all your work in the classroom." Like Rob, she decided to design her own field of concentration and included in her plan a practicum in a city welfare office during the fall semester of her junior year. Martha's three months as a case worker were disastrous. "I felt totally incompetent. I'd had no training. I was really bummed out by the fact that people felt just because I was from the department that I had power and that I knew everything." Living by herself in a rooming house, hassled by her male boss, Martha became very critical of the welfare system. "The client has almost no choice but to be a child. That's the fault of our whole society 'cause it's looked upon as bad to be unemployed, to ask for help." By the end of the practicum, Martha had concluded that "to work in the department of public welfare or in most human services is merely to propagate an already shitty system. I cannot keep putting on band-aids." She returned to campus primarily because she "didn't want to deal with the hassles of quitting — with the censure I would get from my family." In the fall of her senior year, she became a freshman counselor; her success at helping new students navigate their first weeks of school was gratifying, but Martha feels that she has "outgrown" the university. Recently she has been thinking about living on a farm with a group of friends after graduation, trying to become self-sufficient so they won't have to take "shit jobs" and be part of the system. But Martha feels that "nothing is definite until it happens. I'm not putting anything out of the question."

Despite her disappointments, Martha feels that college is going to turn out to have been worth the investment of time and money: "I do for the simple reason that I like the way I'm growing, and I know I wouldn't have grown this way if I hadn't gone to college." Martha admires the woman who taught her women's studies class. "She's always growing and always reading new things — she's not stagnating. She helped us a lot in getting us thinking you have the right to be a bitch, and it's sorta like you should be proud of it." Martha is trying to be an outspoken feminist herself, "growing all the time, learning all the time," saying what she thinks instead of what people want to hear, and risking the painful encounters that result. "I like the fact that I can be honest with myself and with other people. I think once you stop growing, you can just forget it — you start rotting away in a rut someplace."

Martha's stress on personal growth and her rejection of a specific career goal are unusual, but everybody who has gone on from Milltown to further schooling draws a sharp contrast between the growth and change they see in their own lives and the stagnation they see in the lives of their peers who went straight to work and have continued to live in town. These college youth have revised their views of life in Milltown: the familiarity and friendliness are still cherished, but more as abstractions; more salient now are the limitations. Ben Smith, whose college life is full of academic and financial hardships, finds comfort in comparing himself with his old football buddies, who are working at blue-collar jobs and spending their evenings drinking beer at the club. "It's funny. Everyone who's in there every night — all they do is bitch about doing it every night, but they're still there every night." When Sally Virgilio leaves the New Hampshire town where she is working as a nurse to visit home, she sees "the kids I was friends with in high school. Some of them are still back there where I was before, doing the same things we did while I was in high school, which is surprising to me — that you can spend all that time doing things the same."

The young women who postponed their plans for career training or dropped out of school early on have stayed in Milltown: Liz Erkila is married and working in the office of the local computer firm; Alice Wisnowski is engaged and working as a bank teller; and Doris O'Hare went to business school for a year but found it a waste of money and is back working at the gas station where she worked in high school. All of them are content with their lives, but they share the view of their classmates who have continued in school that they are settling for less than they might have attained, and they view their lack of long-range goals as a sign that they are not developing successfully. Asked how she has changed since high school, Doris replies: "That's the whole trouble. I haven't changed. I don't take on any responsibility or anything — just happy-go-lucky. It's good in a way, but some-time you have to change; sometime in your life you gotta start taking on some responsibilities." Since leaving business school, she says, "every three or four months, I start getting itchy. I find a couple of schools, I write down the names, I call them up. By the time I get the stuff, I don't want it any more." Alice is happy with her "day-to-day" life, but "the thing I hate myself for right now is not going to nursing school like I had planned." And Liz, who still talks wistfully of pursuing a career in special education, and applied to a community college after she had worked for a year, explains, "I got accepted there, and then I decided to get married instead, I guess." Homeowners now, Liz and her husband need her paycheck for their living expenses; going to school is something she believes she can no longer afford. Liz too sees herself as having changed little since high school and says that she would advise a new high school graduate "to think about it and find out what they really want, to make sure that they get into something that they really like. It's better for people to know what they want."

Milltown college youth now have a perspective on their parents' lives that is similar to their views of their friends who remained in Milltown. Their parents' lives seem more circumscribed, their views more narrow than they appeared to be when, in high school, many of these young people viewed their parents as ideal role models. To Barbara Natti as a high school senior, her family was the most important thing in her life, and she attributed her successful adolescence to skillful parenting; now she sees her parents as "an influence in that they're holding me back." Barbara views the restrictions her parents enforced during high school as "for my own good," but she is infuriated by their inability to understand that she is now capable of deciding what's in her own best interests. During a psychology course in her first year at nursing school, Barbara learned that "the objective of parenthood is release"; thus far, she has been unable to persuade her parents to agree, particularly when the issue is spending the night at her boyfriend's house. In dealing with her parents, Barbara tends to follow her own inclinations without "making waves." As she explains, "Why should I cause a lot of static when they have six kids to worry about!" Her strategy is a common one among Milltown students, who have discovered that keeping their parents "sort of naive" about aspects of their lives that differ from Milltown conventions makes it possible for them "to get along fairly well" when they are at home. Like Rob, Barbara feels "guilty about being independent. I hope that once I've gone through breaking away, I can go home and really have fun again." These Milltown youth are engaged in a slow break-away, gradually easing themselves into more independent positions without provoking direct confrontations.

Even Martha, intent as she is on speaking her mind regardless of the consequences, has concluded that arguing politics with her parents is "just not worth the effort. Try as I might, I cannot have them open their minds—I've finally given it up. It makes it easier to live together." Martha still respects her parents, particularly for their efforts to understand and accept the changes in her, and she "will do my best to try not to hurt them, but I'm still going to do what I want—I'm still going to go to Europe on my bicycle whether they want me to or not." Martha is wary of getting her mind "locked into one set," a condition she sees in her parents and older people generally. She finds everything more complicated than she once thought: she feels that she should tell people what she thinks no matter who they are, yet she has been taught to respect authority and age. Besides, she feels sorry for her family. "They always thought of me as that happy-go-lucky little one, and it's sort of hard for my parents to accept the fact that I'm sick of being that type of a person. They're really cool people, and they really try to understand."

As a high school senior, Hank Groblewski was the only Milltown youth who believed that his parents had failed to bring him up properly. He resented their constant bickering and their inability to recognize how responsible he had become. Now his father's drinking has been acknowledged as a serious family problem, and his mother has gotten a divorce. Hank admires how well his mother is handling her new situation, and she, in turn, is proud of Hank's success in college, holding him up as an example to the younger children in the family:

They resent the fact that I'm doing so well, at
least in my mother's eyes. If I tried to discipline
them or anything like that, they'd say, "Oh,
here's big-deal-Hank," and I think that I'd best
not aggravate the situation. I wish I could do
something. All the time I feel responsibility for
these kids, but at the same time I have to keep my
distance to a certain extent — maybe I've
convinced myself of this – to absolve myself of the
responsibility.

Now Hank imagines that he may even have benefited from
growing up in his family, "because you just get exposed to
things a lot sooner than you normally would. Before I saw the
way they acted and I just resented things that I didn't like, but
now I look for the motivation, the reason for doing things the
way they do, which changes things a lot. I don't necessarily
have to agree with their reasoning, but at least I can understand it."

Understanding their parents' limitations rather than
condemning them for their shortcomings is characteristic of
these Milltown youth. They have come to identify themselves
as part of a younger, less tradition-bound generation and see
their parents' attitudes as reflecting their specific historical
context, as Cityville youth did when they were high school
seniors. But unlike Cityville youth, who now feel as politically alienated as their parents do, these young people of
Milltown believe that their generation's broader perspective
may reverse the negative direction in which society is heading. Their new sense of their generation as tolerant and open
to change has been influenced by experiences at work, where
they encounter hostility from older workers who want to stick
to old-fashioned ways. For instance, although Sally Virgilio
likes her work as a nurse in a small New Hampshire hospital,
she is frustrated by the outmoded treatment methods being
used there. "They're very backwards, not like a city hospital.
The nurses don't have so much responsibility, and they are
really fearful of the doctors." Sally has learned to cope: "If it's
just a nurse that's using a backward method, then I'll use my

own technique because I can do that — they can do it the way they want, and I'll just do it my way. But if a doctor is doing the treatment, and you think there's a better way to do it, then your hands are tied." But she believes that the hospital is changing, "because we're all like younger blood coming into this place, and we've got different ideas on nursing than some of the older people there. The more younger people that are working there, the more able we'll be to make changes with up-to-date things."

Sally is one of the few Milltown youth to have completed her schooling and obtained her first regular position. She decided to move out of the state to prove to herself that she could manage on her own. "When you're in school, it's not like being out on your own. I didn't think I wanted to be too close to home — it's so easy, you can just call up on the phone and say, 'What will I do now?'" Like Sally, most Milltown youth see themselves as in a transitional stage of independence. During this time in their lives, career preparation and self-development take precedence, and they consider it appropriate to be self-absorbed, postponing commitments that might constrain their individual growth.

The young man most disaffected as a high school senior continues to see himself as an exception. Ed Gilbert rejects the notion that he is in a transitional stage of life. "A lot of people think, 'I'm in college now, I'm going to go to law school, and then I will be sort of like an adult, I will be out in the world.' Well, I'm out in the world now — I just happen to be in college, that just happens to be my profession right now." Ed sees himself as having traveled farther and faster than his peers: "I find myself feeling like a 30-year-old 21-year-old." Yet when Ed thinks about his social class, he identifies himself "at this stage in my life," as part of the "collegiate class, that class that wants to get ahead, that forward-moving class."

Ed believes that he has moved far from his "little hometown situation" and is proud of never having used being from Milltown "as a crutch to say, 'Gee, I could have done this if I came from another school.'" His ambitions are more far-reaching than those of his Milltown peers: he expects to become a lawyer and later perhaps go into politics, to be rich

214

and live with "high-caliber" people in a "nice community" near the city. Although he foresees everything in his life "falling into place," Ed has recently realized that he is not as secure as he wishes: "I find I have a need to want to grade myself." He plans to apply to 25 law schools—"I'm sure there is one out of 25 that will take me." Thus, although Ed believes that he "can still do anything that anybody that came from anyplace else can," he has some doubts about how he will measure up in the fast-paced world of "knowledgeable" people he hopes to join.

Ed's self-confidence has been bolstered by his success as a salesman. After high school graduation, he took a summer job selling cookware and became the top salesman in the Northeast. In recognition, his company flew Ed to Bermuda for five days, all expenses paid. During subsequent summers, he has worked as an insurance and encyclopedia salesman and, most recently, has won a 500 dollar scholarship as the top college student encyclopedia salesman in the country.

The morality of his salesmanship is very important to Ed. What he likes most about himself is that he's honest and fair with people. He believes that he sells a lot because "I find myself having a very incredible amount of success having people trust me." In explaining his success, Ed invokes the Milltown virtues of careful preparation and honesty:

> The first thing I've always done was to check out all the different things that are on the market — say, all the encyclopedia companies. I went through all the training programs and picked the one that I thought was the best, and I felt secure that I was selling the best product on the market so I could be really genuinely honest with people. Then I felt that I knew all the lines—all the gimmicks—so I could be successful because I knew all the answers to most people's complaints.
>
> I know the power of suggestion and how to use it and have used it where I find a person wants the product but needs the motivation. I feel that I am doing them a good deed by giving them that motivation.

Like other Milltown youth more appreciative than he of having grown up in Milltown, Ed believes that being honest and trustworthy is the key to helping solve America's problems. He thinks "we can't really legislate morality" because most people don't know "what truth is about and how important it is." He can imagine himself playing a role in helping people become more aware. "Little things get to me, like false advertising. I'd like to see things brought out more. I don't like to see people being deceived." Ed sees his kind of salesmanship as a moral and helpful act:

> I think that people are oftentimes awestruck by
> my approaches because they look at me and they
> go, "Is this for real?" or "Why are you doing this
> for me?" I never left a house without a smile on
> my face even if they had been very, very rude. So
> I feel like I've sold myself and I've changed a lot
> of people even if they didn't listen to me. They
> thought, "Gee, maybe there are still people that
> are friendly and honest."

Milltown youth continue to view the general deterioration of morality in America as a major source of the nation's difficulties, and, like Ed, they vow to live with integrity. As they did as high school seniors, they believe that they are demonstrating moral character in their willingness to work hard to meet the academic and financial demands necessary to achieve their goals.

Many have faced unexpected difficulties and, in overcoming them, feel that they have shown themselves worthy. For example, Larry, struggling to keep up with the course work in his pharmacy program, had counted on more financial aid from his parents. "But my father just didn't want me to go to school for a year, have everything handed to me, and then after a year drop out—and then he's stuck with 3,000 dollars." Larry sometimes fantasizes that "my parents are paying for my school, they set me up in a nice apartment and give me 25 or 50 dollars a week. I'd take advantage of it—it's ly normal, anybody would." Life would have been easier if had not been forced to work his way through college, but Larry feels, "you wouldn't respect your position as much." As it is, he concludes, "I respect my position as a pauper."

These young people continue to identify themselves as members of the middle class — honest, hard-working people "in the middle" who have to work for what they have and so know the value of money. Now they view the middle class as embattled, paying with their efforts for the benefits claimed by those Americans who are grabbing more than they are entitled to. These "cheaters" and "spongers" jeopardize the chances for which middle-class people have struggled.

These Milltown youth tell tales of fellow students who get by through cheating on exams and claiming food stamps they are not entitled to, of people they've heard of who are cheating the welfare department, and of newspaper stories about protest groups who are demanding more than their share. These young people name the poor and blacks as groups in the society with too much power, and they see little value in affirmative action programs, arguing that there is no reason why individuals should be rewarded for past grievances. They also view people "at the top" as having more power than they should and have become much more negative about politicians since Watergate, but they reserve their most serious moral indignation for people who make unreasonable demands and are unwilling to work in their own behalf. From the vantage point of Milltown youth, the people "in the middle" have virtually become an oppressed minority.

Cityville and Townline youth were already disillusioned about the state of American society during their high school years, but Milltown youth saw themselves as loyal, patriotic Americans. Now they view their high school perspective as naive, the product of having been sheltered from reality. Those who have moved out beyond Milltown have discovered that America faces far more serious difficulties than they had imagined, and their faith in its foundations has been shaken. They cannot identify anyone in government who seems either willing or able to set things right, and things seem "out of control" in a more serious way than they had realized. They see big business as the outstanding culprit but think everyone is implicated, and they remain particularly concerned about the deterioration of the environment, which they see as directly linked to declining moral standards. For instance, Helena complains that Milltown's high-tech company "does a wicked job on the Valley River. They dump all kinds of stuff in there. They have all kinds of laws, but you see this green slimy stuff coming in there. It bugs me that nobody does anything about it."

When they think about how "messed up" things are, Milltown youth get upset and they get mad, but most of the time they do not think about these matters. In their view, worrying about things one cannot do anything about serves no useful purpose and may indeed distract one from pursuing what one can influence. So they work at blocking out and ignoring the stream of disconcerting news. Some, like Rob, remain optimistic about America's long-range prospects, still believing that as citizens become more aware, they will reverse the negative trends; others are less sanguine, and their strategy seems to be to convince themselves that they can choose not to take part. As high school seniors Milltowners identified voting as the quintessential act of the good citizen, but a number of them report that they have not yet voted. Although some explain this as a temporary lapse resulting from self-absorption, others view not voting as a way of expressing their disapproval of government and their desire not to be involved in its workings.

Milltown youth are optimistic about their own prospects and do not perceive their hopes as threatened by the nation's difficulties. Their stance toward the society is compatible with their general approach to life: whenever possible, problems are to be avoided or denied — "I don't let things bother me" — but if they must be confronted, the best strategy is to cope with them one by one as they arise, doing the best that one can.

7

Developmental Dilemmas and the Social Identities of Working-Class Youth

In this chapter we draw together the double strands of our analysis, examining the implications of the dominance of the American Dream and the developmental vision for the evolving social identities of the promising working-class youth of Cityville, Townline, and Milltown. We believe that no matter what alternative values these youth pursue, no matter how strong their convictions about the inequities of American society, they are—as adolescents and even more as young adults—liable to judge their efforts on the basis of individual achievement and hold themselves individually responsible for their fates. As a result, although they have strong hopes for themselves, they are unable to assert the legitimacy of their alternative values.

We begin by examining the central revisions these working-class youth have made in their social identities during their first four years out of high school. We then go on to show how their experiences of upward mobility challenge conventional assumptions about the nature of mobility in American society. Finally we discuss the complex process through which these young people have become so vulnerable and our own ideas for how educators might help working-class adolescents deepen their critical perspective on American society, thus becoming more empowered as they pursue their goals.

The Revision of Social Identities

As promising working-class youth completing high school, the young people of Cityville, Townline, and Milltown expected to make their way through difficult, unexplored terrain: they had few financial resources to back them up, and they had set out on paths that had not been traveled by their parents. Their identities as determined, serious people who had already confronted substantial problems gave them hope for the future; Cityville and Milltown youth had set goals they felt were within their reach, while Townline youth focused on finding goals that were worth pursuing.

During the next four years all found the going much harder than they had anticipated. Needing jobs in order to subsidize their educations and independence, they found that work became a central aspect of their lives. Youth from Cityville and Townline worked at low-level, often menial jobs unconnected to their prospective careers, while Milltown youth found jobs as apprentices in the professions they hoped to enter. All these young people believe that they have faced "real world" dilemmas as workers—people who can get and hold jobs, achieve some advancement, survive being fired and laid off, and manage money. They feel that they have developed confidence in their ability to survive the long years of struggle they now see ahead of them, for by the mid-1970s they have seen gas lines form, heard predictions of continued inflation, and experienced a job market much tighter than they had ever imagined.

We explore here the impact of their entry into new social locations of work and study upon their perspectives: where they stand in society, who stands with them, and who is in opposition; their attitudes toward their original communities; and their conception of relations between men and women. We examine as well their interpretations of new political developments, especially the Watergate revelations, and their revised ideas about themselves as youthful citizens of the United States.

220

Cityville:

The way has been much harder than the young people of Cityville anticipated. The young women have discovered that openings for public school teaching jobs are virtually nonexistent, and the young men, that finding the jobs they wanted will require more education than they expected as well as considerable sacrifice. Many of their parents have become ill, and Cityville youth are proud that they could give them financial as well as emotional support.

The lives of Cityville youth remain anchored there, and they still believe that their early relationships in family and neighborhood helped make them determined and caring people. But as they travel into Boston to study and work, they have been stunned and angry to encounter Cityville's reputation as a place of crime and corruption.

The scarcity of the jobs they once considered safe has made their early pragmatism seem somewhat impractical, and they now think of college as the arena in which they developed general interests and confidence that will make them more versatile. As they think back on the choices they faced as Cityville youth and look ahead to the lives of their future children, they have some questions. They wonder whether growing up in a less densely populated community might encourage children to want more for themselves. Yet they believe that wherever they might move, they will remain Cityvilleans. Caring about others is still their central concern, and although they now believe that finding the right jobs will take a long time and much struggle, they still perceive work primarily as a means to continue and create relationships.

These youth feel that working their way through college has taught them important lessons. Although they believe they will find more satisfying work in the long-run, they see their present jobs—typical working-class jobs like those held by their parents' and offering little security, chance for influence, or intrinsic satisfaction—as having helped them become competent and flexible in dealing with difficulty. While they value their college educations, they sometimes regret the continual pressure of being worker-students, envying their non-college-going friends the money they have for cars and vacations and their chance to have a good time without having to prepare for the next day's classes. Some, wishing for the leisure to participate in the intellectual and social life of college, envy affluent students who do not have to rush off to work as soon as the day's classes are over.

As high school students these youth placed themselves and all "the people" on one side of a moral and economic triangle. They deeded a second side to the affluent and powerful, who did not have to struggle and who had impoverished relationships, and a third to those who were so poor that they deserved the help of the others. These youth looked forward to meeting people different from themselves, and they enjoyed their contact with college professors. But the differences they found between themselves and black fellow students made them angry. Sympathetic as high school students to the oppression of blacks, they were surprised to find black peers wanting the same things they wanted, as advantaged as they, and getting special help under affirmative action programs. In these scarce times, these youth see Civil Service quotas for blacks as oppressing people like themselves and depriving black youth of the chance to prove that they could achieve on their own.

The parents of these young people are still perceived as loyal allies. Most Cityville youth continue to live at home and, through negotiation and their financial contributions to the family, have earned the status of adults in their parents' eyes. Busy with work and school, these youth make sure that they maintain their old friendships. Many of the young women have become involved in serious relationships with young men who never wanted to go to college and are working at blue-collar jobs. More than before, these young women believe that realizing their career goals will determine the economic security of their future families and are developing strategies to cope with the problems they foresee. By remaining steadfast in their own ambitions, they hope to inspire their future husbands to seek better jobs. These young

222

women value their emerging capacity to stand up for themselves, instead of being "good girls" who do what others want; they see their boyfriends as unwilling to knuckle under to others, as seeking independence rather than advancement.

Although they still draw hope from being young and starting out, Cityville youth no longer think of their generation as very different from that of their parents. They feel that they have become more realistic than they were in high school about the immutability of the political world and admit their own unwillingness to spend their energy in political action, or even to vote. Those who join in strikes or protests do so because they believe in the principle of standing by their co-workers. Rather than work for large-scale social change, they intend to work at their commitments to the people they care for and to try to alleviate those injustices in their immediate surroundings that might yield to their efforts.

Townline:

Pursuing worthwhile goals as independent young adults was a priority for most Townline youth, as high school seniors, and they are surprised to find themselves spending almost as much time working to support themselves as on their studies and searching. The Irish-Catholic young men who were headed for more Cityvillean lives now find themselves seeking futures that are more complex and singular, and all these Townline youth are saddened that their struggles have not yet yielded promising directions for the future and that they have often had to move back into their families' homes to save money.

They still hope to find work that will enable them to express themselves and their principles, but for now they take the jobs they can find, contrasting themselves, as young people just starting out, with the older people with whom they work and pained by the contradictions between the world they envisioned and the actual conditions of work. Yet they feel that working has helped them become more grounded in reality—the young women, for example, say that their jobs have taught them how much power men wield over women. Those few in elite universities who work in school-related jobs to supplement their scholarships not only feel estranged from their more affluent classmates, but also worry that their insulated campus lives have compromised their ability to function in the real world.

Townline youth have found few allies in their struggles and maintain little contact with the few sympathetic adults and peers they knew as high school students. They think of themselves as moving alone, having little in common with other students or workers, and when they move back into their parents' homes, they maintain as much distance from their families as they can. Their search for worthwhile goals has yielded more questions than resolutions, and although they are relieved to have survived difficult times, they are more unsure of themselves than ever.

Now they think of themselves as being not from Townline, but as loners trying to create lives that are essentially detached from any place. Although they no longer think much about their early lives in Townline, they are reminded of old angers when they meet people who believe the prevailing stereotype of the community as a place where only wealthy people live, or when they think about more affluent Townline peers, who, they are certain, are having much easier lives. They are grateful that their Townline educations and accents are superior to those of their fellow working-class students in college; these advantages give them some badly-needed comfort.

Although they still value their complex understanding of social problems, they have not found political strategies that seem viable. They still find it hard to give up hope completely, but now they see no reason to hope: the masses seem as credulous as they did before, the ruling class just as arrogant, and former radical activists even more naive and implicated in the system. These young people's determination not to become part of an unjust socioeconomic system compounds their difficulty in finding work that makes sense.

Having a family seems less undesirable now, but the young women of Townline struggle with what they have learned at work about the power of male bosses. They see the connections drawn by feminists between the inequities they suffer and the fact that they live in "a man's world." They feel that it takes too much energy to fight the subservience of their roles at work and also the traditional sexual ideals of the young men to whom they find themselves attracted and conclude that they should postpone involvements. The young men of Townline also agree with feminist analysis, but they have come to feel that men are being accused of something that is not really their fault. They do not think of themselves as personally oppressing women and see themselves as more likely to be losers than victors in sexual relationships. All the young men of Townline hope to find, in the distant future, the right women to understand and share their struggles, but the Jewish young men still believe that conventional family life is one way of "selling out."

Milltown:

Milltown youth looked forward to college as an exciting but frightening first step toward the careers they sought. At first they found their apprehensions justified, but they soon learned to cope with the diversity and anonymity of college life and worked hard to make their studies relevant to the careers they sought.

They see themselves making slow, steady progress toward goals that will take longer to reach then they anticipated. Some focus completely on their studies, part-time jobs, and apprenticeships, while others add the newer goal of personal growth and change to their ambitions for themselves. But all continue to see their vocations as the central arena through which they will express who they are and make their contribution to society, and they regard the difficulties they face as appropriate to their apprentice status. They see themselves now at a transitional moment in their lives and look ahead to a time when they will have completed their training and be free to enjoy the professions and the freedom they have earned.

Although they still see Milltown as a good place for children to grow up, it now seems parochial and too restricted for people like themselves to live in for the rest of their lives. Now they look upon peers who remained in Milltown as stuck, and view their parents not as role models but as traditional people, set in Milltown ways and unable to accept the changes their children have made in their life-styles. As they focus on their life and work at college, these youth feel neglectful of their parents, to whom they owe so much, and conceal from them aspects of their own lives that would be upsetting.

Their difficulties in paying for their educations seem like good training for the new realities they envision. They still identify with those "in the middle," but now they see the middle class as embattled, the fruit of their hard labors threatened by welfare cheaters and groups who are protesting that they have not received a fair deal. These young people look back on their previous political views as naive: now they believe that the problems of American society are more deeply rooted and that the illegitimate power of those at the top also threatens middle-class interests. Though shocked at the revelation of the Watergate cover-up, they feel that such abuses of power are likely to occur again.

In college they encountered feminism, which led the young men to imagine that their future marriages will be more egalitarian than their parents', and the young women to question their previous expectation that their lives will change depending upon the men they marry. These young women embrace their career goals with determination, and young women who did not go to college see themselves as having turned away from their one chance to make something more of their lives.

Milltown youth have become more pessimistic about social reform, and they try not to think about politics. They still intend to live morally as individuals and hope that other citizens will become educated into an awareness of the need for decency. When they do settle down, they may vote or try to figure out how to become involved in social issues. For now, they will spend their energies working harder and longer than they expected to prepare for their careers.

226

Social Location and Social Class: The Meaning of Upward Mobility

What we have learned about the evolving social identities of the young people of Cityville, Townline, and Milltown complicates the terms of long-standing debates on the meaning of upward mobility for working-class people in America. These debates have centered on the question of whether moving up necessarily leads to marginality, alienation, and status anxiety. (See Beeghley, 1978; Jackman and Jackman, 1983; Knutson, 1972; and Lipset and Bendix, 1959).

Early research stressed the gulf between working-class and middle-class life, arguing that becoming upwardly mobile turns working-class youth into young adults trapped in the margins between two worlds, viewed as alien by their working-class peers and the middle-class people they emulate (Gans, 1962; Kahl, 1953). Later data have been interpreted as challenging this view, demonstrating instead that upward mobility has become a value for all Americans, and that the differences between social classes should be seen not as sharp cleavages but as variations along common cultural dimensions (Douvan and Adelson, 1966; Turner, 1964). From this perspective, individuals experience mobility as a gradual and comfortable acculturation and end up with attitudes and behavior that fall midway between those of people at their origins and people at their destinations.

Elements of both perspectives are present in the more complex argument made by Sennett and Cobb in *The Hidden Injuries of Class* (1972), which we discussed briefly in Chapter 1. They accept the view of mobility as a widespread cultural ideal that leads individuals moving up from blue-collar to white-collar status to believe that they are enacting the American Dream. Yet at the same time, it is impossible for them to escape the feeling that fundamentally they have failed. Why is this so? Sennett and Cobb argue that mobile working-class individuals internalize not only the values of their own class but also the dominant values of American society, which judge working-class life to be inferior. Upwardly mobile working-class individuals aspire to do middle-class rather than manual work, but do not respect such work. Thus, they become trapped in a double bind that, when they succeed, prevents them from ever fully accepting their new status. No matter how successful they are, they are doomed to disrespect themselves for joining the ranks of those who look down upon working-class people.

What we have learned about the implications of specific community contexts for the evolving social identities of working-class youth makes us skeptical of the value of searching for the one generalization about upward mobility that may be most accurate for the most people. We suggest that more is gained by asking questions that acknowledge the specificity and contingency of working-class experience: under what circumstances does the pursuit of mobility lead to feelings of marginality? Where and how does it occur with ease? And when with a mixture of feelings?

The working-class youth of Cityville interpret upward mobility as cementing rather than severing their ties to their parents' lives and values; they experience many difficulties in pursuing their goals, but not feelings of betrayal. They differ from the adult men portrayed by Sennett and Cobb in several important ways: they have grown up among family members of several generations but not in the close network of extended families characteristic of inhabitants of the urban village; they interpret their parents' jobs as products of the scarce possibilities available during the Great Depression, rather than as the honest work appropriate for members of the working-class; becoming ambitious was a major achievement for most of these adolescents, a sign that they had fulfilled their parents' hopes that they would be persons of character. Being able to go to college meant that they had simultaneously to differentiate themselves from the masses of Cityville youth and to remain connected to their less ambitious friends. Pursuing their ambitions places these youth under the pressure to succeed in school, work, family relationships, and friendships — but not that of entering alien worlds.

The occupations they headed for when they were high school seniors were not all that elevated, and most considered their eventual career destinations less important than their personal goals of being hard workers who remain anchored in the "we" of Cityville life. The few who aimed for the highest-status professions have become commuters to private, residential universities, and—like Kahl's "common man boys" and the marginal youth of Gans's urban village—have begun to sever their Cityville connections, allying themselves with other college students who are headed for similar careers. But most of these Cityville youth attend state-supported colleges with other worker-students who are also juggling multiple demands, and they return each night to their homes in Cityville, resuming their lives with friends and negotiating the privileges of adult status with their parents. They interpret encounters with professors and other professional people as helpful to their growing confidence and versatility but also as tangential to their lives.

A sharper shift in values is part of the experience of pursuing upward mobility for the working-class youth of Milltown. Their need to travel into the city or go away to college led them to view moving up as also moving out, and their original identity as loyal Milltowners, insulated from the rest of the world, has given way to their sense of having more in common with other college students. Although they originally minimized the differences between themselves and other Milltown peers, they have begun to characterize their friends who remained in Milltown as stuck in limited routines of living and thinking. Yet upwardly mobile Milltown adolescents continue to maintain the early distinctions they drew between people who come from places like Milltown— people "in the middle"—and people from wealthier, more materialistic and alienated communities. And although they feel that their perspectives have expanded, they remain like their parents in valuing decency and hard work. Enjoying their new sophistication, they try to avoid confrontations with their parents and continue to regard towns like Milltown as perennial sources of wholesomeness for children lucky enough to be born there.

The interpretations of the experience of upward mobility created by Cityville and Milltown youth support the claims made originally by Berger (1960), and extended by

Hamilton and Wright (1975), that the major cleavage in the American class structure is now between the dominant upper and upper-middle classes on the one hand and the combined working- and lower-middle classes on the other. These adolescents feel similar to all those people whom they view as ordinary, decent, and hard-working, and they do not intend to step across the fault lines that divide their world from that of wealthier people whose values they consider false. They define the ground they want to cover so that while representing a successful move up in terms of financial security and the inherent interest of the work, it remains safe and familiar in terms of social and moral outlook. We see no reason to doubt that if they are successful in the terms they have set, they need not disrespect themselves or suffer from marginality. But we note that when they fail, they are likely to blame themselves — a development we will later discuss.

Upward mobility has placed the working-class youth of Townline in a much more vulnerable and exposed position. Their experience of lowered status and social rejection during high school, their own rejection of the values of wealthier peers, their parents' relatively low status in their community and inability to understand their children's lives — such realities underlie the belief of these adolescents that the future is uncertain and that there are few moorings to which they can anchor their ambitions. During their high school years, they felt unique, living in the margins between the groups they perceived and separate from life in their families and neighborhoods; during the next four years, they became even more anomalous, lonely and unsure of themselves. They thought of themselves as individuals, not part of any group. They neither identified with other working-class youth nor believed that others shared their situations. Because the distinctions they draw between themselves and their wealthier, more materialistic peers are crucial elements in their social identities, they find it difficult to articulate goals for themselves without stressing that they do not value financial success. If they do move up, they may well feel like traitors to their original values, though not perhaps to their original class, because they have no strong sense of class-identity.

The Preemptive Power of the Developmental Vision

Another lesson we draw from the evolving social identities of these working-class youth is that no matter what alternatives to mainstream values they pursue, they are vulnerable to judging themselves by the values of what we have termed the *developmental vision.* This ideal portrays adolescents as choosing among multiple options and growing into adulthoods of free-standing, self-contained individualism. Prolonging early ties with family and community is viewed as constraining their freedom to develop and to pursue their own best interests. We pointed, in Chapter 1, to the congruence between this vision and the American Dream: the individual is the brave explorer, usually male, leaving behind the bonds of the settlement to make his own way.

According to mainstream theory, working-class youth are developmentally disadvantaged because their families both lack the resources to provide them with sufficient opportunities for self-discovery and value loyalty to the group above individual freedom of choice. Working-class values are viewed as more primitive than middle-class values, based in a culture that, because of economic scarcity and traditional mores, values stability over progress, authoritarian relationships over democratic ones. Middle-class and upper-middle-class life, abounding in economic and thus psychological options, is viewed as generating the democratic individual, who is confident that the political world will respond to the actions and interests of self-directed individuals.

In contrast, we set forth the concept of an evolving social identity that sees individuals as continually defining themselves in relation to others, positioning themselves in the social world and drawing conclusions about their possibilities from their interpretations of social experience. Thus, we believe that the individuals who see themselves as independent or self-made are expressing a cultural value rather than a reality: the experience of individuality is, like all experiences of self, socially constructed. From this perspective, the belief that those individuals and social classes who succeed economically and politically are likely to be more developed, psychologically or politically, than those who fail is an ethnocentric judgment, expressing the values of those who dominate and functioning to justify the status quo.

Once we step outside the ethnocentrism of mainstream judgments of development, we can see many forms of positive development taking place in the lives of the working-class youth of Cityville, Townline, and Milltown. From the scarcity of options in their lives these young people conclude that they must become active improvisers on their own behalf and find new ways of using what is available to them. In response to unexpected difficulties, they revise the ground plans for their futures and prepare for the long run.

We see as positive the developmental route taken by Cityville youth. Developing through *engagement with others*, these young people value interdependence rather than separation; they work to strike a balance between their individual ambitions and their deep commitments to others; and they define individual success as the ability to enhance one's relationships. Becoming responsible rather than moving on is important to them, and they believe that it is a sign of maturity that they have become increasingly able to nurture their siblings and parents, to respond to the needs of neighbors and friends. Gaining independence is important to them, but they accomplish this task within their relationships rather than using them as points of departure. These youth perceive their relationships to others not as ties that constrain their individuality but as the matrix within which their individuality acquires meaning.

This developmental route offers possibilities not only for individual growth but also for the life of families, neighborhoods, communities, and the world. American society has given undue credence to the notion that individuals who pursue their own best interests thereby promote the general welfare; there is ample evidence that the democratic vision of numerous interest groups vying in the public arena results not in some balanced consensus and just distribution of resources but in the promotion of the interests of those who start out with more money and power.[1] Our survival may well depend upon a better balance between self-directed action, as it is celebrated by the developmental vision and the American Dream, and action on behalf of others, as enacted in the lives of Cityville youth. The Cityville ideal of interdependence seems to us congruent with a vision of the just society as one in which the needs of the least powerful and favored are protected from exploitation. One indicator of a society's achievement might well be the extent to which its citizens conceive of the common good as requiring care for those in need.[2]

Individual Responsibility as a Source of Hope and Self-Blame

We see these developmental strengths, but we also see how difficult it is for these youth to recognize the legitimacy of values and paths that are not part of the developmental vision. It may well be that there are now few communities isolated enough and few religious groups determined enough for their children to grow up with a firm conviction that alternatives to mainstream values are worthy enough to base their lives on.

Certainly the values of the developmental vision were part of the social identities of the young people of Cityville, Townline, and Milltown throughout their adolescence. As they move from their communities into college and work, hoping to create successful lives, they become even more vulnerable to judging themselves on its terms. Most important in this dynamic is their belief that they are individually responsible for their fate, which fuels their hope for the future while weakening their awareness of what they have in common with others who have limited power and resources.

Their sense of solidarity with others is of two kinds. The first is interpersonal: their sense of being like others in their immediate surroundings and of sharing with them common origins and values. The second is structural: their sense of sharing group interests with others in a society where some people start out and remain far ahead of others.

In Cityville working-class youth start out making no distinction between the two kinds of solidarity. They believe that their commitment to their relationships makes them part of "the people" and also sets them apart from the competitive, selfish "them," who dominate the politics and economy of the nation. These youth intend to remain different from "them" by staying away from arenas in which they might fall under "their" influence. They believe that they can escape becoming implicated in or part of the system "they" dominate by not wanting wealth and power, except the power to succeed in their individual lives, which they believe they can have without stepping on anyone else.

As we see, this formulation poses a serious dilemma. It prevents them from recognizing the competing interest groups in the arenas they enter after leaving high school, the systemic underpinnings of the value conflicts they face whenever they work and study in contexts that are governed by mainstream values and standards. When they face difficulties, they do not look for structural explanations. Although they are ready to attribute the failures of their parents and other people they know to poverty or historical circumstance, they believe that their futures are up to them as individuals. They have accepted the value of individual efficacy and responsibility set forth by the developmental vision, and they judge their achievements by its standards without realizing that these are the standards valued by "them."

We see this dynamic most poignantly in the life of Barbara Lockhart, the young woman who gave up her aspiration to become a doctor when she was a junior in college. As we observed in Chapter 6, Barbara, in explaining her career change, does not give herself credit for making the right choice when she attended her dying grandfather during his long hospital stay and neglected her course work. She takes her loyalty and caring for granted. She does not criticize the university system or her adivsors for not recognizing her difficulties. Nor does she apply to herself the charitable explanation that she would make for anyone else. Instead, Barbara blames herself. "I guess I didn't have what it takes," she explains. "I guess I just got lazy."

We do not argue that nursing is an unfortunate choice of profession for Barbara: it will give her the chance to express the caring and responsibility she feels for others, it will keep her involved in medicine, and it will advance her far above her mother's status as a welfare recipient. Our concern is that from her point of view, she has not chosen nursing but accepted it by default. Barbara, gifted and committed, working 50 hours a week at two jobs in addition to being a student, believes that she must not have tried hard enough and begins her career a failure in her own eyes.

For the working-class youth of Townline we see a different sort of developmental dilemma. They long for a world where peace and justice make it possible for people to be caring in their relationships, yet these young people have experienced very few alliances in their own lives. They leave high school with a structural analysis of the unequal life-chances of groups in society, learned in part from social studies classes and the ideology of the radical movement. But they do not apply this analysis to their own situations: rather than seeing their difficulties as part of the struggle between social classes in Townline and the larger society, they feel that they move alone and that they can escape the tangle of injustice, materialism, and corruption they see in society by remaining thoughtful questioners. But they cannot find career goals that correspond to their values, and they cannot want to move up without feeling that they have bought into the materialism they despise. The more difficulties they face in making their way in the years after high school, the more confused and despairing they become. They have little sense of themselves as personally oppressed by the society they criticize, and find it difficult to feel allied with other working-class youth they encounter, because they feel special—both by virtue of having grown up in Townline and because of their commitment to self-understanding. They identify with the plight of other workers but feel that they themselves are not really or merely workers. Their belief in the unlimited freedom that individuals can attain through thinking for themselves gives them reason to believe the central tenet of the developmental vision — that individuals should free themselves from others' influence and proceed on their own. Instead of feeling oppressed, they feel confused, vulnerable to self-blame.

Milltown youth left high school with a strong sense that everyone in their home town shared the same goals and values. But because the central Milltown value stressed the personal efficacy of disciplined, hard-working individuals, those who left Milltown for college also left behind their sense of home-town commonality, embracing the strand of the developmental vision that sees individuals moving up and away and regarding peers who remained in Milltown as having been left behind. As high school seniors, they viewed their counterparts in the wealthy suburbs and urban ghettos as unfortunate because they had not had the advantages of Milltown teaching and caring; now, having faced some difficulties themselves, they are more likely to regard people on the bottom as demanding what they have not earned. They justify success on the basis of individual morality linked to hard work and interpret failure as a sign of a deficiency in character. Milltown youth who did not leave town blame themselves for failing to move onto the track of individual growth.

In Their Own Realms of Reality: The Politics of Working-Class Youth

Another potential source of self-blame lies in the political arena. The working-class youth of all three communities feel themselves to be much more alienated from political concerns and activity than they were as high school seniors. They are still critical of the government and social policies, but they have found themselves thinking less about issues that were raised in high school social studies classes, and blame themselves for not voting.

The Watergate revelations confirmed what Cityville and Townline youth already believed about corruption in national politics. Cityville youth drew their low expectations about political behavior from the machine that governed their city for two decades, from the extension of a federal highway through Cityville neighborhoods despite local protests, and from the firing of a popular social studies teacher. The election of a reform mayor made little difference to the political interests of their parents. Four years after high school, these young people have given up their sense of themselves as part of a liberal and politically involved younger generation; not voting or even keeping up with the news, they have concluded that their parents were right to think that expecting things to change, even in themselves, is pointless.

For Townline youth, politics is one more aspect of life that has turned out to be more complex and overwhelming than they imagined it would be. In high school their anger about injustice and materialism in American society coincided with the school's generally radical atmosphere, but they felt marginal to the student movement, whose leaders were protected from the negative consequences of their actions, and skeptical that a system that had been so successful at indoctrinating the masses could be changed. Four years later, the unexpected challenge of making enough money to support their schooling makes them wonder more than ever whether they or anyone else can escape the materialism they hate, and their heightened sense of the futility of political action increases their general weariness and sadness.

The Watergate revelations shocked Milltown youth, who had believed in high school that the nation's problems stemmed from the greed of a very few politicians and that if the political interest that their parents and other Milltowners expressed through participation in town government were moved to the larger sphere, America's basic strengths would continue. Three years later they have come to see their earlier optimism as naive, for the country's difficulties appear fundamental, based in complexities that these youth have little hope they can either understand or change.

The classic view among mainstream political scientists has been that the sense of political powerlessness is an identifying trait of working-class and poor people, whom they depict as projecting the insecurities of their personal lives upon the political arena.[3] These youth blame themselves for their political alienation, feeling that they *should* — if they knew more, had more time, were properly motivated—vote and be more involved in the general political life of the nation. Our view differs both from the classic stereotype and from these young people's own assessments of their political inadequacy: we believe that they have ample reason to be indifferent to conventional party politics but find evidence in their social identities of another sort of positive involvement.

Most of these working-class youth believe that the political realm is controlled by "them"—people whose social status, personality, and mode of relating to others is different from their own. "They" include not only professional politicians but also all those people whose economic interests they serve. These young people see "them" as motivated by different desires and operating by different rules. Their perception of separate rules at work for wealthy people and for ordinary people like themselves is fundamental to their view of society: they are critical of the inequities in the socioeconomic system, and they consider that system virtually unchangeable.

And yet many of these youth do act to effect social change in the public arenas in which they live and work. If we distinguish between conventional politics—with a capital P—and a small p politics linked with the spheres that these young people define as significant to them, we can understand the political worlds in which they act and take risks.

We see this distinction made by the young nurse from Townline, Suzanne Baer, whose life we discussed in Chapter 6. The world of conventional politics she has decided to ignore; the hospital where she works, however, she describes as "my own realm of reality." It is the setting for her social action. There she takes a stand in opposition to discrimination against minority patients, even when doing so puts her at risk. She sees these actions as integral to her definition of a good nurse and thus as part of her professional as well as personal identity.

Many of the working-class youth of Cityville, Townline, and Milltown take part individually in what might be called "small p politics." Youth from Cityville and Townline share Suzanne's indignation about injustice and make efforts to help people in need. Family and neighborhood are often arenas for the concerns of Cityville youth, who characterize their actions as simple decency rather than as expressions of more abstract social goals. When these young people take public, collective steps — joining a picket line, initiating changes in the college curriculum, joining friends to design a neighborhood playground — they define their actions as efforts to improve conditions in the lives of people they care about. Many Townline youth have more general analyses of the problems of capitalist societies, including sexism and racism, and when they act — as Suzanne does, and as Danny Genzuk did in helping his Puerto Rican co-workers learn English — they are likely to act on behalf of people at the bottom of the social order. Milltown youth who have embraced career achievement without questioning the contexts in which that achievement will occur, link their work to the social welfare: as nurses, pharmacists, teachers, naturalists, they think they will be contributing to the betterment of society.

Because all these working-class youth agree with the definition of the good citizen as one who believes and participates in the mainstream political process, they believe that they are not good citizens and that they have become apathetic and alienated as a result of their own laziness. We wish they could acknowledge the legitimate reasons for their indifference to electoral politics and link their actions in their own realms of reality to their societal criticism and concerns.

On Supporting Working-Class Youth in Their Struggles

We see the vulnerability of these working-class youth in mainstream society and wish that they placed more value on their efforts on behalf of others and their critical outlook on social problems. We wish that their efforts on their own behalf could be fueled by a sense that their struggles are shared by others. We see that when they make broad judgments about the inequities in the life-chances of different socioeconomic groups, they give structural explanations; yet when they think about their own lives, they think of themselves not as members of those groups but as individuals whose will and effort will determine their fate.

Their anger at inequalities of opportunity is expressed when they discuss the workings of society at large; the hope they draw for their personal lives stems from their commitment to individual efficacy and responsibility. This gap between the levels of their social analysis gives them hope but also, we believe, dooms them to self-blame when they do not succeed. As long as they feel that their lives are exempt from societal rules, unconnected to ongoing political and economic struggles, they will find little justification for the failure of their own attempts.

We have asked whether it is possible for them to focus on the difficulties faced by working-class people trying to make their way and still retain their adolescent hopefulness. Can we help them understand and name the conflicts between their own values and those of the developmental vision so that they can become more active in choosing their own directions and less likely to blame themselves for where they end up? Will it be possible for them to ally themselves with others in similar stituations as they attempt to make their own way? [4]

Our work points to the need for a complex awareness on the part of educators of working-class youth. First, they should recognize that becoming upwardly mobile is a legitimate personal goal for young people starting out from positions of relative powerlessness. Moreover, helping these youth arrive at a colletive sense of what they are undertaking is likely to make them more resilient in their struggles. [5] For many of them, as well as for us, cooperation and concern for others are primary values. They start out with a conception of development that defines interdependence rather than competitive individualism as an ideal end-point. Helping them see that their self-interests are linked to group-interests and intersect with the interests of many others in society will, we believe, give them more energy in their struggles and reduce eventual self-blame.

Let us illustrate these thoughts with specific examples.

240

Like Barbara Lockhart, the young people of Cityville take their values so much for granted that they do not name them or credit themselves when they make choices on the basis of interpersonal relationships rather than individual achievement. Further, because they do not foresee the inevitable conflicts between their values and those of institutions like universities, they are not prepared to fight for recognition of the legitimacy of their values and their struggle to move up while they maintain their nurturing relationships. If they were better prepared for such conflicts and had a sense that their struggles were shared by other young people, they might be better able to defend themselves. Barbara might expect her professors to know her well enough to ask why her lab reports suddenly stopped; or she might feel entitled to meet with her advisor and ask how she could make up her work; or she might choose to do exactly what she has done but recognizing the conflicts she faced and not feeling that she is becoming a nurse because she is lazy.

Suzanne Baer needs to recognize that she is taking risks as she fights for the rights of minorities at the hospital and that her struggle is not only a personal one but also a struggle for power that is being waged by others in similar institutions. If she did, she could see the connection between the morality of her action and the political welfare of the nation and feel proud that she is actively involved rather than ashamed that she has never voted. The isolation of Townline youth compounds their confusion about what work is meaningful to do. If Suzanne, and Danny Genzuk, helping his fellow factory workers, imagined that they and others were working separately and also as part of a larger effort to chip away at the wrongs of an unjust society, they might not feel so helpless. Through a sense of collective effort they might see that they start with similar hopes and from similar circumstances and in fact have group interests that are different in scope but not necessarily in kind from those of the minorities they are trying to aid.

If we do not recognize the personal implications of our societal criticism, affirm the validity of our own ideals, and link ourselves to the larger struggle against inequities, we all

241

remain vulnerable to the vision and values that dominate. It is our hope that if working-class adolescents become more aware of their collective lack of power, they will develop a more complex view of the dilemmas they face, form alliances with others who share their ideals, and be better able not only to respond to unexpected assaults upon their hopes, but also to join the struggle for a more just society.

Notes

Preface

1. Flacks (1967) and Keniston (1968) were major proponents of the view that student protest was an expression of the highest ideals of contemporary youth. Gadlin and Garskof (1970) contains an interesting collection of research studies and essays from that era. Rothman and Lichter (1978) have severely criticized the ideological assumptions and methodological flaws of research on the protest movement.

2. Prominent proponents of the *embourgeoisement* thesis include Bell (1965), Mayer (1969), and Wilensky (1964); major critiques have been written by Goldthorpe et al. (1968), Hamilton (1972), Massey (1975), and Rinehart (1971).

3. There has been considerable controversy in the status attainment literature as to whether working-class youth benefit from growing up in high-status contexts. It is important to realize that "benefits" are always defined in terms of conventional upward mobility. Early findings (Turner, 1964; Wilson, 1959) seemed to indicate that attending a middle-class school raised the aspirations of working-class students and converted them to middle-class values. However, in later studies, with more adequate controls for individual variation, high-status contexts have had only negligible effects on the ambitions and attainments of

working-class youth. (See Alexander et al., 1979; Hauser, Sewell, and Alwin, 1976; and Kerchoff, 1974 for comprehensive reviews.)

4. Barker and Gump (1964) and Miel and Kiester (1967) present contrasting positions on the advantages and disadvantages of growing up in small or large communities.

5. In Cityville the sample consisted of one-fifth of the members of the senior class with 115+ IQs. In Townline an effort was made to draw half the sample from those seniors with 115+ IQs whose fathers had blue-collar jobs and half from those seniors with 115+ IQs whose fathers had white-collar and sales jobs.

    In Milltown almost every senior with an IQ above 115 was interviewed; thus, the sample includes children of the professionals who service the town. In drawing the Milltown portrait, the interviews with these young people were not included.

    The actual distribution of fathers' occupations in each community was as follows:

Father's Occupation	Cityville	Townline	Milltown
Unskilled and semi-skilled blue-collar	7	6	9
Skilled blue-collar	9	7	4
White-collar and sales	4	6	2
Business and professional	—	1	5

6. We reinterviewed fifty-seven of the sixty young people in the original sample. The Milltown follow-up interviews were conducted first, closer to three rather than to four years after the initial interviews.

Chapter 1

1. To protect anonymity and confidentiality, we use fictitious names for individuals and places, and have changed minor details that might lead to their identification.

2. Lane's (1962) pioneering work on the "latent political ideology" of working-class men was a rich resource for us. One of the few political psychologists to explore the meanings working-class people create out of the circumstances of their lives, his distinction between latent and forensic ideology inspired the distinction we make in Chapter 7 between "large *P*" and "small *p*" politics. Lane's belief in the central role of social reference points in the development of the individual self helped us envision how the context of a particular community might influence adolescent development.

3. Bronfenbrenner characterizes much of contemporary research on human development as "the study of development-out-of-context" (1979, p. 21). He is one of the few developmental psychologists with a conceptual framework for analyzing the role of settings, and he has embarked on a research program comparing the specific contexts in which key developmental transitions take place.

    Barker has made the most systematic effort to document the nature of interaction in different kinds of behavior settings (1968; see also Barker and Gump, 1964). Through detailed observations of the daily patterns of behavior of children and adolescents in a range of settings, he and his students have developed a model of relations between settings and interaction patterns.

4. Community studies from *Elmtown's Youth* (1949) to *Middletown Families* (1982) have looked at class differences in socialization patterns and school experience in an effort to understand how community stratification perpetuates itself. Here, as in much survey research, the interest is in looking at the differences between middle-class and working-class youth rather than in exploring the diversity of working-class experience (see Caplow et al., 1982; Douvan and Adelson, 1966; Hollingshead, 1949; and Jennings and Niemi, 1975).

5. Textbooks on adolescence reflect the dominant per-

spectives in the field. Invariably they portray working-class youth as held back by their parents' values and socialization practices. See Grinder (1978), one of the most popular and respected texts, for a typical example.

6. For detailed analyses of the flaws of passive transmission models of socialization, see Jennings and Niemi, 1975; Merelman, 1972; and Solomon and Steinitz, 1979.

7. The search for context-free generalizations about the meaning of social class is a doomed enterprise, for, as Mishler (1979) convincingly demonstrates, meaning can only be understood in context.

8. Connell and his colleagues' emphasis on economic dependency and political powerlessness as defining features of working-class existence parallels our own conception. They reject static definitions of class membership derived solely from occupation; instead, they explain, "By 'working class' we mean, broadly, people who have common interests because they are dependent for their living on a wage or a wage substitute (such as a pension) and don't have means of gaining larger shares of the social product through ownership of capital, power in organizations, or professional monopolies" (1982, p. 159).

9. Elder's pioneering research on the differential impact of the Depression on children in different age cohorts and social classes pointed the way toward placing development in a historical context. He emphasizes that "each generation is distinguished by the historical logic and shared experience of growing up in a different time period, and by the correlated activities, resources, and obligations of their life stage. Particularly in times of rapid change, individuals are thought to acquire a distinct outlook and philosophy from the historical world, defined by their birthdate, an outlook that reflects lives lived interdependently in a particular historical context" (1974, p. 15).

10. Connell et al.'s elaborated example of the interweaving of gender and class is particularly instructive:

"The joint presence of gender and class, say for a working-class boy, means a relationship between processes. It means that the construction of his masculinity goes on in a context of economic insecurity, or hard-won and cherished security, rather than economic confidence and expansiveness. It means that his father's masculinity and authority is diminished by being at the bottom of the heap in his workplace, and being exploited without being able to control it; and that his mother has to handle the tensions, and sometimes the violence, that result. It means that his own entry into work and the class relations of production is conditioned by the gender relations that direct him to male jobs, and construct for him an imagined future as breadwinner for a new family. And so on" (1982, p. 181).

11. Block (1973) discovered through analysis of longitudinal data from the Oakland and Berkeley studies that middle-aged women's occupational histories revealed a significant negative association between occupational commitment and sex-role socialization. Indeed, there was an inverse relationship between upward occupational mobility and femininity ratings. Only women who diverged from traditional sex role stereotypes were likely to advance in status. And Gallatin concluded from her review of research on adolescent development that boys tend to be more "ambitious, assertive, realistic about the future and purposeful," whereas girls are more "passive, modest, vague about the future, and retiring" (1975, p. 245).

12. As Douvan and Adelson put it, "What the girl achieves through intimate connection with others, the boy must manage by disconnecting, by separating himself and asserting his right to be distinct" (1966, pp. 347–48). Fifteen years later, in a review article in the *Handbook of Adolescent Psychology* on "Identity in Adolescence," Marcia proposes, "Perhaps it is time to take Douvan and Adelson seriously. The predominant concerns of most adolescent girls are not with occupation and ideology. Rather they are concerned

with the establishment and maintenance of interpersonal relationships. Adolescent boys are encouraged to make life decisions that will often lead to increased interpersonal conflict with both authorities and families. The experience of such conflict can be an identity confirming event. However, if an adolescent girl, who is expected to become proficient in interpersonal relationships, creates such tension and conflict by her decisions, she may take this as disconfirmation of the success of her identity formation" (1980, p. 179).

13. Anyon provides a cogent analysis of the developmental tasks faced by young women. From her perspective, "gender development involves not so much passive imprinting as active response to social contradictions. Thus, for girls, gender development will involve a series of attempts to cope with—and resolve—contradictory social messages regarding what they should do and be. Girls are presented not only with ideologies regarding what is appropriate behavior for themselves as females (for example, nurturance of men and children in a domestic situation, submissiveness and non-competitiveness with men outside the domestic situation, and sexual submissiveness), but also with ideologies of what are appropriate means in US society of achieving self-esteem (for example, through success in the non-domestic, competitive world of work). These two sets of ideologies, as others have noted, are in direct contradiction" (1983, p. 19). (Also see Baruch and Barnett, 1975; Broverman et al., 1972; and Horner, 1971).

14. Thus, for example, Turner (1964) in an important study of adolescent ambition asks young women simply to write in the names of the careers they are interested in pursuing and then inquires in detail about the occupations they hope for in the men they marry. Beeghley (1978) notes that patterns of female occupational mobility are very different from male patterns because of the effects of discrimination and marital mobility. Huber (1980) has criticized researchers

for ignoring women in the major status attainment studies.

15. The recent flurry of interest in psychic deprivation theory as an explanatory model for social class differences in political socialization is the latest indication of the continuing strength of deficiency models of working-class development. For extreme examples of this line of reasoning, see Davies (1977), Knutson (1972), and Renshon (1974).

16. The vision we are describing is a male one; the emphasis is on autonomy and an ethic of individual rights, and the presumption is that the good society can be achieved if individuals pursue their own interests and form alliances with others on the basis of common interests. See Gilligan (1982).

17. The assumption that there is a developmental progression from egocentric concern with oneself to an ever-widening concern with others is critical to those who see political development as paralleling personal growth. Thus, Jeanne Knutson claims, "All of Maslow's self-actualizers were 'democratic people in the deepest possible sense'" (1972, p. 89). This assumption has come under increasing attack from critics of unidimensional developmental schemes, particularly those who have become disenchanted with Kohlberg's stages of moral development. See Hogan (1975) and Sampson (1977) for insightful critiques.

In addition, a growing body of evidence demonstrates that the assumption of unidimensionality in measures such as Rotter's Internal-External Control scale and Campbell's Political Efficacy scale reflects "a conservative view that links personal competence and effort to the belief that the system is just in its allocation of rewards" (Gurin, Gurin, and Morrison, 1978, p. 275). Gurin and her colleagues found in analyzing data from a national probability sample that for political conservatives, personal control and belief in the responsiveness of the system were both highly interrelated and predictive of political behavior, but for liberals and blacks, personal control scores were unrelated to political behavior, and, indeed, those with an external control ideology were more likely to participate in political action.

18. The frontier is one of the most pervasive of American motifs. Although it is now generally recognized that the frontier offered less opportunity than was originally claimed, the individual seeker is still seen as living out what is best in America. Blau and Duncan (1967) did indeed find a relationship between geographic mobility and occupational mobility in their major study of status attainment and mobility patterns. The explanation they give for the association is that people move to places where jobs are available.

19. For us, Erikson's work is the quintessential statement of the developmental vision, albeit a very complicated version. In his earliest writing, "Reflections on the American Identity" in *Childhood and Society*, he stressed the dynamic polarities in the American character — "migratory and sedentary, individualistic and standardized, competent and co-operative, pious and free-thinking, responsible and cynical" — but singled out the element of autonomous choice as essential to the process of identity formation: "The individual must be able to convince himself that the next step is up to him and that no matter where he is staying or going he always has the choice of leaving or turning in the opposite direction if he chooses to do so" (1950, p. 245). Although he worried then about whether the tendency toward the increasing give-and-take in American families would diminish the possibility of adolescents rebelling against their fathers and challenging authoritarian trends in society, the activism among adolescents in the sixties and early seventies persuaded Erikson that "the ethical potential of youth" could be fulfilled here (see Erikson, 1968, 1970).

20. For a thoughtful portrayal of images of mobility in American mythology, see Strauss (1971).

21. Gallatin (1975) provides a good summary of the evidence relevant to the continuity versus conflict debate about the nature of the adolescent experience. She concludes that there is scant empirical support for fundamental questioning as a modal experience and that most adolescents accept their parents' views about important life decisions.
    The debate about whether mobility rates have been higher in America than elsewhere is a longstanding one. See Beeghley (1978) for a good summary of the literature.

22. Joseph Adelson has been one of the most vocal critics of the "strain toward generalization" that characterizes most research on adolescent development; he has noted that the field has little to say about adolescents who are neither from the same upper-middle-class backgrounds as researchers nor exotic enough to draw their attention (see Adelson, 1970, 1979).

23. A very different and, from our perspective, far more promising tradition of work on the socialization of working-class youth has emerged in Britian. There, Marxist sociologists, interested in the role of cultural forms in social reproduction, have done participation-observation studies of youth groups in an effort to understand how their members make sense of their situations and "negotiate" with the dominant culture (see Mungham and Pearson, 1976, and Willis, 1977).

24. Perhaps the most widely cited books about American working-class values have been *The Urban Villagers* (Gans, 1962) and *Class and Conformity* (Kohn, 1977). The former emphasizes the role of the peer group, the latter the significance of work conditions, but both subscribe to the idea that working-class life is antithetical to self-direction. Thus, Kohn claims, "The essence of higher class position is the expectation that one's decisions and actions can be consequential; the essence of lower class position is the belief that one is at the mercy of forces and people beyond one's control, often, beyond one's understanding" (p. 189).

Rubin (1976) purports to draw a more sympathetic portrait of contemporary working-class life, yet her characterization still singles out restriction and frustration as its dominant features.

25. Keniston (1970) coined the phrase "tenuously included" in an effort to account for class differences in student participation in protest activity. Erikson (1970) included working-class adolescents in his "apolitical vocationalists" category, and Havighurst (1975), drawing on Yankelovich (1972), classifies them among the "practical-minded" as opposed to the "fore-runners."

26. Knutson's claim that affluence and psychic competence are inevitably correlated is not supported by careful reviews of the evidence. For instance, Sniderman (1975) found little support for the widespread assumption that social status and self-regard are strongly related; his comprehensive review of the literature on social-class differences in self-esteem revealed only small correlations between measures of self-esteem and status indicators such as occupation, education, and income. In a similar vein, Schwartz (1973) concludes that the relationship between social class and alienation is weak at best and may be disappearing altogether as alienation becomes a more pervasive phenomenon in American society.

27. Pease, Form, and Rytina contrast "evolutionary liberalism" with "structural realism," which holds that "distinct classes emerge as a consequence of socially created arrangements that maintain economic, political, and social inequality" (1970, p. 128). They attribute the popularity of evolutionary liberalism among American sociologists to its congruence with dominant ideological currents in American society.

28. Miller and Riessman's (1961) original response to Lipset and Bendix (1959) remains a relevant and powerful critique. Hamilton (1972) provides the most thorough refutation we have discovered of the assertion that poor and working-class people are more au-

thoritarian than rich and middle-class people. He concludes that the poor may have a greater commitment to equality than any other group.

29. Kolson and Green (1970) point out that questionnaires that measure political trust, efficacy, and involvement are often phrased in terms so unrealistic and general that it is difficult to take them seriously. Faced with this kind of situation, young people often try to figure out what the adults in authority want them to say. The superior performance of middle-class children on these measures must surely reflect, in part, their greater skill in figuring out what the teacher wants to hear and their greater willingness to provide the "right" answers.

30. A classic statement of this viewpoint can be found in Lipset: "The lower-class individual is likely to have been exposed to punishment, lack of love, and a general atmosphere of tension and aggression since early childhood—all experiences which tend to produce deeprooted hostilities expressed by ethnic prejudice, political authoritarianism, and chiliastic transvaluational religion" (1963, p. 114).

31. Connell and Goot's trenchant critique of political socialization research lays bare the problematic nature of the "community of meaning" assumption. We have found their analysis of the connections between methodology and ideology particularly useful. They argue that standardized questionnaires ask for agreement or disagreement: they provide no opportunity for subjects to tell their questioners what they really think of their questions. The questions presuppose the existence of a social world in which the interests of all coincide and there is no necessary conflict between the pursuit of individual or group interests and the promotion of the general welfare. These questions continue to be used despite evidence that they mean different things to people in different social circumstances. Connell and Goot ask, "Is it really surprising that working-class children as a group feel less able to

affect or influence a capitalist state?" (1972–73, p. 183).

32. Recognition of the culturally based as opposed to universal nature of the developmental vision is becoming more widespread. See Gilligan, 1982; Riegel, 1979; Sampson, 1977; Simpson, 1974; and Sullivan, 1977 for a variety of perspectives on this point.

33. Parkin's distinctions among the dominant, subordinate, and radical value systems provide a useful starting point. He defines the dominant value system as "a moral framework which promotes the endorsement of existing inequality"; the subordinate value system as one that promotes accommodative responses; and the radical value system as one that advances an oppositional interpretation of class inequalities (1971, p. 812). He contends that these three meaning systems compete in the marketplace of ideas, with the dominant value system having the advantages of institutional support and perceived legitimacy. Working-class values are influenced by all three meaning systems, and within-class variations depend to a considerable extent on differences in access to the competing value systems.

    In Parkin's view, subordinate value systems arise in local working-class communities and represent modifications of dominant values in response to the existential conditions of working-class life, whereas oppositional interpretations are rooted in mass working-class political parties, and their availability depends on those parties' visibility and power. He views the "we-they" distinctions of the subordinate value system as part of a parochial interpersonal meaning system, in contrast to the radical value system's analysis of class conflict as a systemic feature of the political economy of the nation-state.

34. We agree with the critics of reproduction models — both the conservative and radical versions thereof — who contend that these models are too mechanistic: through their claims that people's fates are determined by forces beyond their influence or control,

reproduction theorists deny the potency of individual agency and the possibility of social change through radical education and consciousness raising. (See Apple, 1982; Fine, 1983; and Giroux, 1983.)

Chapter 5

1. In the early seventies the dominant value system was under attack by left-wing activists who sought to provide a systemic analysis of the ways in which the American Dream served to bind the subordinate classes to the existing system and to obscure the perpetuation of inequities by the privileged classes. Thus, in Parkin's (1971) terms, an oppositional meaning system was available to working-class people. The accessibility of that meaning system varied among the three communities: Townline youth had direct access to radical interpretations through activist students and teachers at the high school, whereas Cityville and Milltown youth received such messages primarily through the media and thus through the filter of commentators with some allegiance to the dominant meaning system.

2. Barker and Gump (1964) found that small high schools provide greater opportunities for student participation because there are many leadership positions — in school government, extra-curricular clubs, athletic teams — relative to the number of students available to occupy them. These opportunities in "undermanned settings" seemed to contribute to students' positive feelings about their high school experience.

3. The contrast Milltown youth draw between their safe, healthy environment and the dangerous, unhealthy city supports Sennett's claim in *The Uses of Disorder* (1970) that isolated, homogeneous communities heighten the adolescent propensity toward purified identities.

4. Milltown youth's belief in the autonomy of Milltown

life is reminiscent of the "Springdalers'" belief in their town's independence from political and economic forces in the larger society (Vidich and Bensman, 1960).

5. Elder, drawing on Barker's concept of an "overmanned behavior setting," argues that the politicization of youth in the early 1970s may be explained in part by their membership in a relatively large cohort that was entering a depressed labor market. He contends that the historical context exaggerated "traits commonly attributed to adolescence as a social category — a no-man's land without self-defining productive roles, a position of marginality and low integration relative to the larger community" (1981, p. 189).

6. Our finding of support for more expressive life-styles among Townline and Cityville youth is consistent with results of national surveys (Yankelovich, 1974). Resistance to "the new morality" in Milltown is not surprising, given the educational, class, and regional variations in receptivity to changing values.

Chapter 7

1. Not surprisingly, there are substantial variations among high-, middle-, and low-income people in their beliefs about the opportunity structure and distribution of power in American society. Generally speaking, the higher the income, the greater the belief in the equity of the status quo: for instance, high-income respondents were more likely to believe that plenty of opportunity is available and that power is distributed among many different groups in society. Also, the higher the income, the more frequent the agreement with the statements "poor people don't work as hard as rich people" and "poor people don't care about getting ahead." And, finally, the higher the income and education of the respondents, the less they believed that all groups should have equal power (Huber and Form, 1973).

In a similar vein, research evidence demonstrates greater support among working-class than among middle-class people for social welfare policies aimed at alleviating the hardships of people at the bottom of the socioeconomic ladder (Feagin, 1975).

2. Michael Lewis (1978) argues convincingly that the ideology of the American Dream, through its individualization of success and failure, inevitably entails derogation of people in trouble. He provides a detailed account of the ways in which Americans struggle to maintain their distance from society's failures in order to convince themselves of their own relative success. Also see Ryan (1971) for a cogent analysis of the multiple sources of victim-blaming in American society.

3. Psychodynamic theories of political efficacy have been seriously challenged by Langton (1980), who concluded after critically reviewing major studies that there is little support for family primacy in political learning. In his own research on competing predictors, Langton found generalized personality dispositions the weakest determinant of the decision to participate.

    Also relevant to the traditional claims of working-class alienation is the finding that political alienation has become pervasive in America. Distrust in government increased dramatically between 1964 and 1974. For instance, the percentage of a national sample who "trust government only some of the time" increased from 22 to 61, and the percentage agreeing that "government is run by a few big interests" increased from 29 to 65 (Abramowitz, 1980).

4. In stressing the importance of being able to "name" one's reality and to forge alliances with those who share one's interests, we draw on Paulo Freire's pioneering work, *The Pedagogy of the Oppressed* (1970).

5. In their attempts to find meaningful collectivities for adolescents to claim, we would caution educators to be attentive to the differences among young people from different communities and the distinctions that

are meaningful to their social identities. Feminists, for example, might assume that everywhere, young women will place a higher value on nurturing than young men and will be more likely to give up their career plans to care for sick parents. But in Townline young women were encouraged by guidance counselors as well as their mothers to fight against their sense of responsibility for their families and to focus instead on pursuing their own careers. Cityville young men, on the other hand, might well choose, like Barbara Lockhart, to be with their grandfathers in the hospital rather than working in their labs. Community analysis complicates radical feminist and class analysis. If Barbara had grown up in Townline, she might have been encouraged to remain in the pre-med program, but had she grown up there as an Irish-Catholic, she, and her male peers, might well have relinquished the dream of becoming a doctor once they entered high school and found themselves placed "at the bottom of the top."

References

Abramowitz, A. I. 1980. "The United States: Political Culture Under Stress." In *The Civic Culture Revisited,* edited by G. A. Almond and S. Verba. Boston: Little, Brown & Co.

Adelson, J. 1970. "What Generation Gap?" *New York Times Magazine,* Jan. 18: 10ff.

Adelson, J. 1979. "Adolescence and the Generalization Gap." *Psychology Today,* 12:33ff.

Adelson, J. 1981. *Handbook of Adolescent Psychology.* New York: John Wiley.

Alexander, K., and Eckland, B. K. 1975. "Contextual Effects in the High School Attainment Process." *American Sociological Review* 40:402–16.

Alexander, K. L., et al. 1979. "School SES Influences—Composition or Context?" *Sociology of Education* 52:222–37.

Anyon, J. 1983. "Intersections of Gender and Class: Accommodation and Resistance by Working-Class and Affluent Females of Contradictory Sex-Role Ideologies." In *Gender, Class and Education,* edited by S. Walker and L. Barton. New York: Falmer Press.

Apple, M. W. 1982. *Education and Power.* Boston: Routledge & Kegan Paul.

Barker, R. 1968. *Ecological Psychology.* Stanford, Calif.: Stanford University Press.

Barker, R., and Gump, P. 1964. *Big School, Small School.* Palo Alto, Calif.: Stanford University Press.

Baruch, G., and Barnett, R. 1975. "Implications and Applications of Recent Research on Feminine Development." *Psychiatry* 38:318–27.

Beeghley, L. 1978. *Social Stratification in America: A Critical Analysis of Theory and Research.* Santa Monica, Calif.: Goodyear.

Bell, D. 1965. *The End of Ideology.* New York: Free Press.

Berger, B. M. 1960. *Working-Class Suburb.* Berkeley, Calif.: University of California Press.

Berger, P., and Berger, B. 1971. "The Blueing of America." *New York Times*, Feb. 15:23.

Blau, P. M., and Duncan, O. D. 1967. *The American Occupational Structure.* New York: John Wiley.

Block, J. H. 1973. "Conceptions of Sex-Role: Some Cross-Cultural and Longitudinal Perspectives."*American Psychologist* 28:512–26.

Bronfenbrenner, U. 1979. *The Ecology of Human Development.* Cambridge, Mass.: Harvard University Press.

Broverman, K., et al. 1972. "Sex-Role Stereotypes: A Current Appraisal." *Journal of Social Issues* 28:66–68.

Caplow, T., Bahr, H. M., et al. 1982. *Middletown Families: Fifty Years of Change and Continuity.* Minneapolis: University of Minnesota Press.

Connell, R. W., Ashenden, D. J., Kessler, S., and Dowsett, G. W. 1982. *Making the Difference.* Sydney, Australia: Allen & Unwin.

Connell, R. W., and Goot, M. 1972–73. "Science and Ideology in American 'Political Socialization' Research." *Berkeley Journal of Sociology* 27:166–93.

Davies, J. 1977. "Political Socialization: From Womb to Childhood." In *Handbook of Political Socialization,* edited by S. Renshon. New York: Free Press.

Douvan, E., and Adelson, J. 1966. *The Adolescent Experience.* New York: John Wiley.

Elder, G. H. 1974. *Children of the Great Depression.* Chicago: University of Chicago Press.

Elder, G. H. 1981. "Adolescence in Historical Perspective," In *Handbook of Adolescent Psychology,* edited by J. Adelson. New York: John Wiley.

Erikson, E. H. 1950. *Childhood and Society.* New York: Norton.

Erikson, E. H. 1958. *Young Man Luther.* New York: Norton.

Erikson, E. H. 1968. *Identity: Youth and Crisis.* New York: Norton.

Erikson, E. H. 1970. "Reflections on the Dissent of Contemporary Youth." *Daedalus* 99:154–76.

Feagin, J. R. 1975. *Subordinating the Poor: Welfare and American Beliefs.* Englewood Cliffs, N.J.: Prentice-Hall.

Fine, M. 1983. "Perspectives on Inequity: Voices from Urban Schools." In *Applied Social Psychology Annual IV,* edited by L. Bickman, Beverly Hills, Calif.: Sage.

Flacks, R. E. 1967. "The Liberated Generation: An Exploration of the Roots of Student Protest." *Journal of Social Issues* 23:52–75.

Freire, P. 1970. *Pedagogy of the Oppressed.* New York: Herder and Herder.

Freud, A. 1958. *The Ego and Mechanisms of Defense.* New York: International Universities Press.

Gadlin, H., and Garskof, B. 1970. *The Uptight Society.* Belmont, Calif.: Brooks-Cole.

Gallatin, J. 1975. *Adolescence and Individuality.* New York: Harper & Row.

261

Gans, H. 1962. *The Urban Villages: Group and Class in the Life of Italian-Americans.* New York: Free Press.

Gilligan, C. 1982. *In a Different Voice.* Cambridge, Mass.: Harvard University Press.

Giroux, H. A. 1983. *Theory and Resistance in Education.* South Hadley, Mass.: Bergin and Garvey.

Goldthorpe, J. H., et al. 1968. *The Affluent Worker: Political Attitudes and Behavior.* Cambridge: Cambridge University Press.

Grinder, R. 1978. *Adolescence.* New York: John Wiley.

Gurin, P., Gurin, G., and Morrison, B. M. 1978. "Personal and Ideological Aspects of Internal and External Control." *Social Psychology* 41:275–96.

Habermas, J. 1970. *Toward a Rational Society.* Boston: Beacon Press.

Hamilton, R. 1972. *Class and Politics in the United States.* New York: John Wiley.

Hamilton, R., and Wright, J. 1975. *New Directions in Political Sociology.* Indianapolis: Bobbs-Merrill.

Handel, G., and Rainwater, L. 1964. "Persistence and Change in Working-Class Life Style." In *Blue-Collar World,* edited by A. Shostak and W. Gomberg. Englewood Cliffs, N.J.: Prentice-Hall.

Hauser, R. M., Sewell, W. H., and Alwin, D. F. 1976. "High School Effects on Achievement." In *Schooling and Achievement in American Society,* edited by W. H. Sewell, R. M. Hauser, and D. L. Featherman. New York: Academic Press.

Havighurst, R. J. 1975. "Youth in Social Institutions." In *Youth,* 74th Yearbook of the National Society for the Study of Education, edited by R. J. Havighurst and P. H. Dreyer. Chicago: University of Chicago Press.

Hogan, R. 1975. "Theoretical Egocentrism and the Problem of Compliance." *American Psychologist* 30:533–40.

References

Hollingshead, A. 1949. *Elmtown's Youth.* New York: John Wiley.

Horner, M. S. 1971. "Femininity and Successful Achievement: A Basic Inconsistency." In *Feminine Personality and Conflict,* edited by J. Bardwick. Belmont, Calif.: Brooks-Cole.

Huber, J. 1980. "Ransacking Mobility Tables." *Contemporary Sociology* 9:5–8.

Huber, J., and Form, W. H. 1973. *Income and Ideology.* New York: Free Press.

Jackman, M. R., and Jackman, R. W. 1983. *Class Awareness in the United States.* Berkeley, Calif.: University of California Press.

Jennings, M. K., and Niemi, R. 1975. *The Political Character of Adolescence: The Influence of Families and Schools.* Princeton: Princeton University Press.

Kahl, J. A. 1953. "Educational and Occupational Aspirations of 'Common Man' Boys." *Harvard Educational Review* 23:186–203.

Keniston, K. 1968. *Young Radicals.* New York: Harcourt, Brace & World.

Keniston, K. 1970. "What's Bugging the Students?" *Educational Record* 51:116–29.

Kerchoff, A. C. 1974. *Ambition and Attainment.* Washington, D.C.: American Sociological Association, Arnold and Caroline Rose Monograph Series.

King, P. 1979. "Pathways to Adulthood from a Small Town: Milltown Youth, 1972–75." Ed.D. dissertation, Harvard Graduate School of Education.

Knutson, J. 1972. *The Human Basis of the Polity.* Chicago: Aldine-Atherton.

Knutson, J. 1974. "Pre-Political Ideologies: The Basis of Political Learning." In *The Politics of Future Citizens,* edited by R. Niemi. San Francisco: Jossey-Bass.

Kohn, M. L. 1977. *Class and Conformity.* Chicago: University of Chicago Press.

Kolson, K. L., and Green, J. J. 1970. "Response Set Bias and Political Socialization Research." *Social Science Quarterly* 51:527–38.

Lane, R. 1962. *Political Ideology.* New York: Free Press.

Lane, R. 1973. "Patterns of Political Belief." In *Handbook of Political Psychology,* edited by J. Knutson. San Francisco: Jossey-Bass.

Langton, K. P. 1980. *Political Participation and Learning.* North Quincy, Mass.: Christopher Publishing.

Lewis, M. 1978. *The Culture of Inequality.* Amherst, Mass.: University of Massachusetts Press.

Lipset, S. M. 1963. *Political Man.* Garden City, N.J.: Doubleday. ————————

Lipset, S. M., and Bendix, R. 1959. *Social Mobility in Industrial Society.* Berkeley: University of California Press.

Marcia, J. E. 1980. "Identity in Adolescence." In *Handbook of Adolescent Psychology,* edited by J. Adelson. New York: John Wiley.

Marin, P. 1972. "The Open Truth and Fiery Vehemence of Youth: A Sort of Soliloquy." In *The Prospect of Youth,* edited by T. Cottle. Boston: Little, Brown & Co.

Massey, G. 1975. "Studying Social Class: The Case of 'Embourgeoisement' and the Culture of Poverty." *Social Problems* 22:595–607.

Mayer, K. 1969. "The Changing Shape of the American Class Structure." In *Social Stratification in the United States,* edited by J. Reach, L. Gross, and O. Gurrslin. Englewood Cliffs, N.J.: Prentice-Hall.

Merelman, R. M. 1972. "The Adolescence of Political Socialization." *Sociology of Education* 45:134–66.

Miel, A., and Kiester, E. 1967. *The Short-Changed Children of*

Suburbia. New York: Institute of Human Relations Press, American Jewish Committee.

Miller, J. B. 1976. *Toward a New Psychology of Women.* Boston: Beacon Press.

Miller, S. M., and Riessman, F. 1961. "Working Class Authoritarianism: A Critique of Lipset." *British Journal of Sociology* 12:263–76.

Mishler, E. G. 1979. "Meaning in Context: Is There Any Other Kind?" *Harvard Educational Review* 49:1–19.

Mungham, G., and Pearson, G. 1976. *Working-Class Youth Culture.* London: Routledge & Kegan Paul.

Nelson, J. I. 1972. "High School Context and College Plans: The Impact of Social Structure on Aspirations." *American Sociological Review* 37:143–48.

Parkin, F. 1971. *Class, Inequality and the Political Order.* London: Macgibbon and Kee.

Pease, J., Form, W., and Rytina, J. 1970. "Ideological Currents in American Stratification Literature." *American Sociologist* 5:127–37.

Renshon, S. 1974. *Psychological Needs and Political Behavior.* New York: Free Press.

Renshon, S. 1975. "The Role of Personality Development in Political Socialization." In *New Directions in Political Socialization,* edited by D. C. Schwartz and S. K. Schwartz. New York: Free Press.

Riegel, K. F. 1979. *Dialectical Psychology.* New York: Academic Press.

Rinehart, J. W. 1971. "Affluence and the 'Embourgeoisement' of the Working Class: A New Look." *Social Problems* 19:148–62.

Rothman, S., and Lichter, R. 1978. "The Case of the Student Left." *Social Research* 45:535–609.

Ryan, W. 1971. *Blaming the Victim.* New York: Random House.

Rubin, L. 1976. *Worlds of Pain*. New York: Basic Books.

Sampson, E. E. 1977. "Psychology and the American Ideal." *Journal of Personality and Social Psychology* 35:767–82.

Sampson, E. E. 1978. "Scientific Paradigms and Social Values: Wanted—A Scientific Revolution." *Journal of Personality and Social Psychology* 36:1332–43.

Schwartz, D. 1973. *Political Alienation and Political Behavior*. Chicago: Aldine.

Sennett, R. 1970. *The Uses of Disorder*. New York: Knopf.

Sennett, R., and Cobb, J. 1972. *The Hidden Injuries of Class*. New York: Alfred Knopf.

Simpson, E. 1974. "Moral Development Research: A Case Study of Scientific Cultural Bias." *Human Development* 17:81–106.

Sniderman, P. 1975. *Personality and Democratic Politics*. Berkeley, Calif.: University of California Press.

Solomon, E. R. 1977. "Ideological Development in Cityville Youth, 1972–76." Ed.D. dissertation, Harvard Graduate School of Education.

Solomon, E., and Steinitz, V. 1979. "Toward an Adequate Explanation of the Politics of Working-Class Youth." *Political Psychology* 1:39–60.

Spady, W. 1976. "The Impact of School Resources on Students." In *Schooling and Achievement in American Society,* edited by W. H. Sewell, R. M. Hauser, and D. L. Featherman. New York: Academic Press.

Strauss, A. 1971. *The Contexts of Social Mobility: Ideology and Theory*. Chicago: Aldine.

Sullivan, E. V. 1977. "A Study of Kohlberg's Structural Theory of Moral Development: A Critique of Liberal Social Science Ideology." *Human Development* 20:352–76.

Turner, R. 1964. *The Social Context of Ambition*. San Francisco: Chandler.

Vidich, A., and Bensman, J. 1960. *Small Town in Mass Society.* Garden City, N.Y.: Doubleday.

Wilensky, H. L. 1964. "Mass Society and Mass Culture: Interdependence or Independence." *American Sociological Review* 29:173–97.

Willis, P. 1977. *Learning to Labour.* Westmead, England: Saxon House.

Wilson, A. B. 1959. "Residential Segregation of Social Classes and Aspirations of High School Boys." *American Sociological Review* 24:836–45.

Yankelovich, D. 1972. *The Changing Values on Campus.* New York: Simon & Schuster.

Yankelovich, D. 1974. *The New Morality: A Profile of American Youth in the 70's.* New York: McGraw-Hall.

Index

271